ARDENS ~ Co.DOWN.

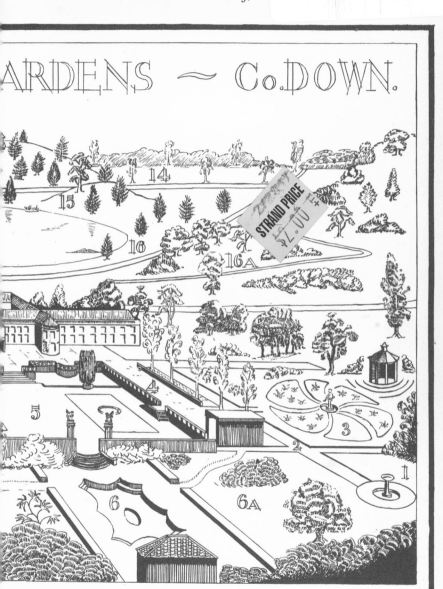

*Touring the Gardens
of Europe*

Touring the Gardens of Europe

by

DOROTHY LOA McFADDEN

Wheel Tour Maps by WINFIELD BARNES

DAVID McKAY COMPANY, INC.　　　　New York

To my husband—
My favorite companion abroad or at home

TOURING THE GARDENS OF EUROPE

COPYRIGHT © 1965 BY DOROTHY LOA MC FADDEN

LIBRARY OF CONGRESS CATALOG NUMBER: 65-18547

MANUFACTURED IN THE UNITED STATES OF AMERICA

VAN REES PRESS   •   NEW YORK

ACKNOWLEDGMENTS

I AM very grateful to my parents, who introduced me to the joys of traveling in Europe —as well as of gardening—in early childhood.

So many people have contributed suggestions for this book that it is difficult to list them all. May I extend very special thanks to Miss Elizabeth C. Hall of the New York Botanical Garden for reading the entire manuscript and checking all botanical names. Also to the following experts who so kindly spent some of their valuable time in making special lists of historical gardens for me: Mr. J. M. de Casseres and Mr. C. Sartori of the Netherlands Ministry of Agriculture, and Jonkheer Dr. H. W. M. van der Wijk of the Netherlands Government Service of Ancient Monuments; the Marchese Giuseppe Roi of Vicenza, Italy; and Professor Francisco Caldeira Cabral, President of the International Federation of Landscape Architects, Lisbon.

In Europe, the following have been most helpful in making suggestions and taking me to gardens: Belgium: M. René Pechere, landscape architect. England: Miss Marion Jennings of the British Travel and Holidays Association, also Mr. D. L. Harmshaw of the same organization in New York City. France: Mme. Beaupere of the French Horticultural Society; and M. and Mme. René Lauret. Germany: Herr

Direktor Encke of the Palmengarten, Frankfurt; Herr Horst Hammler and Frl. Elizabeth Goering of the German Gardens Association; Herr Friedrich Kockerols of Hannover; and Herr Hans Schirmer of the German Central Tourist Association. Holland: Mr. G. C. Miga, and Mrs. J. J. van Ortmeerssen. Ireland: Mrs. J. Cooper-Foster of the National Trust Committee for Northern Ireland. Norway: Mr. Per Wendelbo of the Botanical Garden, Bergen. Portugal: Mr. Francisco José Gentil Berger. Scotland: Ilay Campbell, Esq.; Sir Angus Cunninghame Graham and Mr. J. E. Robson of The National Trust of Scotland; and Lady MacMillan of Langbank. Spain: Dr. L. H. Arnaud, former Cultural Attaché of the U.S. Embassy. Sweden: Mr. Tor Nitzelius of the Botanical Garden, Gothenburg. Switzerland: Dr. Werner Ness. Wales: Mrs. M. R. Nicholls of the Northern Wales Horticultural Society.

Among the people in the United States who made suggestions or showed me their pictures of European gardens, I would like to express my appreciation to: Julia Berrall, Dr. Benjamin Blackburn, Marget Cochrane Cole, Mrs. Leonard H. Colville, Mrs. Willam M. Cooper, Raymond M. Dinsmore, Mary Anna Heile, Mrs. Helen Hull, Mrs. Herbert E. Ives, Joseph Junkin, Mrs. George Kennan, Alice Dustan Kollar, Mrs. Ezra Laderman, Mrs. Charles MacFarlane, Mr. and Mrs. Alfred Mausolff, Mrs. A. J. Mautner, Harriet K. Morse, Margaret Perry, Mr. and Mrs. Hermann G. Place, Mrs. Edward W. Roessler, Mrs. Ruth Smiley, Mrs. Donald B. Smith, Mrs. C. L. Snowden, Jr., George Taloumis, Leon Washington, Beryl Webb.

I am grateful to Dr. Frederick G. Meyer for his bulletins.

Finally, this book could never have been written without the generous people who share the beauties of their grounds with others, so I give my sincere thanks—to people who have gardens!

DOROTHY LOA MCFADDEN,
MENDHAM, NEW JERSEY.

CONTENTS

HOW TO USE THIS BOOK

*T*HE gardens of Europe vary widely in character from country to country. That is one
reason for reading this book: to study the kinds of gardens
available, and then decide which you would enjoy most. If
you are a flower lover, don't go to the formal green gardens
of France or Italy, but select those in countries that offer
really colorful bloom. If you are interested in trees, in my
lists are arboretums that will charm you. If you are studying
landscape design, there are many famous examples for you
to see.

In making the selection of gardens for this book, I have
arbitrarily omitted what is often called "the landscape garden," introduced in England during the 18th century and so
enthusiastically copied all over Europe that many gardens
that would have been historically interesting were destroyed
in the process. These landscape gardens are what we would
call parks—vast expanses of lawns, trees, lakes, so artfully
designed that they look as if nature had planted them, although actually the hills, valleys, and lakes are man-made.
There are only a few examples included in this book. Otherwise I have chosen to concentrate on the formally designed
garden, the informal flower garden, or, in the case of public
parks, only the areas given over to specialized gardens, such
as plantings of roses or iris, or rock gardens.

In the descriptions of gardens, I have only occasionally referred to their history, their former owners, or their designers. You will find this information in the books listed in "Suggested Reading About European Gardens." Before taking any conducted garden tour, or while planning your own trip to Europe, do plenty of reading in advance.

You will, of course, be using other guidebooks for information about the sightseeing in each place. My personal favorites are the books by Fodor and those by Sidney Clark. Use these also in selecting hotels and restaurants. I have mentioned a few here and there that I happen to have enjoyed particularly, or that have lovely gardens.

I have traveled in Europe since I was a child, and have specialized in visiting gardens during some twelve months of travel in the last five years, taking color slides for lectures to garden clubs. While planning these trips, I found that the information I needed about kinds of gardens to see, hours of opening, people to get in touch with in order to see them, directions for reaching them, was so scattered and difficult to find that I realized a book was needed to help other garden lovers plan their trips more easily. The kind of information that I have wanted and found lacking is gathered together in this book. Here is what you will find:

COUNTRIES

You will find separate chapters describing many gardens, for most of the countries of Europe. In the cases of Austria, Belgium, and the Scandinavian countries, however, you will find the gardens listed and described only in the "Key to Gardens," except in a few cases where they fitted into the chapter on "Follow Your Garden Hobby Abroad," or the chapter about "Flower Shows."

In trying to locate gardens by using road maps, I found that some of the smaller places where the gardens are located could not be found. Since most tourists would be going to such smaller towns by car, and using the regular road maps, I decided to list these gardens at the nearest town that *is* found on such a map, indicating how far this is from the actual garden. For example, in the "Key to Gardens," you will find Rousham House listed under "OXFORD (near): 12 miles north off route 423 at Steeple Aston," because Steeple Aston is not on most road maps, but Oxford is easy to find.

As you read the chapter about gardens in each country, you will find a town name, as well as the garden name, in italics. These are the names to look for in the "Key to Gardens" and in the Index.

KEY TO GARDENS

This is a listing of gardens open to the public in each country, including the days and hours and best seasons for visiting. You can look them up here either by town or by the name of the garden. If there is a page reference, this refers to a longer description in one of the chapters. The lists are also keyed for easy selection of gardens with various specialties—roses, alpines, etc. The size of the garden or number of plants is mentioned as often as possible, to give you an idea of how much time you might want to spend there. The most important or interesting gardens of each country are marked with a "bullet" (•).

WHEEL TOUR

This is a name I invented for an easy way to visit gardens. You stay in the "hub" town at the center and radiate out from there, like the spokes of a wheel, to other gardens within a thirty-mile maximum radius, traveling by car, bus, or train. During my own travels I have found that the way to save one's energy was to stay in each place at least three days (or even longer), if possible. This gives you a feeling of relaxation and saves the wear and tear of constant packing for one-night stands. *You will find Wheel Tours listed at the end of each country, in the "Key to Gardens," and marked on the maps.* Since not all gardens are open daily, you will probably not be able to see *all* of those included in one Wheel, but can make a selection. Choose them from the "Key to Gardens," selecting them by days open, best season, and their appeal for you.

MAPS

The maps in this book are really charts, planned for use with regular road maps. The towns having gardens are given in their geographical relation—to each other, to key cities, and to the hubs of Wheel Tours. Use them together with the "Key to Gardens" to plan your tours.

EXPLANATION OF SOME GARDEN TERMS

You will find some of the following terms, used by landscape designers and garden historians, throughout this book:

KNOT GARDENS: Victorian flower beds, designed in patterns like embroidery, sometimes called "mosaiculture."

PARTERRE: A level garden, usually designed to be seen from the house, divided geometrically, the design made by low clipped hedges and colored sand or gravel, occasionally brightened by flowers.

TOPIARIES: Clipped shrubs, usually box or yew, in geometrical shapes, or even simulating animals, people, or furniture. (See

 xii

chapter on "Follow Your Garden Hobby Abroad" for more details.)

ORANGERIES: Glasshouses, or rooms, where the potted orange trees and other tender plants are wintered over.

For other and more detailed explanations, see the Shell Garden Guide (listed in "Suggested Reading About European Gardens").

A WARNING

Please remember that the days and hours when gardens are open may change from year to year, so it is always wise to check with your hotel porter about changes in garden-visiting regulations before going any distance. Use the annual listings and other sources that I have suggested under "Useful Information" at the end of each chapter, to get up-to-date data. Watch out for local holidays, as these affect garden openings. Even the plantings in the gardens may be changed quite readily, or the garden may suddenly no longer be open to the public. Please remember the possibility of such variations!

chapter 1

GARDEN TOURS OF EUROPE

*F*OR the tourist who has been "doing" the indoor attractions of Europe, garden-touring is a refreshing contrast. Walking on earth or grass paths is delightful after maneuvering over cobblestones and sidewalks. In the cool north you will welcome the warmth of sunshine; in hotter climates, revive in the deep shade of old trees. If you are traveling with children, here at last there are areas where they can roam about outdoors.

Best of all, a love of gardens brings strangers together quickly. If you know the Latin names of plants, even a difference in languages will not keep you apart, as you identify your favorites with fellow tourists.

If you are a garden club member, be sure to find out about the services offered by your federation, or the projects sponsored by it abroad that you might see. The Garden Club of America, for example, has a "Visiting Gardens" card available to its traveling members, which admits them to certain private gardens not otherwise open to the public. A courtesy service is also offered to certain foreign visitors wanting to see gardens in America. There is an Interchange Fellowship for English students of horticulture, sponsored by this organization, and a slide service for members, such as the set of pictures of American gardens given to the Museum in Bath, England.

The National Council of Garden Clubs has a World Gardening Committee. This is the outgrowth of a letter-writing project, sponsored by former President Eisenhower's People-to-People Program, to bring together garden lovers throughout the world. I am still corresponding with and visiting some of the people in Europe whom I first met by answering a few of these letters. Various clubs, through the World Gardening Committee, have sent flowering trees and plants to other countries. One traveling member made a gift of seeds and a flower-arranging calendar to FLARE (Flower Arranging in Europe) on the occasion of its first flower show in Frankfurt, Germany. Slides of American iris were sent to Florence, Italy. Other traveling members have served as judges or exhibitors at English flower shows, representing the National Council.

There are many ways in which you as a garden club member can promote friendship among peoples of other nations, if you will keep your eyes open as you travel about and be ready to tell of your organization's activities and interests. Take along sample copies of your club program to show, your federation yearbook, and such aids to foreign visitors coming to America as the National Council's booklet, *Your Invitation to Visit American Gardens,* which lists all those open to the public. As you meet your fellow gardeners abroad this way you can form lasting friendships.

Everywhere you will find ideas to adapt to your own garden at home. Whether you want to study the over-all design, the shapes of flower beds or pools, the color combinations, or the individual plants, if you choose your country right, you will have a wonderful time. If you like gardens, you will never be bored, no matter how many you see, for no two are alike. Your main problem will always be one of selection. Wherever you go for other sightseeing, you will be able to fit in a visit to a nearby garden. Or you may want to plan an entire trip to one or more countries with gardens as the main feature. If you prefer conducted tours, there are a number of these to choose from that feature gardens. They are listed at the end of this chapter.

If you have some flower specialty that you would like to follow around Europe, read the chapter on "Follow Your Garden Hobby Abroad" for suggestions. If you are interested in formal landscape planning, go to France or the Italian villa gardens. But avoid those if your passion is flowers, for they are rather severe green gardens; book a tour through England, or one at tulip time in Holland, instead.

Another important consideration in garden-viewing is the time when you make your trip, particularly if you can make a choice. Study the "Key to Gardens" listings to find out when to see flowers at their best. At the end of almost every chapter, I have listed tourist offices and other sources, under "Useful Information," to which you can write in advance for help in planning your trip.

Think, also, about the weather and temperatures you prefer. During winter the entire Mediterranean coast is a mecca for flower lovers. Even farther north, there are some warm pockets where gardens are lovely very early in the spring or in late fall: on Lago Maggiore in Italy, for example; or the islands of Brissago, belonging to Switzerland; or even the island of Mainau, in Lake Constance, south of Germany. Cornwall and the Scilly Isles are the warmest spots in England. And there are flowers in bloom at Inverewe, in the north of Scotland, in February—but I doubt whether you would brave that region then unless you are a rugged type. In the Canary Islands, however, the best season of all is from November to June.

Now let's consider the advantages and disadvantages of three kinds of garden tours.

The Dovetailed Tour: On this type of tour, you simply fit gardens into your regular sightseeing whenever possible. Use the "Key to Gardens" at the back of this book to find out what gardens are available in or near the towns and cities on your route. Refer to the maps to find out what Wheel Tours might be possible, seeing gardens from one central point, radiating out in all directions. Or use the maps to take in gardens along the way when going from one point to another. Do lots of reading and map-planning before you start, for it is always disappointing to find out, after you come home, that you missed a lovely spot nearby just because you didn't know it was there.

You will also have to send for some of the booklets, mentioned at the end of many chapters under "Useful Information," that give up-to-date information as to when gardens are open. Otherwise you will be frustrated by turning up at a locked gate on the wrong day. The disadvantage of a "dovetailed tour" is that you may have little time for gardens when too much else has been planned, and that those you would enjoy most do not fit the itinerary. But with careful planning you can see many fine gardens in this way, as I do on my husband's rather tightly organized business trips.

The Individually Planned Garden Tour: If you are planning a tour with friends who also enjoy visiting gardens and who have no fixed appointments to fit in, you will have a glorious time. Study this book to decide which gardens all of you would enjoy most. Consider the season of the year, and days when the gardens are open, before making up a tentative schedule. Then take this framework to your travel agent, who will help you with transportation, distances, hotels, and other details. Allow plenty of time for each garden, for the great advantage of a personally planned tour is that you need not feel rushed.

Try to stay as often as possible in a comfortable hotel in

the "hub" city of a Wheel Tour, so that you can return to it every night. This is much more restful than unpacking and settling in a different hotel each night. If you rent a car to drive yourself, or employ a driver, it will make your tour very flexible. But it is perfectly possible in any country to work out ways to see many gardens if you travel by bus or train.

Don't be afraid to tour alone. I have traveled all over Europe by myself, including Russia, with no difficulties whatsoever. The great advantage in traveling by yourself is that you can stay as long as you wish or move on when you feel like it. Talk to fellow tourists, and especially to all the local people you meet, and you will never be lonesome. You will find many a kindred soul while looking at gardens.

The Conducted Garden Tour: Many people prefer booking a "package tour" from an agency, since all planning, transportation, baggage handling, and tipping is then taken care of by the courier. A number of tours of this sort go to the gardens of Europe. Some of these trips are listed below.

Before settling on such a tour, study the agency's literature carefully, with your own preferences and habits in mind. Consider first of all who is leading the tour. It should be, and usually is, an expert horticulturist, landscape architect, or other garden specialist. If the leader comes from a botanical garden, you will be given very expert and detailed information about the plants in each place. If it is a landscape architect, you will hear all about the history of each garden and how the different owners added to or subtracted from it through the years, and you will learn a great deal about the designing of gardens. Some couriers are particularly interested in the architectural details and sculpture of historic gardens. Others are full of interesting information about trees. Be sure of your own interests and try to select the right tour to reconcile with them. If you go with one of the

English-led groups listed below, learn the Latin names of plants and flowers before you go, or take along a handy reference list, for the British use only botanical names in identification.

Perhaps most important of all is a study of the tour schedule to see whether it fits your pace of travel. A garden tour entails a great deal of walking. Are you prepared for this? On a conducted tour you will have to keep up with a large group of tourists who may want to stay a longer time in each place than you do, or on the other hand, may want to rush through it too quickly to suit your taste.

If you are an ardent shopper or browser, is there enough unscheduled time allowed for such pastimes, and does that fall during shopping hours, or on Sundays and holidays when stores are closed, as one of my friends discovered on her tour? How much time is allowed for sleep, or for breakfast? If you don't like to be hurried, don't go on a conducted tour at all, for schedules are usually strictly observed.

The great advantage of a conducted tour is, of course, that all travel details are taken care of by someone else, and all costs can be figured in advance. You need do no planning, no worrying about transportation, baggage, or tipping, what hotel to stay in, or where to eat. If you are at all timid about traveling, this is the solution.

Another advantage of conducted tours is that the agencies are able to arrange for visits to many private gardens that you could not otherwise see, and for lectures and luncheons with the horticultural experts of other countries. Most important of all, you will have a guide with you at all times to tell you the history of each garden, to point out special features, and to identify plants.

The following list of tours from which you might choose is only a sampling; a check with your travel agent will always bring you up to date. Also, tours change from year to year, and new ones always come into being. Since I have not gone on the tours that follow, I cannot endorse them through personal experience, but am simply listing them for your investigation, to show what is available.

If you are a member of an organization such as The Garden Club of America, The National Council of State Garden Clubs, or a state Horticultural Society, you will find European Garden Tours that they sponsor offered in their monthly bulletins. Others are organized by garden magazines or individual garden lecturers.

CONDUCTED GARDEN TOURS FROM THE UNITED STATES TO EUROPE

JEAN BERKE TRAVEL SERVICE, INC., 518 Fifth Ave., New York 36, N.Y.: Currently this agency is offering its fifteenth series of annual garden tours led by horticultural experts. There are six different tours, some of which can be taken consecutively: one to Portugal, Spain, and Italy; another to Holland, Belgium, France, and England; another to the British Isles; another to Scandinavia and Germany; another to Central Europe, including Liechtenstein; and, lastly, a Mediterranean Art and Garden Tour.

LINBLAD TRAVEL, INC., 1 East 53rd St., New York 22, N.Y.: This agency is currently offering a five-week garden tour, led by a horticultural expert, to Scandinavia.

WILLIAMS WORLD TRAVEL LTD., 75 East 55th St., New York 22, N.Y.: Garden tours arranged for and sponsored by The Garden Club of America. Their latest tour covers England and Wales. Each group led by a horticultural expert.

CONDUCTED GARDEN TOURS THAT START IN EUROPE

Arrangements for taking these can be made in advance by mail.

From England

BRITISH RAILWAYS, 630 Fifth Ave., New York 16, N.Y.: One-day tours to Holland at tulip time, from London and return.

ERNA LOW TRAVEL SERVICE LTD., 47 Old Brompton Rd., London S.W.7, England: Garden tour of England; also Alpine Flower Enthusiasts' Tours to Austria and Switzerland to see the wildflowers blooming in the mountains.

GALLEON TOURS LTD., Eccleston Court, Gillingham St., Victoria, London S.W.1, England: Seven-day garden tours of England and Wales, some of them led by garden experts.

HAROLD INGHAM LTD., 15 St. John's Rd., Harrow, Middlesex, England: Garden tours led by horticultural experts, to European Garden Exhibitions, to the Italian Lake Region, etc.

HISTORIC HOMES AND GARDEN TOURS LTD., 39 Beauchamp Place, London S.W.3, England: Special garden tours around London or throughout Great Britain, for large groups in buses or for a few tourists by private car with or without driver and guide. Can include private gardens not open otherwise.

PANORAMA HOLIDAYS, 161 Church Rd., Hove, Sussex, England: Four-day excursions to Holland at tulip time, from London and return.

YACHT HOLIDAYS LTD., 85 Buckingham Palace Rd., London S.W.1, England: A choice of cruises on modern motor ships lasting 5–10 days, to Holland and the bulb fields, in April and May.

In France

FRENCH HORTICULTURAL SOCIETY (Société Nationale de Horticulture de France), 84 rue de Grenelle, Paris VII, France: Write to Mme. Beaupere (an Englishwoman) for information about joining the Society and participating in short garden tours.

In Ireland

NATIONAL TRUST, NORTHERN IRELAND COMMITTEE, 82 Dublin Rd., Belfast, 2, Ireland: Annual membership of $5.60 entitles you to participation in a number of garden tours of Northern Ireland and in the Republic of Ireland.

ROYAL HORTICULTURAL SOCIETY OF IRELAND, 16 St. Stephen's Green, Dublin, 2, Ireland: Membership in the Society, $3 annually, will enable you to participate in garden tours of Ireland.

In Scotland

The National Trust for Scotland, 5 Charlotte Square, Edinburgh 2, Scotland: Annual membership of $2.80 makes you eligible to participate in many excursions to gardens and castles in Scotland; also in the exciting ship cruises that visit private gardens on the coast and islands of Scotland or Ireland each year.

Scotland's Garden Scheme, 26 Castle Terrace, Edinburgh 1, Scotland: Special bus tours to castles and gardens, particularly during the Edinburgh Festival in August.

In Switzerland

Any Travel Agent can book you for one of the "Gardens of Switzerland" tours. This is a six-day tour beginning in Geneva and ending in Zurich, and can be arranged for two people or larger groups. The tour includes visits to gardens in Geneva, Montreux, Rochers-de-Naye, Interlaken, Schynige Platte (or castles of Schadau and Oberhofen), Locarno and the Islands of Brissago, and Zurich. Details of the tours are available from the Swiss National Tourist Office, 10 W. 49th St., New York 20, N.Y., but arrangements must be made through a travel agent.

chapter 2

FOLLOW YOUR GARDEN
HOBBY ABROAD

RAVEL with a special purpose in mind can be much more interesting than an aimless tour of many countries. If you enjoy gardening, pick out the places where you can see the flowers and plants that interest you most. The "Key to Gardens" at the back of this book is keyed with just this idea in mind. If you are interested in flowers, choose the gardens marked **f**; if trees are your passion, find the ones keyed with **ar**, for these include arboretums and estates with exceptional appeal to the dendrologist. For the serious plant student, botanical gardens are marked **b**; rose gardens are marked **r**; and so on.

ROSES

A whole tour of Europe might be built around its fine rose gardens. Try to plan a rose tour for June. Not that you would see only roses on your trip; there are many great historic houses and castles adjoining these gardens that you would also want to see. The cities in which some of the best rosariums are located also have many fine art galleries, museums, cathedrals, and other goals for your sightseeing.

If you write in advance to the Horticultural Societies in Paris and London (see chapter on "Flower Shows in Europe"), you can plan your tour around the dates of the big Rose Shows there. By consulting the tourist offices of the countries concerned, you can also find out the times when roses are judged in national and international competitions; these go on in The Hague, Holland; Baden-Baden, Germany; Geneva, Switzerland; Rome, Italy; Madrid, Spain; Lyon, France; and one recently was inaugurated at the Château de Roeulx, in Belgium.

France has always been particularly fond of the rose, and there are some beautiful rosariums there. Perhaps the most exciting one in all Europe for the rose fancier is the garden of *L'Hay-les-Roses,* on the outskirts of *Paris,* (pronounced "lay-lay-rose," but write it out for getting directions!). This was begun as a small hobby garden by Mr. Jules Gravereux, one of the founders of the Bon Marché department stores in Paris, when he retired to the country. At first he planted only a small rose garden in his grounds, with a few of the best-known varieties. But as his enthusiasm grew, he began to build his collection by corresponding with every rose grower in the world, and in 1899 he had a special garden designed on his grounds, with the shrubs grouped around statues and climbing over pergolas.

Soon even this garden became too small, and other sections were added, so that today you will see there the most comprehensive rose garden anywhere in the world. You will find a botanical collection of wild roses; a History of Roses in living plants; a group of the old roses of the Orient; all the roses grown by the Empress Josephine, in her garden at Malmaison; a collection of the old Polyantha roses; new introductions developed here at L'Hay-les-Roses; and all the modern varieties. You could spend a long time looking at the documents, books, and pictures in the Museum of the Rose, which tells of this flower in art and industry. If you pick the right day, you may even see a play, with the rose as its theme, presented in the little Theatre of the Rose. After Mr. Gravereux died, his heirs kept up the gardens for some years; then in 1936 they were turned over to the City of Paris, Département de la Seine. They suffered much damage in World War II, but have been restored, and you can still see some 4000 varieties of roses there today.

The roses in the gardens of *Bagatelle,* in Paris, are also justly famous. This is described in the Paris section of the chapter on "France." The French city of *Lyon* has been a mecca for the rose enthusiast for the last century, for it was here that the first Polyantha rose was developed, and a number of other famous roses originated with the growers of this area. You will see three very fine collections of roses in the famous *Parc de la Tête d'Or* (named for a legendary golden head said to be buried here, which has never been found). One is the collection of wild roses and interesting hybrids, 1200 in all, in the botanical garden section; nearby is a small semicircular rosarium in which the annual competition takes place for the best French rose; and the third is the new international rose garden, opened in 1964.

This last is a large park area with modern, natural landscaping, featuring a long pergola. The roses have been planted in groups of 100 to 500, in beds running along the pergola, down the sloping lawns, and bordering a little brook. You will find beds of perennials here and there, and rockgarden plants combined with miniature roses. If you want to get some ideas for the use of roses in other than formal beds, this is the place to study. Or if you wish to look at a great variety of types, the 70,000 rosebushes—among them 331 varieties developed in France—should certainly satisfy you.

In the *Musée Rodin* in *Paris* you will find a wonderful rose garden, as well as many other rose gardens marked **r** in the "Key to Gardens" under "France."

In Belgium you will see a rose garden, in the city of

Ghent, which is a fine example of international friendship. In the *Parc de la Citadelle,* adjacent to the exhibit halls used for the famous Belgian flower show, the "Floralies" (see "Flower Shows in Europe"), you will find a rose garden that was originally planted by France for the 1913 World's Fair. The French government continued to keep up this garden for many years. After it was badly damaged in World War II, the French and Belgian rose fanciers got together to rebuild the garden and have been cooperating in its care ever since. Another fine rose garden may be seen at *Bellecourt.*

In the chapter on "Holland," you will find descriptions of the many lovely rose gardens in The Hague. Others are described in the chapter on "Germany," where the ones in *West Berlin,* at the Island of *Mainau,* at *Zweibruecken,* and at *Frankfurt* are particularly outstanding. The little town of *Uetersen,* near Hamburg, is in the center of the rose-growing region, and boasts a very lovely rosarium in the park, nurtured by the German Rose Society. Other German rose gardens will be found in the "Key to Gardens." If you should be going to *East Germany,* don't miss one of the most famous rose gardens in the world, at *Sangerhausen.*

The city of *Geneva,* in Switzerland, is proud of its many parks and gardens. One of these is the large rose garden in the *Parc de la Grange.* This was developed after World War II, partly in an effort to stem the rising tide of unemployment. Beginning in 1944, men were hired by the city to lay out the grounds and plant some 12,000 shrubs of 180 varieties of roses. The garden lies within a beautifully landscaped park, with the deep-blue waters of Lake Geneva as a foreground, the snow-crowned Alps looming behind. It is a fairyland picture at night when it is artificially illuminated, and makes an exquisite stage setting for occasional plays that are presented in the rose garden itself—dramas written around the theme of this favorite flower.

The municipal rose garden of *Rome* is described in the chapter on "Italy"; there is a fine one described under "Portugal" at the Crystal Palace in *Oporto*, and one in *Madrid*, in the chapter on "Spain."

Heading north now on our rose tour, we will come first to *Copenhagen*, Denmark. You will find a new rose garden here in the *Valby Park*, southwest of the city near the coast. You enter through a pergola covered with climbers and come to a circular garden surrounded by hedges, with grass paths. There are 11,800 rosebushes here, including 3200 of the Polyanthas and 300 climbing varieties. Nearby you can see the trial gardens where Danish growers are testing various types for suitability to this climate.

There are so many lovely rose gardens in the British Isles that it would be impossible to list them all. Those in the parks of *Aberdeen*, Scotland; *Regent's Park, London; Roath Park*, in *Cardiff*, Wales, are particularly famous, as are those of the Botanic Gardens of *Kew* and *Wisley*, in the *London* area. If you are particularly interested in old-fashioned roses, which are becoming so popular again, go to *Sissinghurst Castle, Greys Court, Cothay Manor, Snowhill Manor*, or *Newby Hall*, in England. For tree roses, see the collection of 2000 at *Prestwood Hall*. At *Chilham Castle*, in *Canterbury*, you will find an enormous Banksia rose about 140 years old. At *Bayfordbury*, in Hertfordshire, you will see more of the old roses, and also the National Collection of Rose Species. If you want to see still more, look under the **r** markings in the "Key to Gardens" at the back of this book.

ALPINE PLANTS AND ROCK GARDENS

If you have a rock garden at home and are particularly interested in alpine plants, you will find many places in Europe where you can pursue this hobby. From the end of May into June, you can see wildflowers blooming on the mountains and in the high meadows of Austria, France, Italy, and Switzerland. In May, you will find a great abundance and variety of flowers blooming in the Oberinntal district of Austria, near the Italian border; and in summer, in the Grossglockner Pass of Austria, between Lienz and Zell am See. In the higher reaches, these flower as much as two months later than they do in the lowlands. You will find many varieties of campanula, achillea, ajuga, cyclamen, dianthus, myosotis, ranunculus, Alpine roses, and much more, all growing in mixed bouquets of delicate color schemes.

There is a group tour offered by an agency in England (see chapter on "Garden Tours of Europe") that goes to parts of Austria and Switzerland for the express purpose of seeing alpine flowers. If you like to hike, go to the village of *Zernez,* in Switzerland, and ask at the Hotel Langen when groups are scheduled to go into the Swiss National Park to see the mountain flowers, especially lovely in June. Another such area of botanical interest is *Ben Lawers,* in *Scotland* (see chapter on "Scotland").

There are also a great many botanical gardens with alpinums, and special alpine gardens, which you will find under "Austria," "Italy," and "Switzerland" in the "Key to Gardens," marked **a**, and many rock gardens in other countries similarly marked. The *Jardin des Plantes* in *Paris* has a special section called the "Jardin Alpin," near the Jussieu station of the Métro, with a wonderful collection of plants from the Alps, the Pyrenees, the Himalayas, and even the North Pole. This is open daily from 2 to 5 P.M. The *Botanical Garden* at *Lyon* has some 2000 varieties of alpine plants, including many very rare specimens. This is open daily from May to October. Another interesting garden in France is the *Biological Station and Alpinum* (Station Biologique et Alpinum) in the high Alps. This is located at an altitude of about 6000 feet at the *Col du Lautaret,* which can be reached by car from Grenoble or Briançon about 54 miles distant. This is open from mid-June through September, but the best time to see the flowers is in July. You will find 3000 alpine plants here, among them some of the rarest in the world. There is also a fine collection of mountain plants in the botanical garden and alpinum called *"La Jaysinia"* near Samöens, northeast of Lyon.

One of the biggest and most beautiful alpine gardens in the world is *"Floralpe,"* at *Lac Champex,* Canton of Valais, in Switzerland. You can reach this in forty minutes by car from Martigny, along the road to St. Bernard. Or you can get there on the train that goes from Paris to Milan via Lausanne. This lovely place is 4500 feet up on Mont Blanc. The flowers are at their best in June and July. You will see about 5000 alpine plants from all the mountain ranges of the world, planted in a beautifully arranged rock garden that seems like part of the natural scenery. Some of the plants here have been cultivated for the first time. Some are still unclassified, others are new hybrids, and many are rare in Europe. The pride of the garden is the collection of primula, the most important private aggregation in the world, some 90 species including varieties from China, India, Nepal, Tibet, and other areas of the Himalayas. There are a number of new, unnamed varieties of meconopsis, the beautiful blue poppy, from Tibet. You will see about ten different species of alpine orchids. Be sure to look at the many lath-covered frames where the seedlings are raised, including a wonderful collection of sempervivums. You will be amazed how much there is to see in this two-acre alpine paradise.

Another very lovely place is the *Alpine Garden* (Alpengarten), at *Schynige Platte,* in Switzerland. You can reach this by cogwheel railway from Wilderswil near *Interlaken.* It is located 6,494 feet up on the mountain, with superb views of the Alps, and is open from mid-June to end of September. The height of bloom comes from the end of June to early July, and as in all these high-altitude gardens, you will find that the strong ultraviolet rays of the sun have intensified the colors, as well as developed exceptionally large plants. This garden includes many different types of soil, from the most acid to a chalk base, so that you can study the plants here in relation to their needs and their native habitat. They are Swiss flowers that grow at various altitudes, and many of them have been traced to the days before the Ice Age, when they traveled southward with the glaciers, then gradually grew their way up the mountains again as the ice melted. If you grow rock-garden plants from any of these lovely flower-families—aquilegias, primulas, azaleas, gentians, thistles—you will have a fascinating time seeing their high-altitude relatives here.

In Italy, too, you can visit some exceptionally interesting gardens specializing in alpines. "*Paradisia*" at *Valnontey-Cogne* in Aosta province is part of the national park Gran Paradiso. It lies about 5100 feet high near Cogne, which you can reach by bus or train. Then it is only about a mile and a half to the alpine garden. This is at its best in June and July. Here you will find the flowers that grow all over the western Alps. At *Stresa,* not far from Lago Maggiore, you will find *"Alpinia,"* easily reached on the highroad from town, with many plants native to the Alps. It features some 2000 small plants and over 1000 shrubs. This is a fascinating place from May to September, with something always in bloom. You can also enjoy a splendid view from here of the lake and the mountains.

At *Gardone Riviera,* near Lake Garda, in Italy, you can visit the private garden of Dr. Arturo Hruska, at *Villa Hruska.* This is an outstanding rock garden, planted in a setting of natural cliffs fifty feet high. Here you will see a wonderful collection of plants from the Alps, the Pyrenees, and the mountains of Asia.

In Germany there are also two very interesting gardens devoted entirely to alpine plants. In the suburb of Wuerm south of *Pforzheim,* not far from Stuttgart, you will find an *Alpengarten.* If you are driving, stop at the charming little inn, Gasthaus zur Post, in Wuerm, for a lunch of the local noodle specialty called "Spaetzle"; the waitress will show you which path to take to the garden. This is quite a steep ten-minute climb. If you have passengers who cannot make it, drive up the motor road with them, but as there is not parking space above you will not be able to stay long. The garden is arranged geographically, with alpine plants from all over the world, selected for their beauty and for their adaptability to home gardens. There are over 5000 varieties, and you will see something in bloom at any time. The finest display is in May, when the pink alpine roses (a form of tiny rhododendron) are in flower, as well as the gentians, mountain pinks, and hundreds of other bright little blossoms. June is another colorful month here, with alpine pinks, campanulas, iris, broom, and many others at their height. The famous cottony edelweiss flower blooms in July, as do varieties of lavender, asters, and astilbes. In August you will find many different heathers.

A German alpine garden more difficult of access is the *Alpinum* on the Schachen Mountain, between *Garmisch* and Mittelwald. If you like mountain climbing, it will take you about four or five hours to reach it from Castle Elnau in Klais, for the garden lies at an altitude of 5600 feet. The road is not too good, but the scenery is glorious, with high peaks above you, the dark green forest below. One ardent plantsman made the trip by Jeep from a hotel in Kruen, but admitted it was a hair-raising experience. There is a good inn near the garden, where you can get meals and a rest, and stay overnight if you wish. The garden is open only from July first to September, as it is buried in some nine feet of snow the rest of the year.

For anyone truly interested in studying the plants growing at high altitudes, this particular Alpine Garden is most rewarding. You will find a collection of some 2000 species from the Arctic, North America, the Carpathians, the Pyrenees, the Caucasus, the Himalayas (a particularly fine group), as well as those native to central Europe, all arranged geographically. You will see many flowers in a glorious blue that seems taken from the sky itself. There are Aquilegia alpina, Veronica bonarota, and gentians, from central Europe; other aquilegias, from the Caucasus; Meconopsis grandis, from the Himalayas; a dwarf delphinium, from Bhutan; as well as brilliant blossoms in many other colors.

If you prefer being on lower ground and staying in the more usual tourist centers, you can still see many lovely rock gardens; the one in the *Botanical Garden* of *Berlin-Dahlem* (see chapter on "Germany") is exceptionally interesting. The rock gardens at both *Kew* and *Wisley* in the *London* area have superb collections of plants, but you may not like the ugly, rather overpowering stones, that look like square building blocks, from which these gardens are constructed. In *Hascombe Court*, at *Godalming*, Surrey, you will see a large rock garden as well as many other flowers. The most famous and unusual rock garden in England, perhaps, is that of *Highdown*, in *Goring-by-Sea*. Here you will find a water garden around a pool below a chalk pit, beautifully planted for a long season of bloom. Beginning with the snowdrops and daffodils, the flowers continue in bright procession, the peonies, eremurus, lilies, iris, roses, and cyclamen being particularly outstanding. This garden will give you many ideas if you have alkaline soil in your own garden at home.

In the *Botanical Garden*, at *Edinburgh*, Scotland, you will see a famous rock garden, one of the largest in the world, specializing in plants brought from western and central China.

If you are fond of heathers and brooms, do go to Ireland and visit some of the private gardens around Belfast (see chapter on "Ireland").

Whatever country you wish to travel in, you will find rock gardens to visit if you check the "Key to Gardens" for those marked **a** (for alpine).

CACTI AND SUCCULENTS

Perhaps you have been specializing in cacti and succulents on your sunny windowsills at home, or you prefer traveling in warm climates, or you like to take refuge from bad weather in a tropically heated greenhouse as often as possible while you are traveling. Any of these reasons could lead you to plan a rewarding tour of Europe with cacti and succulents as the central theme.

If you want to wander around in the warm sun and examine the many desert plants with their strange shapes and brilliant flowers, one of the best places to begin would be in the *Exotic Garden* of *Monte Carlo,* where there are more than 6000 varieties. (See end of chapter on "France.") Another famous collection (described in the chapter on "Spain") is the garden of *Pinya de Rosa* at *Blanes* on the Costa Brava of Spain, in which you can study the cultivation of cacti from the seedbeds to their final great size and height.

You can follow this hobby even farther north, for in *Zurich,* Switzerland, strangely enough, you will find the collections and showplace of the International Succulent Society (*Staedtische Sukkulentensammlung;* address, Mythenkai 88), housed in seven greenhouses and a display case outdoors. You can buy an illustrated catalog of all the plants there. This exhibit is open throughout the year, and contains some 4500 different succulents from thirty-two plant families ranging across the world. The *Jardin des Plantes* in Zurich also has some fine big specimens. The *Botanical Garden* of *St. Gallen* has 800 varieties of cacti and succulents, among many other fine collections.

Still farther north, at *Kiel,* Germany, you can see a very

famous collection in the *Botanical Garden of the Christian-Albrechts University,* at Duesternbrookerweg 17. If you understand German, take the guided tour on Tuesday or Friday, between 1 and 5 P.M. You can study some 2000 varieties of succulents here, mainly from Africa, including some cissus plants that are 500 years old. The *Botanical Garden* at *Heidelberg* has a good collection of succulents from Madagascar and South Africa.

In England, visit *Worfield Gardens,* at *Bridgnorth,* in Shropshire, to see a tremendous collection of cacti and succulents. Check on the days and hours for visiting in the booklet, *Historic Houses, Castles and Gardens* (see end of chapter on "England"). Here you will find desert plants from America, Mexico, and Africa, in colored dioramas showing their natural habitats. In addition you will see a good collection of bonsai, the dwarf trees from Japan and China. You will find many cacti and succulents also in the tropical gardens of *Tresco Abbey,* in the *Scilly Isles* (see chapter on "England"). The *Jardin des Plantes* in Paris has some 17,000 varieties in one section of the garden. If you will look in the "Key to Gardens" for the listings marked **c** for cacti and **g** for greenhouse, you will find a number of other places in every country where you can follow this hobby.

CLEMATIS, DAHLIAS, FUCHSIAS, IRIS

We could not possibly list gardens for all the flowers in which you might be especially interested. Here are just a few suggestions that will lead you to some very lovely gardens in which these are featured:

Clematis: Don't miss the collection of 120 different varieties at *Burford House,* in *Tenbury Wells,* Shropshire, England.

Dahlias: The most extensive dahlia show in Europe is probably that in the special arena at *Gruga Park,* in *Essen,*

Germany, where you will see thousands of varieties. The Island of *Mainau,* in Germany, also features this flower in late summer. In Switzerland, you can visit the annual Dahlia Show at *Unter-Enstringen* near Zurich, held in September and October. If you are going to France, where this is one of the favorite flowers, see the Dahlia Test Gardens at *Sceaux* (Seine), *Selestat* (Bas-Rhin), or *Viry-Chatillon* (Seine-et-Oise), or the annual Dahlia Show at Vincennes. There is also a fine display of dahlias in the Jardins des Plantes, in *Paris,* in late summer.

Fuchsias: See the lovely specimens, the educational display, and the instructions for cultivating fuchsias at home, in the *Royal Floral Hall* at *Rhyl,* Wales (see chapter on "Wales").

Iris: In England, there are especially lovely iris gardens at *Kew* and *Wisley;* the *Savill Gardens* at *Windsor;* the *Harlow Car* trial gardens near *Harrogate,* where both the bearded and Kaempferi varieties are tested for hardiness in a northern climate. *Cassiobury Park* in *Watford* (Herts) is famous for its iris, as are *Holland Park Gardens* and the *Royal Park of Richmond* in *London.* There are iris test gardens at *Orléans* (Loiret), in France. In Germany, you will find very lovely iris gardens in the *Planten un Blomen* park of *Hamburg;* and the display gardens of the Bavarian Department of Agriculture (*Bayrische Landesanstalt fuer Wein-Obst-und Gartenbau*) at *Veitshoechheim* near Wuerzburg. Probably the most famous and beautiful garden of all, however, is the *Iris Garden* at *Florence,* Italy (see the chapter on "Italy").

WATER PLANTS

If you have a brook or pond area at home that you want to develop with further plantings, look at the charming gardens at *Annesgrove* and *Mt. Usher,* described in the chapter on "Ireland." For the waterlily enthusiast, I would certainly recommend a visit to *Burnby Hall* at *Pocklington* (Yorkshire), in England, where you will find nearly sixty varieties in the great ponds, planted for color effect, all in bloom at once during the summer. Check the booklet, *Historic Houses, Castles and Gardens* for days and hours of admission (see end of chapter on "England"). You will see many other gardens having formal pools, or brooks and ponds, marked **w** in the "Key to Gardens." If you are planning to make a formal pool, you will be able to sketch many shapes from the gardens in France, Italy, and Spain.

TOPIARIES

Just for fun, if topiary amuses you as it does me, you might tour the gardens of England, particularly, to see the many fantastic shapes. *Levens Hall* at *Kendal* (see chapter on "England") is perhaps the most famous garden of this type, but there are a great many more, marked **t** in the "Key to Gardens." You can even find one in Germany at *Aschendorf*, in the north (see chapter on "Germany").

Among the most comical topiaries I have seen are those at *Mt. Stewart* in Ireland (see chapter on "Ireland"), where there is an Irish harp, a boat with the family riding in it, and a whole parade of animals clipped into the tops of the hedge, all made of Monterey cypress. In Italy, at the *Villa Sciarra*, in *Rome*, you will see very intricate topiary designs of twisted spirals, birds in handled baskets, and others with long tails.

Perhaps you have wondered, as I have, how the gardeners have developed these remarkable topiary figures. Many of them are trained on wires. To make an arch, for example, two trees of the right height will be tied together with wire at the top, the upper branches trained from then on until they meet in the center. To make the fascinating spiral shapes, a heavy stake is driven into the ground against the trunk of a young tree; as it grows, the branches are wound around and around toward the top and constantly clipped of new growth to make them thicker. If you want to make a peacock, fasten two wires to the trunk of a young tree to serve as bases, one for the neck and head, the other for the tail, and keep training the branches over these.

The art of topiary, or "bush barbering," as some have irreverently named it, goes back hundreds of years. Pliny the Younger described the clipped hedges in his Tuscany garden. From Rome, the custom spread to the Far East, to Spain, to France, and finally to England, where topiaries became a tremendous fad. Eventually they became a great subject of controversy, for there were many who made fun of these fantastic, artificial garden figures, to such an extent that the custom died out and many topiaries were destroyed. Fortunately for the garden historian, and for those of us who simply enjoy seeing them, there are still many to be found in the British Isles. If you are a photographer, you will certainly find them a fascinating subject as you travel around.

These are only a few of the garden hobbies which you could follow around Europe. If you will follow the key letters and study the descriptions in the "Key to Gardens," you will find many more subjects that might interest you— ride your hobby and have fun!

chapter 3

FLOWER SHOWS IN EUROPE

*T*HERE are so many flower shows held all over Europe throughout the year that you would be traveling constantly if you tried to see just the majority. You could begin the year in San Remo, Italy, in January, and visit a show somewhere every month after that.

Write to the organizations and tourist offices listed at the end of this chapter for the dates of flower shows that might fit into your trip.

The flower shows of Europe are of two different kinds. There are the horticultural exhibits, where the display is mainly indoors, and emphasis is on recent plant introductions, exhibited in competition by amateurs and commercial growers. The other type is like a great new park, or addition to an old park, which is kept blooming from May to October. Examples of this were the International Horticultural Shows held in Hamburg, in 1963, and in Vienna, in 1964, and the German Flower Shows, which take place in different cities every third year. In some cases you will find indoor exhibits as well as some outdoor demonstration gardens.

Here is a sampling of some of the flower shows you could visit in each country.

Belgium: This is a country with a long tradition in the growing of ornamental plants. Nearly 60 percent of the tuberous begonias, for example, that are imported into the United States come from here. The Indian azaleas grown here are famous throughout Europe. The first flower show ever held on the Continent took place in the city of Ghent in 1809. The Ghent Floralies, held every five years, is one of the finest shows in Europe. Running in 1965 from April 24 to May 3, it has exhibits from many countries. The big Citadel Park has been turned into a vast garden for this event, and the indoor exhibits are in the new Sports Palace. Even when there is no Floralies exhibit in the park, it is well worth visiting for its fine rock garden and rose garden. South and east of Ghent, you can see the house plants grown in acres of hothouses, great fields of azaleas in spring, and begonias in summer.

Denmark: On the island of Funen, about the middle of May, the growers show some 350,000 tulips in Langesø Park, west of Odense. In Jutland at Ribe, about mid-May, a Tulip Festival is celebrated by decorating the houses with tulips and other spring bulbs. In Copenhagen, during the first week in November, you can visit a Horticultural Show featuring chrysanthemums, in the Three Falcons Exhibition Hall.

England: Probably the finest flower show from a horticultural standpoint is the great Chelsea Show, which you can visit for four days in May each year in London. Since every man, woman, and child in England is a gardener at heart, it seems as though everyone on the "tight little island" has converged on these tents for the occasion, and it is sometimes impossible to see the flowers for the people. But if you go early, as soon as the doors open, on the third or fourth day of the show, you will have at least an hour of wandering in comparative solitude, with a chance to take notes and do some photographing. This is the place to study the newest varieties of delphinium, the latest colors in gladioli, or whatever flower you are most interested in. The flower arrangement competition is also completely fascinating. There are usually some outdoor gardens to see as well.

The Royal Horticultural Society, which presents this tremendous show, also offers the public a splendid series of fortnightly flower exhibits in its halls on Vincent Square, London. These begin with house plants in February and end in October with the Great Autumn Show. Many other towns and villages in Great Britain, Ireland, Wales, and Scotland have horticultural exhibits through the year.

France: The second "Floralies Internationales de Paris," in 1964, exceeded in scope and excitement anything done in French flower shows before. Some twenty nations participated, many with actual gardens created in the vast twenty acres of space available in the Palais de la Défense. All exhibits were planned to conform with a general design, so that there was unusual unity of effect, with simulated housefronts as backgrounds, and a series of canals and pools, so that visitors forgot that they were in a building. There was an orchid garden with a rushing waterfall, a tropical garden from South Africa, and others from Monaco, Colombia, and the Ivory Coast. Tahiti displayed thirty-foot coconut palms, and the British showed some of Queen Elizabeth's own orchids.

At Versailles, from the middle of April to the middle of May, there are glorious floral displays with night illumination. At Valenciennes there is an enormous Floralia show each year with international exhibits, under the auspices of the French National Horticultural Society. The same Society also sponsors specialized flower shows throughout the year in Paris. In Rouen, you can see a beautiful Chrysanthemum Show every two years, the even-numbered years. Saverne has a Rose Show and Parade (Corso) in mid-June; Selestat, a great Dahlia Show and parade of floats in August; Provins, a large Horticultural Show in September every two years, on the even dates; and there is an annual one at Rueuil-Malmaison in October. Wherever you go in France, from spring to fall, you should be able to find a flower show for your enjoyment.

Germany: The German Garden Shows (Bundes Gartenschau), which take place in a different city every other year, are quite different from any of the other national shows of Europe, and certainly from anything you can see in the United States. They are planned not merely as a six-month horticultural exhibit for visitors from all over Germany, but as the means of creating a permanent new park, or an extension of an old one, in a city that needs more recreational space for its citizens.

Thus the city of Dortmund, in the smoky coal-mining Ruhr area, acquired the beautiful Westfalenpark through the German Garden Show of 1959. In 1961, Stuttgart's garden show extended the area of its Killesberg Park. And in 1963 the show, which this time was international in character, enlarged and greatly enriched the plantings of the park Planten un Blomen, in Hamburg.

The German Garden Shows are run by an organization of commercial growers, including vegetable farmers, together with the selected city. Costs are met entirely by the city in which the show is held (the 1961 affair, for example, cost some ten million marks), but the income from ticket sales and the shopping and housing of millions of visitors brings a considerable immediate return on the investment.

The plants used in the displays, usually covering about 100 acres, are contributed by nurserymen. At the end of the show, the city buys as many as are needed to maintain the grounds as a public park.

Though American tourists still seem to be unaware of the wonderful attractions of these exhibitions, the Germans themselves attend by the millions. In Stuttgart, for example, 151,000 season tickets had been sold by the time the Garden Show had been open a month, tickets that would bring the same visitors back over and over again until the last chrysanthemum had been enjoyed at the end of October. Practically every garden club in Germany expects to attend such shows in a body, going in chartered buses or special trains. The railroads buy up some 100,000 Garden Show tickets to sell to visitors, as do a great many factories for the benefit of their employees.

And what will you see at such a German Garden Show? You will find an extensive, flower-filled park, no matter whether you go in May, when the thousands of tulips are in bloom, or later on when these have been replaced by annuals, dahlias or chrysanthemums, set in at their blossoming best. You will see demonstrations of small home gardens of every type; exhibits showing how to build paths, how to fertilize, what kind of fences or garden tools are available. You also can walk into small sample houses, such as the Germans place in their rented patches of land where they can spend the weekend close to the soil. (See chapter on "Germany.")

You will find water gardens, rock gardens, Japanese gardens, rose gardens—every imaginable flower specialty in its own area. These shows not only create new parks, they are primarily designed to instruct the owners of small home gardens in everything they might need to know. Each plant is carefully labeled, and there are libraries and picture exhibits on horticultural subjects that you can study. Experts are on hand to consult. When you get tired of wandering around among all this beauty and educational material, you will find secluded areas with benches and lounge chairs designed for quiet relaxation. Children are amply taken care of, with modern playgrounds for various age levels. You will be able to eat at a number of charming outdoor restaurants, or sit in the evening listening to a concert while you watch the synchronized play of illuminated fountains.

The 1965 German Garden Show will be held in Essen, the one for 1967 in Karlsruhe. Don't miss these delightfully different flower shows.

Holland: Every visitor to this charming little country tries to go at tulip time to visit the beautiful flower show at Keukenhof, where the commercial growers display their newest varieties in a park setting. An International Narcissus Show is held in Haarlem in April, and there are many small local shows in various cities in the late summer and early fall. (See chapter on "Holland.")

Italy: There are two flower shows that are particularly interesting here. One is the show in the middle of January at San Remo, which is staged around a central theme each year, such as "Plants and Flowers in the Home." Every iris enthusiast will also want to see the big show and competition in the Iris Garden of Florence (see chapter on "Italy").

Switzerland: You can enjoy a "Camellia Festival" in April and a "Flower Festival" in May, in Lucerne; "Rose Week" in Geneva and in Weggis, in June; and a "Dahlia Show" at Unter-Engstringen, near Zurich, in September to October. Although these are not like the big national flower shows, they are delightful occasions, with fine displays of their specialties. There are also the Swiss Horticultural Shows, held in the big cities at irregular intervals. The first of these was in Zurich in 1959.

International Horticultural Exhibitions: These are held on the Continent at irregular intervals. They are very similar to the German Garden Shows in that they are mainly parks

Flower Parade, Holland (*Anpfoto, Amsterdam*)

developed for future permanent use, with most of the flowers growing outdoors, but the exhibits are prepared by many countries. There was a very fine one held in and around the Planten un Blomen park in Hamburg in 1963, and the largest one ever put together was at Vienna, Austria, in 1964. One of the unusual features at Vienna, which attracted a great deal of attention from horticulturists, was a vertical "tower greenhouse" with potted plants circulating up and down on moving belts, the interior carefully regulated for air, sunlight, and humidity. There is always much to see and learn at the European flower shows. Before planning a trip, be sure to get specific dates for these exhibitions from one of the following sources:

BELGIUM: *Belgian Tourist Bureau,* 589 Fifth Ave., New York 17, N.Y.

ENGLAND: *The British Travel Association,* 680 Fifth Ave., New York 19, N.Y.; *The Royal Horticultural Society,* Vincent Square, London S.W.1, England.

FRANCE: *The French Government Tourist Office,* 610 Fifth Ave., New York 20, N.Y.; *Société Nationale de Horticulture de France,* Madame Beaupere, 84 rue de Grenelle, Paris VII, France.

GERMANY: *Deutsche Gartenbau-Gesellschaft e.V.,* Frl. Elizabeth Goering, Koelnerstr. 142-148, 532 Bad Godesberg, Germany. (Also for information about International Horticultural Exhibits.) *German Tourist Information Office,* 500 Fifth Ave., New York, N.Y. 10036.

HOLLAND: *Netherlands National Tourist Office,* 605 Fifth Ave., New York 20, N.Y.

ITALY: *Italian State Tourist Office,* 626 Fifth Ave., New York 20, N.Y.

SWITZERLAND: *Swiss National Tourist Office,* 10 W. 49th St., New York 20, N.Y.

INTERNATIONAL HORTICULTURAL SHOWS: See Germany, above.

chapter 4

PHOTOGRAPHING GARDENS

HETHER you photograph gardens just for your own pleasure, as a record to show your friends, or for lectures to garden clubs as I do, you surely want to get the best pictures possible.

Of course the ordinary techniques of good photography apply to any specialty: knowledge of your camera's possibilities, choice of correct film, familiarity with special lenses, care in focusing and composing each picture, and so on. Photographing gardens does have some aspects, however, that need a little thought and study.

My suggestions are based on my own experiences and those of my husband, who takes as many garden pictures as I do, and who is our family specialist in black-and-white. These ideas fall into three categories: General suggestions about photographing gardens; gardens in black-and-white; gardens in color.

I. GENERAL SUGGESTIONS

1. DEFINE YOUR PURPOSE: Since you want to photograph gardens, you surely enjoy them yourself—but what is it that you particularly like? Good pictures should express your own

personality. Otherwise you might as well buy postcards, or let someone else take them. What is your particular interest in gardens? Do you like roses best of all? Then give much of your attention in each garden to that flower, with close-ups, so that you can explain the habits and beauties of each variety. Is garden planning your big interest? Then photograph the garden from many angles, showing the paths that lead to a center of interest, the way the garden looks when observed from a height. If you are a tree specialist, pick out the important ones in the garden; show their height compared to a person standing nearby; get a close-up of the bark and leaves. In other words, don't take pictures of "just another garden." Show what interested you most in each.

Or, if you wish to take a less personal approach, try to photograph the features of this garden that make it different from any other. What are its special charms? Is it historically interesting, or Italianate in type, or does it contain a fine collection of one species of shrub? Is it restful? Dramatic? Meant for wandering? Of interest to botanists? Then build your photographing plan around these characteristics.

For practice, before you make your trip, you may want to photograph a series of gardens around one interesting theme. You could take your own or your neighbors' flower beds at various seasons, going back to the same spots each time. Or you might take pictures of gardens in your region open to the public. Such specialization makes for a very interesting album or slide show.

As a final suggestion for those taking pictures to show before clubs, I would like to say this: it is not fair to bill as a "garden lecture" a series of travel slides with only two or three garden pictures thrown in here and there. On the other hand, a program showing only one garden after another, no matter how lovely, can become very monotonous. I try always to insert bits of the countryside, interesting people I saw along the way, even a little sightseeing on the side, if time permits. This breaks up the garden program very nicely, and adds a local flavor—a setting for the area in which you saw these gardens. But it must be done with restraint.

2. TAKE PLENTY OF TIME: To take good pictures, you should not be hurried. Wander around the garden first to get an idea of its size, its outstanding features, the best angles from which to shoot. Then start your photographing, one area at a time, and use plenty of film so that when you get home you can select only the best pictures.

3. USE A STORY-LINE: Try to take your pictures so that whoever looks at them later will feel he has been in the garden, too. First of all, is there a Title Picture you could take, like the sign on the gate with the owner's name—or the garden's, if it is a public one? Is the gate interesting enough to shoot, with a tempting view of the path you are about to enter? Next try to get a picture of the entire garden, if necessary with a wide-angle lens. Now you are ready for medium shots of paths with flower beds, or trees and shrubs from a little distance, or a statue or fountain halfway down. The telephoto lens will narrow the field and fill the picture with a single attractive feature. Finally you can take the close-ups (which so many garden photographers neglect), giving one a detailed look at certain flowers, a piece of sculpture, the tiles around a fountain. If you have a portrait lens, by all means use it for very close pictures of particularly lovely flowers or an interesting leaf. These are the shots that draw a real response from your friends or members of the audience when you show them. They make the onlooker feel he has been right there in person.

4. CONSIDER THE WEATHER: If it rains and you want to take black-and-white pictures—don't. Postpone the trip, for you need sharp shadows. But with modern color film you

can take delightful pictures in a soft rain or a mist. High Speed Ektachrome is the best for these, but I have had good results in Kodachrome also. Have someone along to hold an umbrella over the camera—never mind if *you* get wet!—and try for close-ups showing drops falling down the leaves, or a distant "mood" shot of part of the garden revealed in a mist. If you do have full sun, use a sunshade, if possible, as your best angle may often be shooting right into the glare. Be sure to read your light meter when you are standing out in the open—not in the shade of a tree—and point it at the garden, not taking in too much sky, or you will get wrong exposures. If it is a gray day, a fill-in flash may help you to get close-ups of a flower under a bush. Wind is the great hazard in photographing a garden, and for this the only answer is very fast film and fast shutter speed, and avoidance of close-ups or tripod shots.

5. FIGURE YOUR ANGLES: Never take a garden path head-on, or a square flowerbed facing the exact center. Plan your shots to get interesting compositions, varied angles. It is amazing how many different ways one can photograph the same garden. With two of us doing it together, wandering each his own way, we have never yet had duplicate pictures. Use front or side lighting whenever possible, but don't miss the chance to get the sun shining through a blossom or leaf, by blocking the sun from your lens with a tree or a friend or by using a sunshade. Always try to break up the foreground somewhere when taking a long view, with a large plant or tree branch. Frame your pictures in this way either above or below for real artistry. A plain lawn or pathway makes a dull foreground.

6. FIND A CENTER OF INTEREST: In photographing gardens there is a great temptation, especially when using color film, to forget that each picture must have its own focal point.

Just taking a mass of bloom to show that it *is* a mass is not enough. The flower border must have an outstanding group of plants in the right spot. There must be something at the end of the path worth looking at. A really fine garden will offer you many such vistas and plenty of architectural details, for these are inherent in good landscape design. I can tell as soon as I begin to photograph a garden whether the underlying plan is good, for I will be tempted to stop every few minutes to shoot another view. If you will take time to study the pictures in any well illustrated book about gardens, such as those listed in the chapter on "Suggested Reading About European Gardens," you will find that every place has some definite center of interest, usually architectural: statuary, a summerhouse, a bench, a pigeon-cote or the like.

7. INCLUDE HUMAN INTEREST: It is good to see people once in a while in or around your garden pictures. Not that you want to photograph just when a bus tour has disgorged its passengers and they mill about in your foreground, heaven forbid! But one visitor looking closely at a flower; a gardener at work; the back of a person going through a gate; or portraits of the owners of the garden—all these add the human touch that is so necessary. Some of our most delightful pictures show a dog trotting along the garden path, or a cat asleep on top of the wall, or a peacock preening on the lawn. I was much amused at Warwick Castle, in England, to see two amateur photographers competing for the same picture of a peacock: one had a movie camera and wanted the bird to walk; the other was taking still pictures and kept waiting for the creature to stand still!

8. PHOTOGRAPHING TREES AND SHRUBS: These are difficult to do in color, even more so in black-and-white, for the leaves tend to mass in an uninteresting lump. (A stereo camera is the best solution here.) If you want to show a

particular specimen tree it must stand by itself or else have a very contrasting background to mean anything. Trees that have leaves or needles of different textures can be pictured together if one gets close enough. Shrubs with variegated or light-colored leaves show up well, and blossoming bushes are not difficult. Remember, however, that such flowers and leaves are too small to mean much in a long-shot photograph. Get as close as possible, and take detail shots of individual twigs of foliage or bloom. Whenever you want to indicate size, use a person or a nearby object for contrast. The clipped yews and topiaries so popular in old English gardens are very decorative in photographs, but they must be silhouetted against a light background or sky, or accented with very sharp morning or late afternoon shadows.

9. PHOTOGRAPHING WATER: If there is a pool or pond of any kind in the garden, or a running brook with plantings along the edge, take advantage as much as possible of the reflections in the water. If the surface is too flat, toss a pebble in to get interesting ripples. If it is a well-designed garden, such water interest will add a great deal to your picture story, with flowers and shrubs breaking up the edges of even the most formal designs. Otherwise use an overhanging branch or a figure at a little distance for framing or a focal point.

10. PHOTOGRAPHING FLOWERS: Many of the suggestions above apply to taking good pictures of blooming plants—the need for contrast, the appeal of close-ups. If you are recording a rose garden, for example, don't take only pictures of pink blossoms—get as much variety in color or form as possible, bushes, climbers, tree roses, and so on. If you can get a picture of a bee or butterfly on a flower, so much the better.

11. TAKE PLENTY OF NOTES: Nothing is more embarrassing when showing pictures of a garden, even to one's friends,

than being unable to name the flowers or plants. Keep a detailed notebook, writing down the names of anything you might not recognize yourself when the picture is developed. Also keep a record of the size of the garden, name and address of the owner, which are his own favorites among the plants. Find out where some flower originated, or the greatest number of blossoms that the proud possessor counted on a tree in one year, or anything else that will liven up your story when you show the pictures. Perhaps you have a phenomenal memory and do not need to jog it in this way. Personally, I find keeping a notebook absolutely essential, especially when seeing a number of gardens in succession.

12. EDIT RUTHLESSLY: When you get all your pictures finished and have looked at them yourself, begin to go over them to pick out the ones that would really interest other people. Don't hesitate to throw away any substandard shots —out-of-focus views, dull pictures with no point of interest. Keep as much variety in the series as possible, and then rearrange the order to tell your story in logical sequence. More picture albums and slide showings have been ruined by lack of editing than perhaps by any other single factor.

13. PHOTOGRAPHING GARDENS IN EUROPE: The home gardens in all countries abroad are now acquiring the same modern features because of the influence of books and articles on garden design. You will find the stone terrace or patio, the sunbathing area, the pool, attention to spaces for outdoor living, whether you are in Germany or England, for example. The great trend today is toward the use of shrubs—which need little care—rather than many flower borders.

The great public gardens, however, that you want to photograph during your travels still show distinct national and historical characteristics that have various advantages or disadvantages for the taking of pictures.

English Flower Gardens, with their mixed borders, are excellent subjects for color photography, difficult for black-and-white. Topiaries in the old gardens are excellent for either, but need sharp shadows or bright sky background.

French Formal Gardens show up best in black-and-white, because of their geometrical design. Be sure to shoot pictures from a height, even if only from a bench, to show the pattern of tiny hedges, the bedding plants, and the whole general plan.

Holland's Home Gardens along the canals, or tulip beds reflecting in water, are most effective for photography, as are barge loads of flower blossoms.

Italian Gardens are often on hillsides, offering fine views from both above and below, and vistas to photograph from different levels.

Spanish and Portuguese Gardens consist mainly of potted plants in patios, hanging baskets or pots on walls, vines covering buildings.

In all the European countries don't forget to photograph the boxes of flowers at windows of houses, hotels, and factories, even on railings of bridges, and on lampposts. Also remember the little rented patches of ground for gardens outside the towns.

II. BLACK-AND-WHITE PICTURES

When taking these, you are concentrating on contrast and form, instead of color. If the garden is full of flowers, it is difficult to realize this. Try to think only of the shapes and of dark and light masses. You must visit the garden in the early morning or late afternoon on a sunny day, to get the sharpest contrast of shadows. I am speaking now only to amateurs like myself; a professional will be able to get fine-quality prints even on a foggy day, but this is very difficult in garden photography.

Remember that a plain clear sky in a black-and-white picture is uninteresting. Try to go when there are clouds to break it up, or else shoot low enough to minimize the amount of sky shown. The suggestions I made previously about photographing trees or shrubs are doubly important if you are not using color. Remember in shooting flowers that white ones will show up well, as will light yellow and orange. Green and red will photograph with very similar values, as will a medium blue. Dark blues and violets will come out very dark. It is important to consider these color-value relationships in working for contrast in your pictures. A bright purple flower that you liked may not show up at all if the green leaves near it have the same values.

The great advantage of black-and-white photography is the latitude of results in printing and enlarging. You and your camera shop can tone down or brighten the prints, trim out unwanted parts, make each one as perfect as possible.

III. COLOR PHOTOGRAPHS

Whether you are making prints or slides, in this medium you can let yourself go in recording the colors of a garden. Just remember that your camera can be selective, and you need not take a picture showing two flowers that clash with each other. You can pick out the best color schemes, concentrate on the most pleasing combinations of light and dark, avoid the ugly background when necessary.

When you get your pictures back from processing and have edited the whole series to select the best, look each one over carefully to see what trimming can do for the prints, or masking for the slides. It is amazing how much one can improve one's pictures by leaving out an obtrusive bench, or a flower that is out of focus at the bottom, or the extra people that wandered into your scene. If you want to be really proud of your pictures, be critical and see how you can improve them. You may be an expert at composing a perfect picture in your view-finder. Most of us see some faults that need to be corrected later.

Do take lots of pictures of gardens, if you enjoy seeing them, so that you can sit down with the results on a snowy winter night and have the fun of living the whole experience over again.

USEFUL INFORMATION

There are two useful booklets on travel photography, available at camera stores:

YOUR TRAVEL PICTURES, published by Eastman Kodak Co., Rochester 4, N.Y., price 75¢ (see brief section on Gardens, Flowers and Parks).

VACATION AND TRAVEL PHOTOGRAPHY, by Aarons, published by Amphoto, 915 Broadway, New York, N.Y. 10010. Distributed by Grosset & Dunlap, Inc., price $1.

chapter 5

SUGGESTED READING ABOUT
EUROPEAN GARDENS

EFORE you plan a trip to Europe including visits to gardens, spend some time reading about those you will see and looking at pictures of them. If you are not expecting to travel, but like to read about gardens, these fine descriptions by landscape architects and other horticultural authorities will make you feel as if you were really seeing the gardens in person. Many of these books go into some detail regarding the history of each garden, who designed it, and the festivals or other events that have taken place there. When visiting gardens abroad, be sure to buy the booklets sold at some of the entrances, as these give the history and often list the plants you will find there.

I am also listing here some magazines that will bring you accounts of visits to famous gardens in Europe, as well as articles of practical interest to the home gardener.

Books published in England may be ordered through the British Book Centre, Inc., 122 East 55th St., New York 22, N.Y. Those published in France can be obtained from La Maison Rustique, 26, rue Jacob, Paris VI, France.

The only out-of-print books I have listed are some that

could be found in any American public library with a good garden collection.

HISTORY OF GARDENING

The story of gardening through the ages and information about the various garden designers of Europe can be found in innumerable books, too many to list here. I will only mention two of my favorites:

MEN AND GARDENS, by Nan Fairbrother (Knopf, 1956, $5)

THE STORY OF GARDENING, by Richardson Wright (Dover paperback, $2)

EUROPE IN GENERAL

GARDENERS CHRONICLE, weekly publication ($8 a year from Gardeners Chronicle, Printing House Square, London, E.C.4, England). An excellent magazine for the practical gardener, with frequent articles describing visits to famous gardens throughout the world.

GARDENS AND PEOPLE, by Fletcher Steele (Houghton Mifflin, 1964, $4). A charming, intimate account of the author's visits to gardens throughout the world, his thoughts, opinions, and philosophy. Excellent analyses of the essential qualities that make the gardens of England, France, Italy, and Spain different from any others.

GARDENS OF WESTERN EUROPE, Handbook #33, edited by Frederick G. Meyer (Brooklyn Botanic Garden, 1000 Washington Ave., Brooklyn 25, N.Y., 1960. $1). Brief descriptions of some gardens in fifteen countries, with many black-and-white photographs.

GREAT GARDENS OF THE WESTERN WORLD, by Peter Coats (Putnam's, 1963, $22.95). The most beautiful garden book you could wish for, with 40 color plates and 350 black-and-white. Written by an authority on gardening and landscape architecture, the text is scholarly in its research, delightful in its historical anecdotes. Includes history and description of the finest gardens in England, France, Germany, Holland, Italy, Portugal, Spain, and Wales.

LES JARDINS À TRAVERS DU MONDE, by Jacqueline de Chimay. (Hachette publishers, Paris, France, 1962, $4). A lively account, full of chuckles as well as information, of this well-known French horticulturist's visits to gardens in ten sections of Europe. In French.

GREAT BRITAIN

ENGLISH GARDENS OPEN TO THE PUBLIC, by A. G. L. Hellyer (Country Life Press, London, 1956). Out of print. Beautiful black-and-white photographs and captions describing 144 gardens, of which 53 are open to the public at some time, today. Includes Bodnant, in Wales.

GARDEN OPEN TODAY, by Beverley Nichols (Dutton, 1963, $4.95). An enchanting account by this beloved garden writer of his own garden in England, to which he invites the public if these are people really interested in gardening. Decorated with exquisite line drawings.

INVEREWE, A Garden in the North-west Highlands, by May Cowan (Geoffrey Bles, publisher, London, 1964, $7.65). A delightful account of how this great Scottish garden came into being and grew to its present beauty. With 31 illustrations, most of them in color, and a map and guide to the garden.

JOURNAL OF THE ROYAL HORTICULTURAL SOCIETY, a monthly publication sent to members. (See "Useful Information" at the end of the chapter on "England.") Excellent articles of practical interest to the serious gardener, and occasional very detailed descriptions of famous gardens in Great Britain.

THE ENGLISH GARDEN, by Edward Hyams. (Thames & Hudson, London, 1964, $17.50 plus 35¢ postage). A superb picture book with 188 large plates, 17 of them in color; text tells the history of gardening in England from its beginning with Roman times through today. Includes histories of many of the best British gardens open to the public in England, Ireland, Scotland, and Wales.

THE GARDEN OF THE ROYAL PARK AT WINDSOR, by Lanning Roper (Chatto and Windus, London, 1959, $13.50). 45 color plates and 59 black-and-white photographs, with fascinating descriptions by this eminent garden authority.

THE SHELL GARDENS BOOK, edited by Peter Hunt (Phoenix House, London, 1964, $4.50). With 12 color plates, 120 black-and-white photographs, and 38 line drawings. An excellent guide to the gardens of Great Britain—their historical development and great designers, their characteristics—and the British gardening societies. The "Brief County Guide" at the back unfortunately gives no hint as to which of the gardens described are open to the public; out of 432 gardens listed, about 200 are not open even once a year.

ITALY

GARDENS OF ITALY, by Frances Margaret McGuire (M. Barrows and Co., 1964, $4.95). A personal account of visits to 22 of Italy's most beautiful gardens, with vivid, detailed descriptions. With 13 black-and-white photographs.

GARDENS OF ROME, by Gabriel Faure (Nicholas Kaye publishers, London, 1960). Out of print. 168 black-and-white photographs with a running commentary, originally published in French.

GIARDINI D'ITALIA, by Fiorani (Edizioni Mediterranee, Rome, 1960). Interesting photographs of Italian gardens, some open to the public. In Italian. Obtainable in Italy.

I GIARDINI DI ROMA, by Dr. Elvezio Ricci (published by the Department of Parks, or Servicio Giardini, of Rome). Descriptions of many gardens in Rome. In Italian, with photographs. Obtainable in Rome.

ITALIAN GARDENS, by Georgina Masson (Thames and Hudson, publishers, London, 1961, $18). A gorgeous big book with 211 black-and-white plates, two in color, and six maps. The history of gardening in Italy, and a detailed account of the beginnings and development of hundreds of gardens all over Italy. A scholarly horticultural study, but full of human interest, bringing the stories of the various gardens to life. Includes a list of plants grown in Italian gardens.

THE VILLA D'ESTE AT TIVOLI, by Coffin (Princeton University Press, 1960, $17.50). A detailed description of the designing of this garden, the construction of the famous waterworks.

SPAIN

THE ALHAMBRA, by Washington Irving, first published in 1832. Good to read before visiting this famous place. Editions available at any library.

chapter 6

IRELAND AND ITS
SUBTROPICAL GARDENS

*Y*ou can see much of the beautiful scenery, famous spots, and historical sites in Ireland by visiting its outstanding gardens. We did this—and returned with happy memories of rolling green hills, edged with endless stone walls bursting with ferns and flowers and topped by brilliant yellow gorse (or "furze"), and dramatic vistas of rockbound mountains, among which nestle charming villages.

But most of all, we remember the lush subtropical trees and flowers on the estates we visited. In Ireland, you will be astonished to find palms and tree ferns that you'd usually associate with the tropics. The combination of much soft rain and mist with the proximity of the Gulf Stream makes this country a near-paradise for gardeners. The only problem is to give plants sufficient shelter from the bitter winds of winter.

We began our tour in May, which was recommended to us as the month with the least rain during the flowering season (and we had only two days of it), circling from our starting-point, Cork, to Dublin.

For a shorter trip, you could visit only the many lovely

gardens immediately around Cork, Belfast, and Dublin, and have a good sampling of Irish gardens in their glory.

You will find that the Irish love to talk. My husband discovered that the first morning he went out photographing in Cork. He asked a man on a bicycle the name of a building, and they had a half-hour chat. The Irishman, pausing on his way to work, recited some of his own poetry and told an old fairy tale. This could happen only in the Emerald Isle. Wherever we went to visit gardens, we found the owners or caretakers equally friendly.

From Cork, you can circle out to visit many beautiful estates. Go first to *Fota House* and gardens at *Cobh,* owned by Major and the Hon. Mrs. Bell, where you will see a magnificent collection of rare trees and shrubs from all over the world. Telephone Mrs. Bell at Cobh, when you arrive, for permission to visit (look up her number in the telephone book).

You will see here gardens over a hundred and fifty years old. To enter, you go up a long flight of stone steps, at the head of which is a fine old cedar of Lebanon that you pass as you step onto the lawn. As you wander over the grass, probably trying not to step on the little wild yellow primroses that are naturalized everywhere, you will feel as if you are touring the world. You will find California nutmeg in one spot; in another a Cryptomeria japonica (var. spiralis), some forty feet high, which in China is used to make chopsticks. There is a fine specimen of Rhododendron sinogrande, which after thirty years has just come into bloom and is covered with creamy yellow blossoms with dark spots. There are exotic trees from Australia, Chile, Japan, and elsewhere, that you can spend endless time studying, if trees are your passion.

The plant and flower lover will find an enclosed garden, with a Paulownia platanifolio and a Monkey Flower (Mimulus glutinosus) among the tender plants growing on the walls with other choice treasures, and a thriving little grove of tropical tree ferns, sheltered from the winter winds by many tall conifers.

From Cork, go north to *Castletownroche,* where you can visit *Annesgrove Gardens,* a National Trust property owned by Mr. R. G. Annesley, whom you should write or telephone in advance for an appointment.

The gardens at Annesgrove sprawl over two levels, running along an upper road and down to a riverbed below. As you walk along on the high ground you see glowing in the woods beside you splendid rhododendrons, and exceptionally lovely azaleas that Mr. Annesley raises from seed, among them some particularly fine shades of blue. Nearby, you'll come on a very tall Pieris Forrestii, with new leaves as red and brilliant as our poinsettias. This is quite different from the orangey young growth on our familiar Pieris japonica.

On your left, pause to see the brick-walled gardens. There is a cutting garden on one side in which Mr. Annesley has a rare flower any gardener would envy—the double sweet rocket, which is so difficult to keep. Opposite is a delightful rock garden with a gentle hill behind it covered with heathers in purple and white, pale-yellow broom, and a Berberis, whose stems are a solid mass of double orange blossoms.

Beyond the rock garden you come to a lawn with flowering cherries and an old sundial, from which a path leads to a rustic summerhouse. You can spend much time enjoying the flowers in this peaceful garden.

From here, walk down one of the steep paths leading to the River Awbeg below; there are banks of heather and azaleas on each side, and occasionally a wild anemone. At the bottom, you find flowering cherries spreading their branches over the quiet water near a small weir; clumps of bamboo are nearby, with tall primulas blooming below them. Farther on, masses of lupine, astilbes, and other flowers brighten the shoreline. You can sit on a bench to contemplate this loveliness before you cross a small rustic bridge and go round the house back to the road.

The property has been in the Annesley family since 1606, and it was here that Edmund Spenser wrote his *Faerie Queene*.

From here, drive north a short way to see the prizewinning garden of the Mitchellstown Technical School. The Irish Tourist Board holds a national contest each year to encourage the beautifying of roads most used by travelers. The gardens must be visible from the highway, and prizes are given in many classifications: Community Gardens, Private Gardens, National Schools, Colleges and Technical Schools, Petrol (gas) Stations and Garages, Police Stations, Railway Stations, Hotels and Guest Houses, Thatched Cottage Gardens, and Industrial Premises. Awards of money and certificates are presented to the best in each category in every county, and they arouse great excitement and rivalry. Be sure to obtain a copy of the latest list of prizewinners (see address at end of this chapter) and enjoy as many as possible along your route.

The Technical School at Mitchellstown has won the award for its rose garden, which is why we went there. But to see the garden in all its glory, go there during July or August. Or choose autumn for the dahlia display. It is cared for entirely by the students—boys and girls aged thirteen to seventeen.

If you drive east of Cork, you'll find the unusual gardens at *Mt. Congreve,* near *Waterford,* planted for spectacular display during any season from spring through autumn. Eighteenth-century brick and stone walls enclose four acres here. One garden is planted for May, June, and July bloom. In another, flower borders over half a mile long are planned for color in August and September. In another spot, Michaelmas daisies burst into masses of bloom in September and October. The gardens are wired for music.

Outside the walls you find woodlands with many fine rhododendrons, magnolias, spring-blooming shrubs, and interesting specimens of trees. You'll also discover an enchanted Irish thorn, which is supposed to guard an underground chapel and its treasure. According to legend the tree has power over anyone who tries to interfere with it. The gardens are open every Sunday afternoon or by special arrangement with the Estate Agent, Mt. Congreve, Waterford (write or telephone).

To reach the unusual gardens at Garinish Island, a mile out in Bantry Bay, head west from Cork and plan to headquarter at *Glengarriff*.

You will find nineteen acres of gardens at *Garinish Island,* laid out over fifty years ago by the famous landscape architect, Harold Peto. He loved the Italianate formal garden and created a superb example of this style here, surrounded by the more naturalized wild garden that was so popular in that period. No matter what your enthusiasm, formal or natural, you will find something to cherish here. The gardens today are government property and are beautifully kept under the supervision of an expert head gardener, Mr. Machenzie.

Enter the garden from the boat dock and follow a winding path through glowing camellias, azaleas, and rhododendrons that are backed by exotic trees from Australia and New Zealand. The mild climate of Garinish not only fosters many subtropical plants, but encourages them to grow to huge proportions and seed themselves frequently. Tree ferns thrive here; also the beautiful giant forget-me-not, Myosotidium nobile, with great leaves like a funkia; many varieties of myrtle, cryptomerias, hypericum (up to seven feet tall), and rhododendrons twenty feet high.

Suddenly, the path opens out and you step into the graceful Renaissance loggia overlooking the Italian Garden. Here the severity of the formal design is softened with Irish charm. In spring you see it shimmering with forget-me-nots, with tulips and azaleas reflected in the long pool in the center of the garden. The stone terrace surrounding the pool is relieved with insets of brick designs alternating in open squares and circles, some framing potted Japanese bonsai trees. Heathers, broom, azaleas, encircle the terrace, while tall cypresses bring the flavor of Italy to the background. Opposite the loggia we entered, you will see another, framing a magnificent view of the blue waters of Bantry Bay and the mountain range beyond. The whole region around Glengarriff is noted for its scenery, and the gardens at Garinish are planned to give visitors many lookout points from which to enjoy it.

Leave the Italian Garden and follow the wide grass walks, bordered by heather in all shades from white to purple and by rhododendrons. Everywhere you will see native hollies that give the island its other Irish name, "Ilnacullin," or "Isle of Hollies." The path leads up stone steps to a small pavilion, where you can again revel in the sea and mountain landscape, then down again through rocks, bog, and woods, to a charming walled garden with wide perennial borders. You have been walking in a circle and will pass through the Italian Garden again before taking the boat back to the mainland. Garinish is another garden famous for its ability to inspire literature; here, we were told, George Bernard Shaw wrote his *Saint Joan.*

From Glengarriff, you can quickly reach *Killarney,* where you will surely visit Muckross Abbey. Don't miss the colorful formal flower beds behind *Muckross House,* also the fine rock garden and superb rhododendrons that stud the lawn beyond.

Take a jaunting car through Killarney Golf Course to visit Ross Castle. Here, in late May and June, the swamps are carpeted with bluebells, and later on abloom with sweeps of wild iris and native rhododendron.

We went north from Killarney to Limerick, making two

stops along the way. At *Rathkeale,* you'll find an unusual prizewinning community garden along the highroad. It slopes up steeply, adorned by a cover of evergreens in all shades from deep blue-green to light yellow, with bronze barberries and spring flowering shrubs spotted here and there for contrast.

Just beyond Rathkeale, you will find the little town of *Adare,* "the prettiest in all Ireland," according to the Tourist Board. Along its main street you see picturesque old thatched cottages with colorful front-yard gardens glowing with wall-flowers, forget-me-nots, and primroses in spring, later on with annuals, especially superb sweet peas. You can enjoy not only an excellent lunch at the *Dunraven Arms Hotel* there, but the fine gardens and extensive greenhouses that contribute to keeping this hostel lovely all year.

During the next few days we saw no gardens, for we headed some fifty miles northwest of Galway to the coast of Connemara, where we drove through awe-inspiring mountains, bare except for an occasional thatched cottage. The scenery is magnificent and reminiscent of Scotland, with its lonely moors and deep valleys. It was a proper introduction to County Donegal, still farther north, where we visited *Glen Veagh Gardens,* an amazing green spot hidden inside miles of lonely moors.

We were told that this is the only enclosed deer forest in Ireland, but no one seemed to know why the expression "forest" was used when there are no trees. What a garden lover that first owner of the castle must have been, sixty years ago, even to dream of growing things in such surroundings. You come out of the bleak mountains to see a large stone gate in a long wall. Once within, you are surrounded by exotic trees, flowering rhododendrons, azaleas, and one garden after another, glowing against the cool gray stone of the castle.

A large kitchen garden behind the conservatory end of

the house is filled with flowers, fruit, and vegetables in neat rows, backed by walls covered with blossoming vines. Go through the mossy stone gate at the back and you will suddenly step into a different world—a steep woodland glen with stone steps and dirt paths that lead up an incline. Along the way you walk past ferns, primulas, wild anemones, superb specimen rhododendrons, azaleas, hydrangeas, and old trees that seem to reach right up out of the rocks. The large grassy terrace you finally reach at the top opens onto a wide vista of the castle and grounds, the lake, and the mountains beyond. This, we heard, had been created by the laborious process of hauling rich sod up the long hill in donkey baskets.

As you return to the house, stop briefly at the Roman Garden, a small lawn surrounded by a wall topped with busts of the great of ancient Rome. The rest of the grounds look like an English landscape garden with tropical overtones, for the great lawns are bordered by fine rhododendrons and other plants that grow to unusual size.

Glen Veagh is open to the public only when the American owner, Henry P. McIlhenny, is not there, and then only Wednesday afternoons in May, June, and July. One should write in advance to the Estate Manager, Glen Veagh, County Donegal, for permission, as groups are limited in number. Be sure to ask for road directions at the same time. One of Mr. McIlhenny's dinner guests who had been invited for 8 P.M. got so thoroughly lost in the estate that he didn't arrive until midnight. Written directions or a guide are essential.

Before you leave County Donegal, if you are especially interested in rhododendrons, you must not miss seeing the wonderful collection of the Hooker varieties on the *estate of Lady Leitrim* at *Mulroy*. Be sure to telephone her estate manager for an appointment. The estate is near Mulroy Bay in the northeast corner of the county. The rhododendrons are at their height of bloom in May.

From Donegal you can go directly east to Belfast, but we chose to stop first at the Belleek factory to see the delicate china made, then at Enniskillen and Tempo to visit two beautiful private gardens. This brought us to Armagh for an overnight stop.

Next day, on our way up to the Belfast area, we stopped to see the famous arboretum at *Castlewellan*. It is a must for anyone interested in trees and can be seen by appointment. Mr. Gerald Annesley, the owner, toured the world for eighteen months to find rare specimen trees from New Zealand, Australia, Fiji, Formosa, Japan, and other exotic places with which to stock his arboretum. As they have settled in their new environment they have grown to great size, the way everything seems to do in Ireland, particularly the conifers. There are some fine cryptomerias, and a strange Pseudopanax, from New Zealand, which looks like a giant onion blossom turned into a palm tree. Prince Albert's yew (Saxegothaea conspicua) fascinated us with its pink tips, as did a rare New Zealand daisy tree (Pachystegia insignis) in the small rock garden.

Mr. Annesley, who very kindly showed us around himself, told an amusing story about the great snowstorm of 1961. Four feet of snow had buried many of his tree plantings so that only the tips showed. When a helicopter came circling over on its errand of mercy, the pilot dropped some bales of hay down to this area thinking the tree tops were stranded sheep!

We can happily recommend Crawfordsburn, northeast of Belfast, as a center for operations in this area, since we found all the interesting gardens in easy reach from here. The Old Inn there is charming. The oldest part of the building dates from 1614, and the whole place, though equipped with every modern comfort, is filled with fascinating antiques. Low beamed ceilings look down on gleaming copper and brass on the lounge mantelpiece which is always vivid with flowers.

In the dining room, bare mahogany tables gleam under the light of branched silver candlesticks. The terrace in back is bordered with flower beds.

Our first garden visit from here was to famous *Mt. Stewart* at *Newtownards,* now owned by the National Trust. Allow plenty of time if you go here, for the place is a series of adventures that should be savored slowly. The gardens were designed by the former owner, the Marchioness of Londonderry, in 1921, but they have grown so luxuriously that they seem old and romantic.

We entered between clipped hedges and high shrub arches reminiscent of Spain, to come to the delicately lovely Mairi Garden. This is shaped like a Tudor rose, accented at the far end by a rustic summerhouse. When we saw it in May it was filled with forget-me-nots and white tulips. The color scheme at all times is blue and white. The fountain in the center represents "Mairi, Mairi, Quite Contrary." This little hidden spot has all the charm of an old fairy tale.

Mt. Stewart has a quality unusual in a garden—wit. You see surprising bits of humor throughout, a lilting, quiet Irish chuckle. First there is the Dodo Terrace, a carefully designed resting spot from which one can view the house and the Italian garden. Here four stone dodo birds, the extinct creatures beloved by crossword-puzzle fans, flank a small Noah's Ark, and a rabbit, squirrel, and lizard of stone scamper down the balustrade. Other such creatures peer out everywhere from the tops of walls or behind shrubs, climaxed finally by the topiary animals in the Shamrock Garden.

Before you reach that, however, take time to stroll about in the Italian Garden, which runs the entire length of the front of the great gray stone mansion. Not as dark and severe as a true garden of Italy, it is full of Irish charm and softness and lovely colors. I particularly liked the combination of a sophora tree (native of New Zealand and Chile), with its hanging yellow blossoms, close to the delicate Wedgwood blue of the Ceanothus, which is sometimes called the California lilac. Lucky Californians to have such a pretty thing! You will see many of them in Ireland, often trained like vines onto buildings.

Next, step down at one side into the sunken Spanish Garden, flanked by more tall clipped shrub arches, then on to the Peace Garden, where family pets lie buried. Retrace your steps from here and go through the Lily Wood, and past the Rock Garden, to reach the amusing Shamrock Garden. This delightful spot derives its name from its three-circle shape. Here humor and symbolism run riot. You see one flower bed in the shape of an heraldic crest. The center topiary is a large Irish harp, while a group, cut from the tops of the surrounding hedge, represent the family on a hunting party in a boat, with various animals trailing along behind.

From this fantasy you can return to the house by way of another Sunken Garden, or you can go around the lake and through the famous Rhododendron Walk. Everywhere you go in Mt. Stewart, you will find rare plants, lush growth, and a careful choice of flowers for color combinations and spacing of bloom through the seasons. What an accomplishment in a garden covering eighty acres!

Another famous National Trust garden near here is *Rowallane,* at *Saintfield.* Its main features are the superb borders of choice rhododendrons and the pretty English-type walled garden, but there are also many outstanding trees, which were planted as a shelter from the winds. The grounds were first laid out a century ago, and old bills of 1864 show that the owner, the Rev. John Moore, at that time bought two thousand each of beeches, oaks, and larches, and a thousand spruces, besides many other trees.

The gardens have been planned with great care to include shrubs and flowers and foliage for a long season. Especially famous are the varieties that originated here, including a Viburnum tomentosum, primulas, and hypericum, all bear-

Mt. Stewart, Ireland (*Photo by James L. McFadden*)

ing the name Rowallane. In the walled garden there is a rare white variety of my favorite, Meconopsis superba from the Himalayas.

One of the prettiest parts of the gardens is the Old Wood, where miniature daffodils bloom in early spring, and rhododendrons, Scotch pines, camellias, and heathers give color and interest among the big slabs of rock. I cannot imagine that Rowallane could ever be more beautiful than when we saw it in May at the height of the rhododendron bloom, but reading the garden guide that we bought there, we could see that there would be color throughout the summer and fine fall foliage later on. The individual plants to be seen here, listed at the back of the booklet, would keep a knowledgeable gardener busy and happy for many a day in these lovely gardens.

When we visited the National Trust office in Belfast, the secretary there very kindly made a number of phone calls for us so that we could see some private gardens also. These are usually opened only for charity on certain days of the year. We enjoyed our visit at *Ballyowan House* with Mrs. Phoebe Anderson, at *Drumbeg*, because her garden was so personally planned and evidently much lived-in. Everywhere we found little nooks and benches from which to admire the rock garden and herbaceous borders at different angles.

Guincho, in *Helen's Bay*, a garden to which Mrs. Frazer Mackie devotes most of her time and energies, is another connoisseur's garden with many rare flowers and shrubs that deserve close study. Close to the house are some fine specimens of double gorse and a sophora tree such as I had first admired at Mt. Stewart. The narrow flower borders that circle around to a woods garden contain many special varieties of azaleas, small rhododendrons raised at Guincho from seed, and an exquisite small golden elder, Sambucus racemosa plumoso-aurea—such a long name for a shower of delicate yellow leaves! There are many fine eucalyptus, some raised from cuttings with extraordinary success, a lovely garden of heathers, and a large collection of bamboos. I wished that I might have seen the woods garden earlier in the spring, for Mrs. Mackie has cultivated almost every variety of our delicate little dogtooth violet family (erythroniums), raising them from seed obtained mostly in America. Another favorite of hers, which blooms later in the summer, is the watsonia, many varieties of which were raised here from seed sent from South Africa; this is a tall plant similar to our iris but growing to six feet at times, with scarlet, rose, or white flowers.

Two other private gardens interested us because of their unusual treatment of natural outcroppings of rock. *Creevy Rocks*, the estate of Major D. Anderson, at *Saintfield*, is extensive. All over the front lawn and along grass paths radiating in every direction are beautiful combinations of heathers, small alpine plants, and wild gorse that seem to grow naturally over and around the gray stone ledges. This garden should be an inspiration to those who live in Pennsylvania, New England, or any other rocky, hilly area; here, at home, this type of terrain is often considered a liability, yet it could become an asset if treated like those rocks and rolling hills in the north of Ireland.

At *The Whins,* which Capt. and Mrs. W. J. Miller at *Newtownards* named for the great quantity of wild gorse they found there, the small garden had been developed in much the same way, through the owners' loving planning and hard labor. The various units, which one really could not call flower beds because of their natural effect, are all miniature gardens of heathers, gorse, and small rock plants placed in crevices and around edges of boulders that the Millers found on the place and did not or could not remove. You could stay in this region, visiting the lovely gardens every month from spring to fall and learning about all their rare and unusual plants, without ever growing bored.

The final center of our garden tour of Ireland was *Dublin*. *Glasnevin Botanical Garden,* in the city itself, is justly famous, and rewarding excursions can be made to see the large *Japanese garden* at *Kildare* and the superb gardens at *Birr Castle.* This property of the present Earl and Countess of Rosse has been beautifully planted, as both owners are intensely interested in gardening. Lady Rosse grew up at the famous English garden of Nymans (see chapter on "England") and has used both her horticultural knowledge and many of the plants acquired there. You will find her flower borders and shrubs particularly well planned for color schemes. Lord Rosse's great interest has been in cotoneasters, cherries, flowering crabs, and many other blossoming and ornamental shrubs. The grounds are hilly, making the whole plan of the gardens one of continual surprise and variety.

You will find great drifts of flowers underplanted in many places, beginning with the daffodils and tulip species in early spring and ending with colchicums in the fall. There is a beautiful rose garden, its beds edged with germander (Teucrium chamaedrys) clipped like miniature box hedges. Near the drive there are giant box trees over 34 feet tall, clipped into a "cathedral vault." You will see a particularly happy combination climbing up one of the terrace balustrades and to the third story of the castle: an interweaving of bright-yellow Banksia roses, dusty-pink clematis, and a lavender wisteria. The River Garden alone is so interesting that you could spend hours studying the trees, shrubs, and flowers there. You will also see a nursery where thousands of rare conifers are raised, to be planted later throughout the woodland area. Be sure to allow plenty of time when you visit this delightful place.

The high spots of our trip were the gardens of Powerscourt and Mt. Usher.

Powerscourt, at *Enniskerry,* is now a National Trust property. The Italianate gardens are of a beauty and magnificence that leave one breathless. They were used to great effect as settings in the filming of *Henry V*. The property was owned by the Wingfield family for three generations, and there are splendid old trees throughout the grounds.

Passing a small formal garden, you go through a beautiful wrought-iron gate to a high terrace. Walk along beside the stone balustrade to admire the great urns on the right, filled with geraniums, past which you can glimpse the mountain range. You will be quite unprepared for the glorious view that suddenly opens out as you reach the top of a wide flight of stairs. Nearby, the finely wrought iron railings, painted warm brown and gold, fan out to the sides, surrounding varying levels of terraces that are paved in black and white stone designs. Below you see a large formal pool, framed by statues of two winged horses, part of the family coat of arms. The backdrop to all this beauty is formed by the hazy blue mountains far beyond.

Descend this stair slowly to savor the view from each terrace. You come out on level ground where clipped shrubs and flat flower beds surround the pool. From here you can take a woodland path that goes to the Deer Park. The climax of your walk will be the waterfall, 398 feet high—the highest in Great Britain and Ireland.

If you should be overawed by the beauty of this great place, you may relax in amusement at the story of how the gardens were made. It seems that the formal designs were by Mr. Daniel Robertson. He was conveyed about the place in a wheelbarrow during its construction, grasping a bottle of sherry as he supervised the work of one hundred men with horses and carts. When Mr. Robertson finished his bottle, that was the end of activities for that day. Small wonder that the gardens, begun in 1843, were only completed in 1875.

And now we come to what was for me the loveliest and

most satisfying garden of the whole Irish tour, *Mt. Usher* at *Ashford*. It is the creation of one family of linen merchants, and, most particularly, of Edward Horace Walpole, who took charge of it about 1910, when it was already a half-century old. It is known the world over for its many rare plants. Its fine collection of eucalyptus is the most extensive in Britain; its great Montezuma pine stands eighty feet tall; and there are large numbers of other extraordinary flowers and shrubs. Each item in the sixteen acres of garden has been carefully chosen and placed in relation to every other, for color combinations, variety of seasonal bloom, and selection of perfect growing conditions. Every plant is accurately but inconspicuously labeled. Yet the overall effect, as you wander from one path to another, along the stream, past the brick wall-alcoves built for special shelter, through the flower borders, is that this small paradise could only have been planted by God Himself. There is no straining for effect, no artificial formality, nothing that does not seem as if it had, rightfully, always been there.

We obtained a delightful little booklet on our visit there; in twenty-one pages, it takes the visitor step by step through the entire garden naming each flower, tree, and shrub and pointing out each special feature and view. I can only recommend that every garden lover who visits Ireland should go to this garden, follow each page of the booklet, and enjoy hours of sheer delight.

Of the many countries where I have visited gardens, surely the Emerald Isle is one of the most beautiful and rewarding. Go and see for yourself.

USEFUL INFORMATION

The following leaflets will be helpful to you in planning a garden tour of Ireland. You can send for them in advance. All are free unless otherwise noted.

THE BRITISH TRAVEL ASSOCIATION, 680 Fifth Ave., New York 19, N.Y.: Booklet, "Historic Houses, Castles and Gardens in Great Britain and Ireland," revised annually for dates and hours of opening.

THE IRISH TOURIST BOARD, Baggott Street Bridge, Dublin, 2, Ireland: List of recent winners in the National Roadside Garden Competition. Also list, "Principal Gardens and Historic Houses in Ireland," with current days and hours of admission.

QUEEN'S INSTITUTE OF DISTRICT NURSING IN IRELAND, 48 Lower Leeson St., Dublin, 2, Ireland: List of private gardens open on special days as a benefit for charity.

ROYAL HORTICULTURAL SOCIETY OF IRELAND, 16 St. Stephen's Green, Dublin, 2, Ireland. Membership in the Society is $3 annually, which will enable you to visit certain private gardens on specific days and to join the Society's garden tours of Ireland. Non-members can also enjoy the seasonal flower shows held by the Society; send for a list of dates.

ULSTER GARDEN SCHEME of the National Trust for Northern Ireland, 82 Dublin Rd., Belfast, 2, Ireland: List of private gardens open in Northern Ireland on special days. Membership in the National Trust Committee for Northern Ireland is $5.60 a year; it entitles you to free admission to all the Committee's properties in Northern Ireland, and participation in its garden tours, as well as helping toward their preservation and care.

chapter 7

WALES: GARDENS IN
FERTILE VALLEYS

*T*HE title of that famous novel, "How Green Was My Valley," kept running through my mind as we drove through northern Wales from Holyhead toward Chester, England. The valleys of this land actually are much like the green and fertile farm lands of Ireland that we had just left. Here, however, the mountains are more dramatic, the roads go down more steeply to the little villages nestling below, and the houses, of dark gray stone with black roofs, are more somber. The names of the towns are long, and, to an American, just about unpronounceable.

You could start your tour of northern Wales from Ireland, as we did, taking the overnight boat from Dun Laoghaire to Holyhead and picking up a car there. Your first stop might be in *Bangor,* to see the small but charming garden at *Penrhyn Castle,* with particularly lovely shrubs, and the *Bible Garden,* in the city park, with plants mentioned in the Bible. Then drive on east along the coast to Conway as your first touring center. Or you could reach Conway very easily from Chester, England, or even farther south from Shrewsbury, working your way up through some of the gardens I am going to mention, but in reverse order.

Let's start from Conway, which lies at the top of the long Conway Valley. You can see two lovely gardens in one day if you start for Roewen in the morning, then go back to Tal-y-Cafn when the garden opens there in the afternoon.

You will find a charming little private garden called *Gilfach,* at *Roewen,* just west of Tal-y-Cafn. This belongs to Miss I. Gee, who welcomes visitors there any day except Sunday. An ardent and knowledgeable gardener, she designed her grounds with great taste and vision, the paths winding in gentle curves and leading to various points of interest: the little pool, the summerhouse, and a simple gate over which you will see a glorious panorama of the wide valleys and the mountains beyond.

One of the charms of this little garden is the careful selection of plants for color contrast: the powder blue of a Ceanothus Veitchianus next to Spanish gorse; a fine bush of the Pieris Forrestii with its scarlet-tipped new leaves against its delicate white flowers. Miss Gee has selected her flowers and shrubs to withstand the strong winds that sweep in from the valley, so she has many fine heathers (one, an Australian heath, has grown to ten feet in height), the sturdy little potentillas in both white and yellow, and various varieties of broom. One of the latter, Cytisus A. T. Johnson, was raised by and named for a famous gardener and garden writer who lives close by. In her flower borders, also, you will find only plants that do not need staking, such as the evening primrose, pentstemon, and a native Welsh flower called masterwort (Astrantia major), which has green and white flowers. Among the delights of visiting here are Miss Gee's bubbling enthusiasm for gardens and her willingness to answer questions and give practical advice.

From here you must head east again to Tal-y-Cafn to see one of the truly great gardens of the world, *Bodnant.* This is open on Tuesday, Wednesday, Thursday, and Saturday afternoons from 1:30 to 4:45. Even though you arrive well before opening time, you may find a long line already waiting at the gate. Once inside, however, you soon find out that the gardens are worth hours of standing, if necessary. The setting itself is breathtaking. High terraces look out over miles of fertile valleys to the blue Snowdonia mountains along the horizon.

Bodnant is now a National Trust property, but is still supervised by Lord Aberconway, whose great-grandfather originally laid out the grounds in 1875. Many of the trees were planted a century before that.

The famous Laburnum Walk, near the entrance, was just coming into bloom when we were there toward the end of May. This long archway of laburnums is trained over a trellis so that the hanging yellow blossoms form a delicate ceiling overhead. When the sunlight streams through and also illuminates the pink azaleas along the side, this is a color picture you won't forget.

Walk from here to the East Garden, to enjoy its continuing bloom. It is particularly lovely in spring, with early gentians, iris, Bodnant's own strain of primulas, and tree peonies.

If you then cross the spacious lawn in front of the house, bordered by flowering trees and shrubs, you come to the first of the Italian-style terraces. This one contains the Rose Garden. From here you also get a superb view of the other terraces, the River Conway, and the entire range of mountains beyond.

Just below is the Croquet Terrace, which features a French fountain and pool surrounded by wisteria. In March, the Magnolia Campbellii growing here produces saucer-shaped pink blossoms ten inches across. Everywhere you will see the magnificent rhododendron strains, developed at Bodnant, that have given this garden world renown.

In various parts of the gardens you can see the famous eucryphias, which bloom in July and August, and are fully as exciting as Bodnant's Laburnum Walk. The eucryphia is a shrub some eight to ten feet high, well known in Britain, but originating in Chile. It has four-petaled white flowers, three inches across, that almost entirely cover the plant.

Descend the steps to the Lily Terrace, and you will find yourself beside a formal pool, in which as many as a thousand waterlilies bloom at one time from June to late September. Arching over the water at one end are two ancient blue cedars.

Near the Lower Rose Terrace are a small garden filled primarily with white flowers and another of only tree peonies. The final, and perhaps most striking of all, is the Canal Terrace. The long narrow pool here is bordered with blue and purple flowers—petunias when we were there. At one end is an open-air stage of clipped yews, and at the other a charming old Pin Mill which was moved here in its entirety from Gloucestershire.

From this, the last of the terraces, a path leads through a splendid collection of camellias and magnolias, out onto the top of a ravine, where you come upon a wild garden that riots up and down steep, woodsy paths. You can sit on a bench there and enjoy the sight of great masses of rhododendron blooms pouring down the slopes. Walk down to the bottom, past an old mill, and along the banks of the river, where ferns and azaleas are reflected in the water.

Another drive south through the green Conway Valley will take you to the charming village of Betws-y-Coed. Along the way you can tour little *Gwydyr Castle*, near *Llanwrst*, and enjoy its old garden decorated with topiaries and peacocks. When we admired the birds, the gardener told us that they had become a real problem. They eat up his perennial plants as fast as he puts them in, so now the whole garden will be given over to roses instead. There are many fine trees on the grounds of the castle, one of them a cedar of Lebanon believed to have been planted to commemorate the wedding of Charles I in 1625.

As we started east again in our journey to England, we stopped at the coastal resort of *Rhyl* to enjoy the unique *Royal Floral Hall.* This is a great greenhouse, beautifully planted like a garden, with flower beds along winding paths sparkling with the colors of tropical foliage plants, and brightly-hued cockatoos. You can buy a booklet there that lists the exotic plants and gives hints to those who would like to grow them in their homes. It also includes notes on the best trees and shrubs for a seaside garden and gives special cultural directions for fuchsias.

One section of the greenhouse is devoted entirely to cacti and succulents; another to the glorious little butterfly flowers of schizanthus. Everywhere there are unusual specimens of fuchsias, including an educational display near the entrance. Dozens of different fuchsia flower heads are placed in small vases on the board there, with the name of the variety printed below. There were large and small ones, singles and doubles, flowers of one color or of several shades. A wonderful place for the fuchsia lover!

The Royal Floral Hall is open daily from 10 to 8 and is visited by thousands.

Another favorite spot, if you take this route, is *Plas Newydd* in *Llangollen,* the home of two famous Irish women "who spent their time in friendship, celibacy and the knitting of blue stockings." They were Lady Eleanor Butler and the Hon. Sarah Ponsonby, who left their homes late in the 18th century to live alone in this little cottage, with their faithful maid, who had bought the place for them with her own savings. They must have been ladies of great charm and high intelligence, for Plas Newydd became the mecca of many of the great of that day. Wordsworth, Sir Walter Scott, Madame de Senlis, the Duke of Wellington, De Quincy, and many others came to visit, each bringing a carved ornament as a gift—a collection you can still see there. This must have been one of the most successful of the literary Blue Stocking Clubs so popular with ladies of the period. Our main interest in the place, of course, was the amusing topiary garden. There are eight-sided cones; tall round columns looking as though ropes had been coiled around them; pyramids, large and small, piled one upon the other, and several bird and animal shapes. There is even a clipped couch to sit on. Apparently the ladies had not only intelligence but a delicious sense of humor.

Not far from Llangollen we stopped to talk to the passengers of some gaily decorated canal boats. They described enthusiastically the week they had spent floating forty miles through the lovely countryside, stopping off wherever they wished to sightsee. There were two boats, one of them fitted with an old Diesel engine to pull the other. The passengers slept and ate on board. This would be an ideal way to see some of the gardens of Wales, provided you have plenty of time and the gift of relaxation.

Our personal itinerary took us next to the quaint old town of Chester, from which you can visit a few English gardens, and then south to London. On the way we stopped off at two castles on the border in Wales.

At the first, *Chirk Castle* in Wrexham, we discovered that our schedule, which was limited by business appointments for my husband, didn't coincide with the time when the garden is open to the public. We tried telephoning, but were unsuccessful. So we decided to take a chance and go anyway, hoping to find a gatekeeper to whom we could explain our problem. I wanted very much to see the garden, so that it could be included in this book, and to photograph it for garden-club lectures.

We found the fine old wrought-iron gate stoutly locked, and the keeper's cottage so far inside that we couldn't have been heard had we called out. We were about to turn away when a Land Rover (much like our Jeep) roared up and its driver got out to unlock the gate. Gratefully, I went over and asked if he could help; was there anyone to whom he could speak who would grant us a special permission?

He considered the matter gravely—and then we had a stroke of good luck. "Just a moment," he said courteously, "while I speak to my forester."

My forester! The unpretentiously dressed gentleman, driving his own Jeep, turned out to be Colonel Myddelton, whose family has held the estate for over three hundred years. We snapped up his invitation to wander the grounds at will and photograph whatever we wished.

The lawns beside the castle are surrounded by huge clipped hedges with crenelated tops shaped just like the walls nearby. Cone-shaped yews of a giant size accent the path leading into the gardens. If you walk through the rose garden and across more lawns, you pass deep borders filled with perennials, flowering trees, and shrubs. Nearby is the rustic Hawk House, now the home of white pigeons. A rock garden was in bloom on the hill just behind this. Below the lawns, paths wind through blossoming rhododendrons and azaleas to a spot where a viburnum spreads its white blossoms. From here you can look out over the wide valley and share in the wonderful feeling of spaciousness and peace that permeates the gardens at Chirk Castle.

Farther south, we had no trouble getting into the gardens of *Powis Castle* at *Welshpool.* They can be seen every afternoon except Monday and Tuesday, as they belong to the National Trust. The 13th-century castle is still the home of the present Earl of Powis.

This is a striking garden. Five terraces of Italian design, each five hundred feet long, cover the steep slope below the pink limestone castle. Each level is edged by stone balustrades, urns, and statues, and backed by a warm red-brick wall, under which the flower beds make a colorful display.

Powis Castle, Wales (*Photo from Brit. Travel & Holidays Assn.*)

Growing against these walls are wisteria, clematis, jasmine, and other vines, many forms of euonymus, and the powder-blue ceanothus that I had liked so much in Ireland. In front are heathers, musk roses, iris, and a great variety of other perennials, with tall fuchsias tucked at random into the corners. In July and August, phlox, anthemis, and helenium add their brilliance to the scene.

Marching down the hill at the far end of the terraces is an immense wall of clipped yew over thirty feet high. Here and there along the walks are other yews, one of them cut like a mushroom and used as a summerhouse to shelter a bench. We measured the trunk of one of the yews, found it two feet in diameter, and were told that it was over two hundred years old.

A printed guide details the flowers at each level as you walk down. There are a great many tender plants from the most southern climates—passionflowers from South America, shrubs from Italy and South Africa, flowers from many continents. It was difficult to concentrate on these, however, for we kept looking up to enjoy the glorious view of the mountains and to take pictures from each level. In the flat valley below the terraces there is a hedged formal garden, and on each side paths lead off to attractively planted woodlands. Here again the printed guide can lead one to fine specimens of unusual trees, among them the tallest tree in Britain, a Douglas fir 181 feet high.

On our trip we only nibbled along the edges of Wales. There is even more to enjoy in the center and south of this land if you can take the time on your garden tour there.

USEFUL INFORMATION

Before touring Wales, send for the following booklets, which list the days and hours when public and private gardens can be visited and the admission charged, and give directions for finding them. These are all published annually:

BRITISH TRAVEL & HOLIDAYS ASSOCIATION, 680 Fifth Ave., New York 19, N.Y.: Booklet, "Historic Houses, Castles and Gardens in Great Britain and Ireland." Free.

THE GARDENERS' SUNDAY ORGANIZATION, White Witches, Claygate Road, Dorking, Surrey, England: Booklet, "Gardens Open to the Public," price one shilling plus postage (about 30¢ including postage).

THE NATIONAL GARDEN SCHEME, 57 Lower Belgrave St., London S.W.1, England: Booklet, "The Gardens of England and Wales Open to the Public." Price 2/6 plus postage (about 60¢ including postage).

THE WELSH TOURIST AND HOLIDAYS BOARD, 7 Park Place, Cardiff, Wales: Lists of hotels and other touring information.

chapter 8

ENGLAND–SMALL TOURS TO LARGE GARDENS

ou can probably visit more gardens in England than in any other country of the world. If you saw a garden a day from mid-April to mid-October, you would not even get to all the ones listed at the back of this book! England is the horticulturist's paradise on earth, not only in the number of gardens available to the public, but also in the high quality of their design and their plant content.

The climate in the whole of the British Isles seems made to order for gardeners. The high rainfall, which may at times annoy you in your touring and photographing, and the generally moist, mild air, the long seasons, all are ideal. With primroses blooming in Cornwall in January, and the winter jasmine and Christmas roses everywhere in December, you can find flowers somewhere in England all the year around. If you want to follow the succession of wildflower bloom, buy the little booklet, "Flowers and Their Seasons in Britain," mentioned at the end of this chapter.

April and May are wonderful here. The hawthorn hedges along the country roads are in bloom, the yellow laburnums droop over the walls, and lilacs spread their fragrance everywhere. Watch for the Royal Automobile Club signs or get its maps showing the best routes to take you to the tulip fields around Spalding, the cherry blossoms in the Teme Valley, and the appleblossom sections of Kent.

If you go to Castleton in Derbyshire on May 29th, you will see a flower festival that has been celebrated on this day for over three hundred years. The main feature is a Garland Day parade with a sixty-pound floral pyramid decorating the Garland Queen's horse. The English go slightly garden-mad in spring, working in their own small plots or large estates and climaxing their efforts with as many days as they can spare at the great Chelsea Flower Show in London. (See "Flower Shows in Europe" chapter.)

No matter what other sightseeing you do from earliest spring to late fall, at every historic spot you will see flowers somewhere. Small village gardens, too, are fortunately in front of the houses where you can enjoy them. Even a small patch of soil a foot wide between the housefront and the sidewalk will be filled with gay wallflowers in yellows and browns. Or there will be a narrow trellis supporting a cascade of Paul's Scarlet Climber roses over the front door, just a few steps from the street. The gates and fences are merely frames that you can always look over or through to see a colorful picture.

Away from the villages it is different. In the brick-faced factory town of Northampton, for example, the gardens are behind the attached dwellings. We stayed in one home that had a delightful garden in back only about twenty-five feet wide and perhaps three or four times as long, completely hemmed in by high brick walls. Here were flower beds, a vegetable garden, a small pool, a tool shed and a compost heap, all connected by winding paths and lawn. As we looked out of our second-floor bedroom window, we could see row upon row of such narrow gardens on each side, insuring every family a private retreat outdoors.

Not only are the home gardens and public parks of England full of flowers, but the grounds of hotels and inns are, too. The paths leading up to church doors have their colorful borders. The lock-keepers on the River Thames and the men in charge of railway stations compete annually for garden prizes. Even inside South Kensington Underground Station in London you can see beds filled with flowers, beginning with the daffodils in early spring.

If you want to start a conversation with anyone on your travels, from the milkman to the city sophisticate, just ask whether he has a garden. This is the common ground on which all meet. If you are an ordinary American home gardener like me, however, don't be surprised if the person you talk to makes you feel very small and ignorant. The English know every flower and weed by its Latin name and can tell you the most minute differences between various hybrid varieties of the same family. But don't be discouraged. They have been at this for many more centuries than we.

Next to working in his own garden, I should say that visiting other people's gardens is one of the Englishman's favorite sports. As we all know, much can be learned from studying the seed and plant catalogues in midwinter, or from attending lectures and reading gardening books. But nothing is so helpful—and to many of us, so much fun—as walking about in a friend's grounds, or in a botanical garden, or on a great estate, making notes of the flowers we like and where they seem to thrive best. English men and women do this by the hundreds of thousands. I hope that when you go to see some of their gardens you will chat with your fellow visitors and with the garden owners whenever possible, for you will learn much from them—and perhaps make some lasting friends.

Whether you are just going to be in London for a few days, or are planning a tour of several counties by car, I hope that the material I have compiled in this book will help you to find the gardens you would particularly enjoy seeing. First of all, I would suggest that you send for three booklets before you even start on your travels (addresses are given at the end of this chapter). *Historic Houses, Castles and Gardens* will tell you, for each garden, the days and hours when it is open; the admission fee, if any (usually only 14¢ or 28¢); whether there is a restaurant at or near the garden; and the buses or routes by which it can be reached. It also describes the interiors of the houses and castles that you may see at the same time. *The Gardens of England and Wales,* put out by The National Garden Scheme, and *Gardens Open to the Public,* issued by The Gardeners' Sunday organization, list the dates and hours when certain private gardens are open for charity. All three of these pamphlets are issued annually early in the spring, as dates and places are liable to change each year. That is why I am referring you to these lists, and not mentioning the hours or days when each garden in my book is open, except in a few cases where I have found some that were not included in these booklets.

What the booklets do not do, and what I hope you will find valuable in this book in planning your garden visits in England, is to include some description of the special features of each, and to group them by geographical areas instead of by counties. County lists can be very confusing, as these geographical divisions intertwine in an amazing way. When I tried to find gardens on the road map of England for my own trips, it proved a very difficult task. So I evolved, for use in this book, what I am calling "Wheel Tours." These suggest towns where you might stay for several days, using them as hubs. From these you can radiate out like the spokes of a wheel, traveling by car or bus, to any or all of the gardens in that area that you think you might enjoy, or that fit into your other sightseeing. Thus, if you were to stay in Stratford-on-Avon, for example, in the county of Warwickshire, you could, by using my Wheel Tour, visit delightful gardens within a thirty-mile radius in four other counties as well.

The hub town is only a suggestion, of course. You may like to stay at a different center nearby where you know of a good hotel or inn. To supplement the suggested Wheel Tours in the "Key to Gardens" at the back of this book, I have also included sectional maps for different parts of England, which should prove useful. For the sake of travelers who are driving and using a road map, I have listed the gardens *always* under a town that is marked on such a map. Since Edgehill, for example, where you will find Upton House, in Oxfordshire, is not on a road map, I have listed it under Banbury instead, which is very nearby and easily found.

I must warn you that not all the gardens listed under one Wheel Tour can necessarily be seen on the same day or week. Their opening hours will vary greatly. But each Wheel has a sufficiently large choice so that no matter when you plan to be there, you can see some of the gardens.

In the following sections you will find descriptions of gardens in the Greater London Area and a selection of the more notable gardens in various parts of England. In choosing the gardens of England for this book, I have omitted practically all of the 18th-century landscape gardens that we in America would think of as park-like grounds and not gardens at all. This includes many of those planned by the famous "Capability" Brown, which, through their very art, were made to look as if the trees, shrubs, and lakes had always been there. Although my listings concentrate on the ones that are formally designed or include many flowers, with a few arboretums here and there for the tree lover, there is still a choice of over two hundred that you could visit. The booklets I mentioned above will tell you about many additional private gardens to be seen on special days.

GREATER LONDON AREA

If you will look at our map of the Greater London Area, you will see that we have divided it into two concentric circles, using Oxford Circle, London, as the center. The Inner Circle is within a fifteen-mile radius of this central point; the Outer Circle is drawn within a twenty-mile radius. You can reach any of these gardens by bus or Underground; just ask your hotel or flat porter for directions.

Inner Circle: Working your way from north to south on the map, you would find the following lovely spots: *St. James's Park,* near the center of London, where you can see a wonderful display of flowering bulbs in early spring; lupines in May; geraniums throughout the summer, and then a fine show of dahlias beginning the last of August. Go into the park along Birdcage Walk to see most of the flowers.

If you should go to *Fenton House,* to see the collections of porcelain and old musical instruments, you will find a nice small walled garden there.

In *Regent's Park,* be sure to see Queen Mary's Rose Garden, one of the best rose collections in Britain. There are also a charming small rock garden in an island on the lake, colorful wide flower borders, and a begonia garden. Near the Eastern Gate are the delightful *Hylas or St. John's Gardens,* with wonderful roses and flower borders.

In *Kensington Gardens* what is called the Flower Walk, going past the Albert Memorial, is attractive throughout the seasons. There is a famous sunken garden here between the Palace and Broad Walk, which has wonderful mixed borders of perennials and annuals, at their height in August, but fine from spring to fall.

There is a lovely iris display around the pond and fountains of *Holland Park Garden*.

While you are shopping or in Holland Park, or visiting Kensington Gardens nearby, do be sure to take the elevator in *Derry and Tom's Department Store* to see the roof gardens there. This is an amazing place. You can wander around in three gardens covering one and three-quarters acres. You will see a Spanish Garden with a pool, colonnades, and plants in terra-cotta pots. The Woodland Garden, with tall trees, ferns, even a little brook, will make you feel as if you were far out in the country. The Tudor Garden is a formal design, with brick walls and archways like bits of an old mansion. It is only when you come to an occasional round peephole and look out over the rooftops of London that you realize you are actually on top of a city building. There is a terrace restaurant where you can have lunch or tea while enjoying the greenery.

Going out just a little farther on the western edge of London now, we come to *Kew Gardens*, the Royal Botanical Gardens, famous throughout the world. These are open daily from 10 A.M. to 8 P.M., and you can certainly spend a whole day looking over even a small part of the plantings in the three hundred acres. There are special gardens of azaleas, bamboos, herbs, iris (nearly an acre), rock-garden plants, rhododendrons, and roses. Among the annuals, the collections of sunflowers and asters are the largest in the world. Wander in and out of the eight greenhouses to see the ferns, orchids, succulents, and a splendid example of the enormous waterlily, Victoria regia. There is also a cool house with alpine varieties. Lest this description deceive you, however, most of Kew Gardens will seem like a vast natural park as you walk through its many paths, for much of it is devoted to expanses of lovely lawn bordered by fine old specimens of every variety of tree that could possibly be introduced to this climate. Each tree is well marked, so if this is your hobby, you will be blissfully happy walking around Kew Gardens for days on end.

Not far from Kew is the *Royal Park of Richmond.* You can see many fine varieties of iris near Richmond Gate and the Terrace Gardens. Or if you enter from Kingston Gate, or Robin Hood Gate, you will come to the Isabella Plantation, with heathers, rhododendrons, water plants, and various exotics.

In case you would like to see the garden designed by the author of many delightful books, Beverley Nichols, telephone him at Sudbrook Cottage, *Ham Common,* for an appointment (telephone, Kingston 5087). This is his own flower-filled place, which he has described in *Garden Open Today,* recently so popular in America. It is a fine example of the English genius for creating an effect of wide vistas in a very restricted space, something that many of us have to contend with in our own grounds. Although quite new, the garden already gives the impression of great maturity. Incidentally, some of the features in the garden are constructed of bricks made by Daniel Defoe when he was writing *Robinson Crusoe.*

In this same vicinity are the wonderful old gardens at *Hampton Court Palace,* begun by Cardinal Wolsey in 1514. Start your explorations at the East Front of the palace, where you will find the enclosed Tudor Garden and the Baroque Garden. From there you will reach the South Terrace and go along the Broad Walk, which is a formal garden on the grand scale, with glorious blooming borders almost half a mile long. Now you reach the wooded Dell, with primroses and daffodils in early spring, or gleaming varieties of lilies later on. Circling back, you reach another series of delightful spots—the formal Privy Garden; the Knot Garden, of low flowers in intricate designs; the Pond Garden; the Herb Garden, with its tiny box hedges; and finally the Great Grape Vine, which was planted in 1769. This once bore 2200 bunches of grapes in a year, but even now, at its advanced age, is still producing some 650 clusters.

Now you are near the famous Maze, and can try your luck at reaching the center and then coming out again. Beyond this is a large Rose Garden in what was formerly the Tilt Yard, where knights of old held jousting contests. One of the shrubs here is called the "gooseberry bush rose," and there is also a bearing pomegranate tree. The gardens are at their very best in mid-May, but are certainly worth seeing at any time. Do try to visit the palace by yourself, not on a guided tour, so that you can take your time to explore the lovely surroundings.

On the eastern edge of our Inner Circle on the map, you will find *Greenwich Park.* You will probably want to take the boat on the Thames, anyway, for this excursion to *Greenwich* to see the former Royal Observatory and the ship "Cutty Sark," so linger there a little longer to enjoy the Flower Gardens. They are northeast of the National Maritime Museum as you go toward "The Wilderness," with its Deer Park. The Flower Gardens are well named, for here you will see vivid perennial borders, many roses, and at the end of August, a fine display of dahlias.

A bus excursion to *Eltham,* just a little south of Greenwich, will bring you to *Avery Hill Winter Garden.* This is a group of three greenhouses. The cool one is filled mainly with camellias. In the temperate-zone house, you can see brilliant primulas, showers of delicate schizanthus, and masses of chrysanthemums. The last one is a tropical house, where there are banana trees producing fruit, and other exotic plants and flowers. This would be a wonderful place to visit on a rainy day or when the weather is cold. Since it is not listed in the booklets mentioned above, I must tell you that the glasshouses are open Monday through Friday from 1 to 5 P.M.; Saturdays, Sundays, and Bank Holidays, April through September, from 11 A.M. to 5 P.M., from May through August, 11 A.M. to 6 P.M. Since opening hours for any garden change at times, you might telephone the Avery Hill Winter Garden at Eltham to make sure these hours are still in effect.

OUTER CIRCLE

Now we will start looking at some of the gardens in our Outer Circle of the Greater London Area, none of them more than twenty miles from London's Oxford Circle.

On the western perimeter, you might like to stop at the town of *Egham*, for a meal at *Great Fosters Hotel*. This has a delightful big garden planted in the old-fashioned style, with beds in patterned curves edged with small clipped hedges, filled with flowers and pudgy topiaries. Beyond that there are also a nice rose garden and some mixed flower borders.

About three miles farther northwest, you come to the *Royal Palace* at *Windsor*. If you have chosen your day right, you may be able to see the Queen's own garden at Frogmore, for this is open to the public twice a year for the Garden Scheme. It is a quietly lovely garden (or must be so when masses of visitors are not there), with azaleas, lilacs, and other shrubs flowering on mounds around a lake. But whenever you go, you will be able to visit Windsor Great Park, with its three justly famous horticultural attractions—the Valley Gardens, the Kurume Punch Bowl, and the Savill Gardens. All of these are open from 10 A.M. to 6 P.M. (in autumn and winter, till sundown). Try to see the *Valley Gardens* in the spring, when the rhododendrons and azaleas are out, or you could enjoy the great display of hydrangeas later in the summer. There is autumn color in the trees later on, and then, if you should happen to be in London in midwinter, do go to the Winter Garden and see flowers blooming there even at Christmas. The Valley Gardens alone cover two hundred acres.

The Savill Gardens in Windsor Great Park are among the most beautiful "natural" gardens in the world. True, there are some more formal types included in the area—mixed flower-and-shrub borders, thirty-five feet deep; a rock garden that overflows with bloom in spring; the rose garden featuring many of the oldest favorites; and a wall of brick from bombed-out buildings of World War II, surrounding and protecting many very tender plants. But it is the park-like surroundings, meandering among brooks and hills, that are perhaps loveliest of all. In early spring there are natural-ized bulbs and primulas and a whole Alpine Meadow full of flowers. There are magnolias and cherries in full bloom, and then, most spectacular of all, there is the *Kurume Punch Bowl*. This is a valley of vibrant color from the end of April to mid-May; here thousands of Kurume azaleas cover the slopes on each side. The colors have been carefully selected to blend into one another, each mass of some fifty to two hundred specimens of one variety shading into the next. It is a breathtaking sight. See it first by circling the top of the ridge and looking down on these waves of color from each end. If you cannot visit any other garden around London, don't miss this one. If you have gone out to see Windsor Castle on a conducted bus tour, just leave your companions and spend the rest of the day in Windsor Great Park. You will have no trouble getting back to London alone, for there are many kinds of transportation.

If you should be driving out from London on your way to Oxford, you could make Windsor one of your stops along the way. You could also take in any of the three gardens following, for they are just north of there and would not be far off your direct route.

Once a year, the Royal Garden of *Coppins*, at Iver, just two and a half miles southeast of *Uxbridge*, is open to the public for the Garden Scheme. (See their annual pamphlet for date.) This is the property of the Duchess of Kent. There are naturalized daffodils and other bulbs in spring, a walled garden with fine perennial borders, and a very colorful sunken garden.

At *Stoke Poges* there is a particularly appealing cemetery called the *Gardens of Remembrance*. Stop at the Church Cottage and ask for permission to visit it. The gardens are beautifully designed, including a parterre garden of flower "embroideries," a heather garden, a water garden, and several rock-garden sections.

Just west of here, near *Maidenhead*, is *Cliveden*, the home of American-born Lady Astor, now administered by the National Trust. The gardens here are open on regular days of the week. The grounds reach down to the River Thames, so this is one of the many gardens you could visit if you hired a cabin cruiser, as we did one summer, to prowl upstream at our own deliberate pace, stopping wherever there was a historic spot, a quaint village, or a garden open to the public. We slept on the boat, (a Maidline Cruiser accommodating four), did our own navigation, cooked our breakfasts and lunches in the neat little galley, and had dinner at a different inn each night.

The gardens near the house at Cliveden are designed in the grand formal style with low patterned flower beds. There are also a rose garden, a Japanese-style water garden, and fine flower borders enclosed in boxwood hedges. There are beautiful views of the river from various points, and hybrid rhododendrons and other shrubs and old trees.

Now, let's continue our survey of the gardens within easy reach from London by moving on clockwise to the north. If you should want to drive to Cambridge, from London, you could see any of the following gardens on the way by making only a slight detour. *Cassiobury Park*, in *Watford*, is famous for its display of iris in May. At *Hatfield*, there is an extraordinary garden at *Hatfield House*, which would be worth a special short trip out from London. It is one of the few surviving authentic gardens in England that are now the same as when they were laid out in the first half of the seventeenth century. It is a formal garden in the great traditional style, with beds in front of the house designed around a circular motif. Those at the side are developed in more elaborate scroll patterns, edged with tiny hedges, and filled with flowers for the various seasons, the centers dotted with tree roses and other taller specimens. The palace, once the home of Queen Elizabeth I, can be visited along with the gardens almost every day of the week.

About five miles from here is *Fanhams Hall,* at *Ware,* the property of Westminster Bank Staff College. There is a Japanese Garden here well worth seeing, as it is one of the very few of its kind in England. It is sometimes open to the public for charity, but if you are anxious to visit it, go there and ask the Principal of the College for permission.

From here, I suggest that you swing around to look at the gardens to the southeast of London. If you are going to visit Canterbury, these would be along the way, and there would be others beyond the twenty-mile radius, which I am using here, that you could look up in the "Key to Gardens" in the back of the book, or find by studying the map of the Greater London Area. Kent and Surrey, particularly, are teeming with delightful gardens, so that you might like to plan a special tour of these counties.

Within our twenty-mile radius, however, I suggest, first of all, *Lullingstone Castle,* at Eynsford, two miles south of *Farningham,* where there are lovely heathers and a special herb garden. Now you are on the road to *Sevenoaks,* where you will find *Chevening,* and can enjoy the formal gardens, rose garden, and mixed flower borders when they are open on special days for the Garden Scheme. Another five miles, and you will be at *Squerryes Court* in *Westerham.* The gardens here are open regularly, and are particularly charming in early spring when the daffodils and shrubs are in bloom, but also later on, when there are rhododendrons and perennial borders to enjoy.

At *Edenbridge,* only a few miles southeast, is *Hever Castle.* This is a complete change from the gardens you have just seen, for here there are an elaborate formal Italian design, topiary chessmen, a small rose garden, a maze, a rock garden, a grotto filled with ferns, and good mixed flower borders. Outside the formal areas there is an orchard with daffodils naturalized under the trees, a place of color and fragrance in the spring.

Completing our clockwise swing around London, we now come to three gardens southwest of the city. The first of these, the famous *Wisley Gardens,* north of *Ripley,* should not be missed by anyone interested in plants. This is the showplace and experimental station of the Royal Horticultural Society, open every weekday to non-members, on Sunday only to members of the Society. Particularly outstanding are the collections of alpines, heathers, primroses, rhododendrons, and roses. There are many trial beds where you can compare different varieties and new introductions of some plant. The gardens are so beautifully landscaped, however, that you will forget they are mainly for horticultural research, and you can wander about the 150 acres merely enjoying the colors or exploring the greenhouses if you wish. The magnificent perennial border, twenty feet deep, is perhaps the finest you will see anywhere.

Near *Dorking,* at Bookham, is *Polesden Lacey,* a National Trust property. Here you can enjoy an 18th-century garden of clipped hedges and mixed flower borders on various terraces from which you get distant views of the surrounding countryside. At *Guildford,* about fifteen miles west of here, there are two attractions. One is the estate of *Albury Park,* belonging to the Duchess of Northumberland. There are splendid old trees and fine shrubs, and terraced gardens

Roof Garden, Harvey's Dept. Store, Guildford (*Ludi Photographers*)

with lovely flower borders. On High Street, in Guildford itself, there is a unique roof garden on top of *Harvey's* Department Store. This is quite different from the one at Derry and Tom's, in London, for when you step out from the elevator into this area 120 feet above the ground, you will see a large water garden dotted here and there with flowering islands, fountains, cascades, and stepping stones. There are several hundred goldfish and other ornamental fish swimming about in the pools, including rainbow trout up to eighteen inches long. The five islands and the boxes along the railings on both sides are kept full of flowers from about Easter to the end of September. There is a charming terrace where you can enjoy refreshments during store hours, and from various viewing platforms you can look off over the rooftops at the green hills of Surrey.

SOME OF THE MOST NOTABLE GARDENS IN ENGLAND

Four of these were included in the section on the Greater London Area above: Wisley Gardens; Kew Gardens; the Savill Gardens, at Windsor; and Hampton Court Palace. Now we are going to travel all over England looking at some of the particularly famous and interesting gardens. This was a difficult list to narrow down; it could be a great deal longer, and when you go, you will probably see others that you like so much you feel they should have been included. I could not describe all the two-hundred-plus listed in the back of this book, so here are a variety from among those considered the finest.

I would suggest that you start south of the Greater London Area, where there are four not far apart.

One of the great gardens of England (some call it the most beautiful of all) is that of *Sissinghurst Castle*, at *Cranbrook*. It is the joint product of its owners, the great garden writer and designer, Sir Harold Nicolson, and his late wife, the author known as Victoria Sackville-West, who chose the flowers and plants to go into the gardens.

Although beautifully planned as a whole, with fine views and centers of interest carefully placed, the grounds are actually laid out like parts of a house in separate units, each devoted to a particular color scheme or season, an enchanting place filled with ideas for those of us who cultivate flower gardens at home. In the Rose Garden, for example, where the old, but short-lived, varieties are featured, there are also plantings of iris, peonies, tall eremurus, and yuccas, to give color and interest for a longer time. From here you will enter a pleached lime walk that frames the Early Spring Garden, the borders filled with delicately lovely small bulbs and primulas from March to mid-May.

When you step into the Herb Garden, you will suddenly breathe in pungent aromatic fragrances, for you will actually be treading upon paths of thyme, or sitting down to rest on a stone bench covered with growing scented herbs, something the Elizabethans used to do in their gardens. Another feature here is the lawn just outside the Herb Garden, which is made entirely of thyme, a very successful invention of Miss Sackville-West. Turn back now toward the castle, and you will come to what is probably the most beautiful spot of all, the White Garden. I do hope you can see it in June when the white roses, regal lilies, and baby's breath (gypsophilia) shimmering below are roofed over with showers of almond blossoms. Before you leave, be sure to see also the quaintly appropriate Cottage Garden in front of the South Cottage, its beds glowing with flowers in shades of red, yellow, and orange. What a beautiful memorial these gardens are to Miss Sackville-West, surely one as important and lasting as her writing. How grateful we must be that the public is allowed to come here every day in the week to be inspired by such pictures of living beauty.

Sheffield Park Gardens, at *Uckfield,* is a very attractive place owned by the National Trust. Try to see it in May, to enjoy the naturalized daffodils, bluebells, and gentians, the magnificent rhododendrons and azaleas. There are many unusual trees and shrubs to admire, and a number of lakes and cascades, with some starry waterlilies in late summer. Even in the fall the gardens are colorful with many flowers.

A garden at Lower Beeding, near *Horsham,* is famous *Leonardslee,* open regularly in May, when it is at its height. Be prepared to take some long walks here, for there are a hundred acres of beautifully planted woodlands, streams, and ponds. The magnolias and camellias are particularly lovely, as are the azaleas and the rock garden, but most exciting of all are the superb rhododendrons.

There is the world-famous garden of *Nymans,* at *Crawley.* This is really a very fascinating group of separate gardens. One is almost circular, surrounded by walls. It is full of rare trees and shrubs, as well as a spring-blooming border and others featuring summer flowers. There are many amusing topiaries, some even shaped like open-work globes. There are also a very fine rose garden with old-fashioned roses, a rockery that was one of the first to be made in England, a heather garden, and an extensive arboretum with rare conifers and other exotic trees and shrubs including magnolias, camellias, and rhododendrons. In another part of the garden you will see a pergola with a Wisteria multijuga that has blossoms almost three feet in length; this was raised from seed brought from Japan. It is one of the oldest of its kind in England. Nymans is a beautiful place at any time, but especially so in spring and summer.

Between here and Tunbridge Wells there is also another place of special interest to garden lovers: *Gravetye Manor Hotel,* at *East Grinstead,* which was the former home of the great horticulturist and landscape designer, William Robinson. His own gardens here have been kept as much as possible as he had them—an oval formal garden, a kitchen garden of similar shape, and flowering trees, azaleas, rhododendrons, camellias, magnolias in profusion. A very interesting Elizabethan garden has also been added. Spring and autumn are the best seasons to see these historically interesting grounds.

Traveling north of London, we will go to Oxfordshire. Practically every bus and railway tour from London takes in *Blenheim Palace* at *Woodstock,* so you will surely be seeing the garden here. The very fine parterres of clipped box and the formal pools will remind you of the stylized gardens of France—outdoor rooms for the entertaining of hundreds of people of royal or noble birth, whose elegant pastel silks and satins must have lent beautiful color to the green designs of the gardens.

Not far from Oxford, at *Steeple Aston,* there is another fine formal garden at *Rousham House.* This includes thirty acres planned in the romantic landscape style with cascades, temples, and long vistas. There are also a charming rose garden and a walled garden gay with perennial borders.

There are two wonderful gardens not far from Stratford-on-Avon. The first of these is *Packwood House* at Hockley Heath, near *Henley-in-Arden,* owned by the National Trust. It features some fine flower gardens, a sunken rose garden, and 17th-century walls that were heated, even in those days, in order to bring the espaliered fruit that was trained there to earlier ripening. But most fascinating of all are the enormous topiaries, some twenty-five feet high, which were planted over three hundred years ago in a formation to represent the Sermon on the Mount. You will see many topiary gardens on your tours through England, but never another on this theme.

The other garden that you should not miss, *Hidcote Manor,* at *Chipping Campden,* is considered by many to be the most beautiful of the smaller gardens in England. We

Hidcote Manor, England (*Photo from Brit. Travel & Holidays Assn.*)

Americans can be particularly proud of it, for it was designed and made by a fellow countryman, the late Major Lawrence Johnston, at the turn of the century. He was a man of exceptional taste in garden design, and great originality. He did a number of things in laying out these gardens that have been enthusiastically copied ever since throughout England. The first of these was his use of flowering shrubs and trees mixed in with that favorite standby of the English gardener, the perennial flower border. This technique, which gives a lasting effect throughout the seasons with the least possible care involved, has now become so popular that it is a trademark of the modern, labor-saving garden. Another of his innovations, which you will surely notice as you walk about in the different garden units, is the use of many different kinds of hedges instead of walls to enclose the individual sections. There are bronze-brown hedges of clipped copper beech; there are the more usual hedges of clipped yew, and also some of yew and box grown together; there is a shining silver euonymus hedge; and even one that looks like a marble cake, with its flow of interplanted deep-green holly and yew with beech.

Major Johnston apparently liked the old gardens that were planted as "secret rooms," for his grounds are a succession of such private places, each planned with its own center of interest, its own formal or informal paths, its color-schemed plantings to give interest at various times of the year. In one of these, called the Stilt Garden, clipped hornbeams line each side in trim array, their trunks sheared of branches quite far up. There is a fairy-like White Garden, shadowed beneath with forget-me-nots. There are the Red Borders in another place, a Fuchsia Garden all by itself, a Stream Garden of great charm. There are entire borders of old-fashioned roses, or yellow peonies, making wide ribbons of color at your side as you brush by.

Major Johnston was also a great plant collector and hybridizer, so there is much to make one stop and study and marvel. If you have any of the hypericum Hidcote Gold, or the Hidcote lavender, as I have at home, you will greet old friends when you see these here. The hypericum was imported from China by Major Johnston. There is also a famous Hidcote dianthus.

Just before his death some years ago, Major Johnston gave his garden to the National Trust, which administers it jointly with the Royal Horticultural Society.

The lovely cathedral town of Salisbury would make a good hub for a Wheel Tour, as there are many fine gardens in the surrounding places. Most famous of these is *Stourhead*, at Stourton, not far from *Mere*. Although this is definitely what we would call a great park, rather than a garden, I am including this one example of the English "landscape gardens" as this is the very first to have been made, and so historically interesting, as well as being superbly designed.

In 1740, when the grounds were laid out by the great Henry Hoare, he was drawing entirely upon the genius of his own imagination, with no other models to go by. On what were once merely rolling meadows and hills, he created a beautiful picture. There is a lake of twenty acres, made by damming two valleys, surrounded by a forest of pines and beech trees now over two hundred years old. As you walk around the lake, you come to many of the buildings and statuary carefully placed to give interest to the scene—a creamy Temple of Flora, a small replica of the Pantheon at Rome, a Temple of the Sun supposed to have been copied from one at Baalbek, and a beautiful 14th-century market cross that was found in ruins at Bristol. One attraction, which was to be much copied later on, is a mysterious underground grotto with never-failing springs dripping over the mossy stones, and a reclining-nymph sculpture dramatically lighted from above. During May, rhododendrons and azaleas light up the leafy background of the woods; later in the summer, hydrangeas shine out among the trees.

You might stay in Stoke-on-Trent, Staffordshire, to drive out and see the gardens at *Hodnet,* on one side, *Bakewell* on the other. Or you could use two different hubs to include these, but I am sure you won't want to miss either of them. *Hodnet Hall,* in Shropshire, has over sixty acres of landscaped grounds that include a number of special gardens. If you can go there in May, you will see large sheets of naturalized bulbs, as well as rhododendrons and azaleas. Take the delightful winding path along the ponds and canals bordered with Japanese primulas, iris, and other moisture-loving flowers. Later on you can see peonies, magnolias, lilacs, and many roses. The laburnums are magnificent, and there are many unusual trees such as the handkerchief tree, or dove tree, as we call it in America (Davidia involucrata), with its little white squares fluttering in the wind. Though this might be included in the general class of landscape gardens, there are so many colorful areas overflowing with flowers at all times from spring to fall that it is more truly a series of blending flower gardens.

Chatsworth, at *Bakewell* in Derbyshire, is a garden of a completely different type. Many authorities feel that it is the most magnificent and varied of the great 17th-century gardens to be seen in England today, and that the house (which is also open to the public) is the finest example of the great English country houses.

The gardens have passed through the hands of so many owners and garden designers of varying tastes and whims that only an expert would be able to tell you where each part belongs in history. The present owners, however, the Duke and Duchess of Devonshire, have fortunately restored a great deal that had disappeared. They have also added designs of their own inspiration, such as the parterre of miniature box hedges that outlines the plan of the rooms in

Chatsworth House, England (*Photo from Brit. Travel & Holidays Assn.*)

Chatsworth House itself—a delightful idea. The famous Cascades tumbling down over a series of stone steps once inspired Hugh Walpole to an amusing criticism: he said the water destroyed the very use to which stairs should be put! When you look at the Emperor Fountain throwing its great spire up higher than any other in England, you can visualize its initiation to honor the visit of the Tsar of Russia. Besides the splendid formal designs of other days, you can also see a garden of modern roses, a fine rock garden, and lovely flower borders.

If you visit the quaint medieval city of York, you will be within reach of a number of exceptionally fine gardens. *Bramham Park* at *Boston Spa* is another example of the very formal type of design inspired by the French landscape architect Le Nôtre. Here, too, you will see neat parterres, canals, and basins, with lovely blossoming bulbs to brighten the spring picture, and many other flowers throughout the summer. This is open only once a week, but is well worth a visit. The *Harlow Car Gardens,* near *Harrogate,* belonging to the Northern Horticultural Society, are a smaller version of Wisley (see Greater London Area), covering some forty acres. Among the special features here you will see a dianthus garden and another of heathers. There are fine flowering trees and shrubs, roses, rhododendrons, a rockery, a water garden—always something to study and enjoy from spring to fall. Don't miss the *Valley Gardens,* while you are in Harrogate. This is an especially fine public park aglow with color and interesting plantings. The rockery along the winding brook is very lovely. Both these gardens are open every day until sunset.

Newby Hall, at Skelton near *Ripon,* will delight you if you love flowers. There are many different units here—a walled garden with vivid borders; sunken gardens with many of the favorite old roses and spring flowers; a rock garden; a water garden; a Laburnum Walk, with yellow blossoms dripping down overhead as you walk through the archway upon which the trees are trained. The flowers and shrubs have been carefully chosen for color coordination, and there are many places that were planned to light up the fall months. If you go early in the spring you can revel in blossoms in the Orchard Garden. A little later you will ramble along a flowering Rhododendron Walk.

Still farther north than York, up along the west coast at *Kendal*, in Westmoreland, there is the most famous topiary garden in all England, *Levens Hall*. The garden was planted at the end of the 17th century from designs by a Frenchman, for whom the gardener's house is named, Beaumont Hall. The original plans had much more of a feeling of space and dignity than is visible today, for the yew and box shrubs have grown to such tremendous size that many of them are crowded, some even grown together. But there are parts of the garden where you will still see the original intent of spaciousness and grandeur. Levens Hall had a great tradition of hospitality in the 18th century, when a special drink called "morocco," brewed of beer and herbs from a secret recipe, was served from wheelbarrows in the gardens, together with brown bread and butter and quantities of radishes. These Radish Feasts took place in the "Beech Circle."

While you can no longer attend such a repast, you will be delighted by the amusing topiaries and kept occupied trying to guess what they represent. Besides the easily recognized peacocks, cones, pyramids, and other geometrical shapes, there is the Giant Mushroom shape. One looks like a top hat on an open umbrella; another looks like a corkscrew. One is a helmet on a spiral, still another is a huge green lion showing his teeth. There is a doghouse, a chair you can sit on, an arbor with an urn on top. You will see one that may remind you of an egg-beater, and others that are supposed to represent the Queen and her ladies holding cups of "morocco," if your imagination will stretch that far. If topiaries do not entertain you as much as they do me, you can wander among the fine flower borders and enjoy the roses. For more on the history and art of topiary work, you might like to read that section in the chapter "Follow Your Garden Hobby Abroad." Levens Hall is certainly the supreme example.

Your travel plans may take you to the south of England, however, rather than to the north. Perhaps you have planned a trip down through beautiful Devon to the King Arthur country of Cornwall. You will find a number of the finest gardens in all Britain there.

Two of these are at *Yeovil*, in Somerset, and both belong to the National Trust. At *Montacute House*, you will find one of the best surviving examples of early Jacobean gardens, surrounded by walls topped with a graceful balustrade. Nearby is a sunken garden reminiscent of Italy, with a formal central pool and tall yews, the effect softened, however, by the surrounding flower borders. Many consider these the most perfect formal gardens of their type in the British Isles. The ones at *Tintinhull House*, on the other hand, are semiformal, more intimate in style. There is a whole series of units leading away from the house by a central path, with carefully color-schemed flower borders and shrubs on each side, designed in the modern trend to need as little care as possible. Nevertheless, there is Old World charm in the clematis on the brick walls surrounding the first garden, the conical topiaries along the path, the big terra-cotta flowerpots, and the ancient bits of statuary here and there.

If you drive on toward *Plymouth*, you will come to *Cotehele*, at Calstock, just north of the port city. This is another National Trust garden in the formal style, with terraces bordered with flowers, each level faced with a dry wall overflowing with blossoming rock plants. Be sure to walk beyond this area, however, to see the primulas and meconopsis (that lovely "blue poppy") naturalized along the stream, and the woods garden with fine rhododendrons and other flowering shrubs here and there in spring, hydrangeas later on in the summer. You will see some interesting trees here also, such as the cork oak, which grows so well in Spain and southern France, and in one section you will come on a little herb garden.

At this point you would be about sixty-five miles from *Trengwainton*, just west of *Penzance*. The famous collection of beautiful and unusual shrubs here includes a magnificent array of rhododendrons in a setting of superb views. The walled garden shelters many rare and tender plants that love the sun. The stream is planted with flowers and leafy things that need moisture.

Even though the boat only goes three times a week, do take it from Penzance to the *Scilly Isles* to see the tropical gardens at *Tresco Abbey*. But I must warn you, you will find little or no transportation on the island, and you may have to do quite a bit of hiking over the sand-dune paths lined with gorse. There is a tractor that sometimes pulls a carload of tourists to the gardens, but there are times when it is more urgently needed in the fields. Perhaps the safest thing to do is to join up with a tour group for this trip, with transportation planned ahead.

Once you are at Tresco Abbey, you will think you have landed on the French Riviera by mistake. Here the climate has made it possible for tropical and subtropical plants to thrive. When Augustus Smith, a lifetime bachelor who fell in love with the island, first began laying out his gardens in the middle of the last century, he had mainly the wind to contend with. Against this he planted strong shelters of trees and built a high wall. Soon the tender plants he introduced experimentally began to grow in luscious profusion, and his enthusiasm grew with them. He obtained some from fellow gardeners throughout England, but his best contributions came from the sea captains who made port on the Scilly Isles and soon, learning of his desires, began to bring him rare roots and seeds from all over the world.

In these gardens you can wander the globe, admiring tall palms from the Canary Islands; giant yuccas from Mexico, with flowers at a height of twenty feet; and strange-looking leaves and flowers with even stranger names, from New Zealand, Australia, South Africa, all the places where the climate is hot and always sunny. There is so much variation in form and color among these huge exotic cacti and succulents that you never feel you've really seen enough at Tresco. Fortunately for us, Mr. Smith's great-grand-nephew, Lt. Commander Dorrien-Smith, who now owns the property, has not only seen that it is kept in excellent condition, but allows the public to come there and enjoy it.

These are only some of the high spots of a garden tour around England. If you will study the "Key to Gardens" listings, you will find many more that you may think equally lovely when you see them.

USEFUL INFORMATION

The following organizations have lists and booklets—free unless otherwise specified—that will help you plan your garden tour of England.

THE BRITISH TRAVEL ASSOCIATION, 680 Fifth Ave., New York 19, N.Y.: Booklet, "Historic Houses, Castles and Gardens," published annually with dates and hours when these are open (this includes only some of the private gardens opened on special days for the Gardens Scheme). This is an indispensable handbook, as it also gives directions for getting to the gardens, and where to get meals nearby. Another delightful booklet is "Flowers and Their Seasons in Britain," price 40¢, telling when the wildflowers are in bloom and where. If you cannot get this from the New York office, send for it from the British Travel and Holidays Association, 64 St. James St., London S.W.1, England, including postage.

GARDENER'S SUNDAY, White Witches, Claygate Road, Dorking, Surrey, England: Booklet listing dates when private gardens are opened for this charitable organization; price 30¢ including postage.

THE NATIONAL GARDENS SCHEME, 57 Lower Belgrave St., London, S.W.1, England: Booklet, "Illustrated Guide to Gardens of England and Wales Open to the Public," published annually in mid-March, price 60¢ including postage. This lists over 1000 private gardens and the days when these are open for this charitable organization, also how to reach them and where to get tea. Admission fee is usually only 14¢.

THE NATIONAL TRUST, 23 Caxton St., London, S.W.1, England: For an annual membership of $2.80, you will get free admission to all the National Trust properties; receive a list of these castles and gardens, with up-to-date information on hours of admission; receive News Bulletins and an Annual Report; and you will be helping this worthy organization to preserve these historical properties for the enjoyment of the public. You can also write to them enclosing $3.50 plus postage, for their new National Trust Atlas, with 59 pages of maps of England, Wales and Northern Ireland, showing over 7000 points of interest, including gardens.

THE ROYAL AUTOMOBILE CLUB, Pall Mall, London, S.W.1, England: Free maps showing routes to see the tulip fields around Spalding; cherry blossoms in the Teme Valley; and apple-blossoms in Kent.

THE ROYAL HORTICULTURAL SOCIETY, Vincent Square, London, S.W.1, England: By becoming an annual Fellow in the Society for $5.88, you will get free admission to all the Society's Flower Shows (some twelve events from April to September, including the great Chelsea Show in May); also to Wisley Gardens, where only members are admitted on Sunday; and receive the monthly Journal (see chapter on "Suggested Reading About European Gardens").

chapter 9

SCOTLAND: CASTLE GARDENS

UCH has been written about the beauty of Scotland's mountain scenery, her historic castles, her colorful festivals, but too little has been said about her extraordinary gardens.

Not only are the little home gardens, tucked everywhere, delightful, with their array of primroses, tulips, narcissus, and other flowers in season, but the great smoky cities of Edinburgh and Glasgow are justifiably proud of their green areas and botanical gardens.

The climate of Scotland, like that of Ireland and England, with excessive rainfall and general humidity, has always encouraged gardeners' efforts. In some northwestern sections of Scotland, the warmth of the nearby Gulf Stream (which the Scots call America's Greatest Gift) has even made it possible to grow tropical trees, flowers, and shrubs. Everywhere, the rhododendrons are a spectacular feature of parks and castle grounds.

Many fine homes and castles with beautiful gardens are now owned by the National Trust for Scotland, which is supported by voluntary contributions. The owners of the great estates here, as in all Britain, are heavily taxed and unable to afford the professional help required to keep up these extensive properties. It is fortunate that the National Trust has been able to save many of these historic sites and keep them open for viewing by the public.

Before making a garden tour, write to the National Trust for Scotland for their booklet (see list at end of this chapter); it gives the latest information on hours when each estate is open, as well as directions for reaching it.

Another valuable source of information on gardens to see is Scotland's Garden Scheme, which organizes special days at private gardens for a small entrance fee given to charity. In outlining the suggested tour of Scotland's gardens, below, I have included only a sampling of these. The booklet (see address at end of this chapter) lists over 230 such places each year, giving the special days between April and September when they may be visited, and directions for reaching them. These gardens range all the way from charming small home places to great estates with unique collections of exotic plants.

You will also find invaluable a pamphlet, published every year, called *Historic Houses, Castles and Gardens,* which gives dates and hours of garden openings. (It too is listed at the end of this chapter.) I am referring you to all these publications, which are kept up-to-date, and am mentioning hours for only a few places open daily or not so listed.

We began our tour of the gardens of Scotland by driving up from the Lake District of England. If you do the same, you will make sure to stop at Sir Walter Scott's beautiful castle, Abbotsford, then visit the glorious abbey ruins at Melrose and Dryburgh. There are some lovely gardens in this area that you could include in your itinerary. *Manderston,* at *Duns,* is a great estate where you will see a fine sunken garden, a rhododendron wood, and a splendid greenhouse collection (open a few days annually for the Garden Scheme). Then there is the beautiful Italian Garden and splendid Rose Garden at *Mellerstain,* near *Gordon.* Here you

Mellerstain, Scotland (*Photo from The Scotsman Publications Ltd.*)

will see a unique collection of old and modern roses, and all summer long some fine mixed flower borders. Mellerstain is usually open every afternoon except Saturday. The old towns and enchanting scenery around this part of Scotland, between Kelso and Lauder, are worth a longer visit. You might like to stay at the *Johnstounburn Hotel* two miles north of *Humbie*, a homelike place with wonderful gardens, and visit Edinburgh and neighboring gardens from there. Or you could drive right to the coast, stopping on the way to see old Berwick-on-Tweed, and follow the beautiful shoreline to *Edinburgh*.

Instead of staying in this smoky city, affectionately named "Auld Reeky" even by its citizens, we preferred a delightful homelike inn, *Prestonfield House*, on the outskirts near Arthur's Seat. (If you arrive there in late June, you will enjoy their magnificent garden of tree roses in full bloom. But find out whether they still have the peacocks that screech so early in the morning!)

If you come to Edinburgh in August, for the great music and drama festival, find out about the Garden Tours arranged by Scotland's Garden Scheme to coincide with this.

In Edinburgh, while you are shopping on world-renowned *Princes Street* you will certainly want to stroll through the flower-bordered path along its edge and discover the great *Floral Clock* near the entrance of the park.

Next head for the *Royal Botanical Garden*, on Inverleith Row. This extraordinary collection now covers sixty acres. It was first founded on another site in 1670. The rolling terrain makes this a charming place, with wonderful panoramic views of Edinburgh. Here you will see one of the largest and finest rock gardens in the world, covering four acres. Among its outstanding collections are plants from western and central China and from Tibet. There are particularly fine rhododendrons, primroses, varieties of maple, and heathers. There are beautiful flower borders, a special section for moisture-loving plants, an extensive arboretum, and many greenhouses. Don't try to see everything in this amazing place in one visit, but go back several times. It is open free of charge from 9 A.M. to sunset on weekdays, from 11 A.M. on Sundays. The greenhouses are open from 1 to 5 in the afternoons.

Just outside of Edinburgh are a number of gardens you will enjoy. In the colorful little village of Inveresk, near *Musselburgh,* is *Inveresk Lodge.* This is a small, newly reorganized garden developed by the National Trust as an interesting center for the historic village. There are mixed flower borders, a section with old-fashioned as well as newer roses, and carefully chosen flowering trees and shrubs. At one end there is an old orchard that is a glorious sight in bloom.

Southeast of Edinburgh is *Pencaitland,* where you can see *Winton Castle,* with its terraced gardens and fine display of naturalized daffodils in spring. This is open a few days annually for the Garden Scheme, but can be seen at other times by telephoning the owner, Sir David Ogilvy, for an appointment.

At *Dirleton,* a little to the north, is *Dirleton Castle.* Here you will find attractive flower gardens and a 17th-century bowling green surrounded by ancient yews.

Now that the new Firth of Forth Bridge has been completed, you might like to stay in or near Edinburgh and drive north into Kinross-shire and Fife on several short excursions. Or you could stay in a simple inn at Dunfermline or Kinross, or in the famous golfing center of St. Andrews, and see a number of exceptional gardens from there. In *Dunfermline,* Andrew Carnegie's birthplace, you will want to see the beautiful *Pittencrieff Glen,* of about sixty acres, with flower gardens and greenhouse, one of the great financier's gifts to the town. The little medieval "palace" at *Culross,* near here, also has a nice small garden, and there is a garden at *Stirling Castle* that you will surely visit. Just north of Stirling is *Dunblane,* with a fine garden named *Keir.* This is open on certain days of the week for the Garden Scheme. There is color here beginning in spring, with a fine display of bulbs, rhododendrons, azaleas, woodland, and water plants. Flowers blaze in the borders all summer, and, finally, autumn tints the trees for a special effect.

Be sure to stop at the *Roman Camp Hotel* in *Callander,* if only for a meal, and see their delightful old parterre flower beds that look like a great Oriental carpet. Going north again, you get to *Crieff.* Here, at *Drummond Castle,* you can walk through formal terraced Italian gardens with stairways of natural rock, dating from the 17th century, and see many fine topiaries and old hedges. A unique feature here is the Multiplex Sundial, made in 1630. This is a tall shaft, something like an obelisk, made in carved sections, with an eight-sided block near the center that has a sundial rod on each of its surfaces.

From here, you can head east and stop at *Kinross.* Pick one of the days when the *Kinross House* gardens are open for the Garden Scheme. You will find wonderful deep flower borders here against an old stone wall, with "dividers" of clipped hedges separating the various groups of perennials. If you look straight across the formal Rose Garden to the lake beyond, you get a fine view, framed by a wrought-iron gate at the end of the estate, of Loch Leven Castle on its island. This is where Mary Queen of Scots was imprisoned.

Strangely enough, though *Falkland Palace* is centuries old, its charming garden is completely modern, for the restoration by the National Trust was only begun in 1947, with an old print of the original gardens as a guide. First see the charming little rose garden with edgings of lavender. Next, stop on the paved terrace to look down on the entire garden plan and colors. Try to be there in June, when the famous Great Lupine Border is at its height. This is a bed 126 feet long, in front of a gray stone wall covered with climbing roses. There are twelve different varieties of lupine planted here, with a front edging of German iris, a glorious sight.

Opposite this border is one with all-white flowers, including roses, mock orange shrubs, and many flowering cherries. Another border is entirely blue. At the foot of this flower garden you will reach the entrance of the formal Fountain Garden with its two pools. Stop here a moment and look back toward the castle to get a splendid picture with the flower borders in the foreground. If you are a clematis fancier you will have a delightful time examining the many varieties climbing on the walls of the Fountain Garden, covered with blossoms in all shades of blue, purple, red, pink, and white. Beyond this you will see the only Royal Tennis Court in Scotland, built for James V, in 1539. When you are looking at the magnificently furnished interior of the palace, don't miss the beautiful old tapestries in the long hallway, picturing ancient gardens.

The village of *Leuchars* is well worth visiting for its unique Norman church, which has stood nearly eight centuries. I hope you will be able to plan your tour so that you can be there on the one day when the gardens at *Earlshall*, a small, restored 16th-century castle, are open for the Garden Scheme. You will find an amusing topiary garden full of "chessmen" here, "peacocks," and "pepperpots," and several flower gardens as well. It was one of my favorites on our tour of Scotland, for it has an intimate charm that many castle and estate gardens lack. All the gardens are near the house, instead of being at a great distance, as so many are, and each is framed by hedges to give it privacy.

Most people go to *St. Andrews* to golf, but if you are primarily a flower lover, go anyway, and stay or eat at the famous *Rufflets Hotel* there, in order to enjoy its ten acres of lovely gardens. If you are interested in alpine plants, or cacti and succulents, do stop also at the *University Botanical*

Garden to see the collections there, which also include many interesting plants from the Himalayas.

You can leave the county of Fife by way of the ferry going across to picturesque Dundee and from there drive up into Angus county, where there are four interesting gardens, each within about ten miles of the other. First you will come to *Glamis Castle*, made famous by Shakespeare's play, *Macbeth*, and also by the more recent event of Princess Margaret's birth there. According to legend, the first castle was built here because the fairies said, "Build the castle in the bog, where it will neither shake nor shog." Today you will see no traces of a bog, however firm, in the peaceful royal gardens, both formal in type, at the side of and behind the castle. Tiny hedges of box or clipped yew frame the roses and perennials. The grounds are open on certain days of the week when the Royal Family is not in residence (your hotel porter will tell you this).

Airlie Castle, at *Kirriemuir*, is particularly famous for its topiary garden. The great shapes there are arranged in battle formation like the armies at Waterloo! The garden may be seen by appointment with the owner, the Earl of Airlie.

Guthrie Castle, at *Guthrie*, usually open one day a week, has a delightful walled garden, fine yew hedges, flowering borders, floribunda roses, lilies, and lovely shrubs, in addition to a wildflower section. This is a spring garden, particularly charming at the end of May.

For complete contrast to these (one never lacks variety in garden-viewing!), visit the garden at *Edzell Castle* at *Edzell*. These formal patterned flower beds are just as they were designed in 1604—before the Pilgrims came to America. This is the earliest surviving garden in England and Scotland. The design of the long wall surrounding it is extraordinary. At regular intervals it is recessed into arched niches that display the red-white-and-blue heraldic colors of the first owners, the Lindsays. The niches are framed in red sandstone, painted white inside, and at their centers are blue flowering plants. Above these niches are nesting-holes for birds, each in the form of the Edzell Lindsay star. There are sculptures everywhere, copied from German models of the period. Fortunately, this unusual garden is open every day to the public at certain hours, so even if you are not able to see the others I mention in Angus county, try to get to this one.

Aberdeen makes a good center from which to see the next group of gardens, all of which are within thirty miles of that city. In Aberdeen itself there are fine roses in the parks and an alpine garden and greenhouse at the *Cruickshank Botanic Garden.* Just west of the city at *Drumoak* is *Drum Castle,* with a pretty summer garden of rare flowering trees and shrubs and a water garden.

Among the finest gardens in Scotland is the one at *Crathes Castle* in *Banchory,* where you will find one of the best collections of rare trees and shrubs in Britain. The yew hedges are extraordinary; they are 260 years old, over twelve feet high. The garden itself is divided into eleven square enclosures, each planned to bloom at a particular season or to follow a definite color scheme. The Upper Pool Garden, for example, has trees and shrubs of purple foliage, with red and yellow flowers. Here are a lovely rosy buddleia from India (Buddleia Colvilei), a New Zealand lace-bark (Hoheria populnea), and some honeysuckles from China (Lonicera tragophylla) with four-inch-long yellow trumpets. The Fountain Garden contains blue flowers such as salvia, a Tibetan buddleia, a Hydrangea Sargentiana from China, a fine specimen of Paulownia imperialis. The Rose Garden is surrounded by other unique and lovely flowering shrubs, and here you will find the fascinating handkerchief tree (Davidia involucrata), which has two leafy white bracts that look just like handkerchiefs waving in the breeze framing each flower. The West Herbaceous Border is planted with pink, blue, and

Crathes Castle, Scotland (*Photo from Brit. Travel & Holidays Assn.*)

mauve flowers, and there is another completely White Border sixty yards long. The Trough Garden was carefully designed for continuous bloom from spring to fall. Here you will see many of our famous Oregon lilies, and the Himalayan giant lily (Cardiocrinum giganteum), which reaches eleven feet in height and lasts only one season.

The National Trust, which owns the castle, has published a fascinating illustrated booklet that you can buy at the entrance. This tells the history of the castle itself and its beautiful furnishings and lists a great many of the unusual plants to be found in the gardens.

The gardens of the royal castle of *Balmoral*, at *Ballater*, can be seen on many days from May through July, whenever the Royal Family are not in residence. There are a number of small, individualized gardens very close to the castle, planned so that they could be enjoyed from the windows. Formal geometrical flower beds in one of these units are kept filled with low flowers—usually thousands of pansies in the spring. Queen Mary's Sunken Garden on another side is surrounded by dry walls planted with little alpines, the center beds filled with Polyantha roses interspersed with snapdragons and other annuals for summer color. One garden has beautifully curved steps repeating the lines of the mixed flower borders. There are benches here and there, and all the gardens have an informal, lived-in quality that must be most refreshing to Her Majesty the Queen and the Royal Family when they stay here.

Leith Hall, another National Trust property, at *Kennethmont,* is famous for its splendid flower borders. One planned for early summer features lupines, delphinium, my favorite meconopsis (like a sky-blue poppy), and anchusa. Another with Michaelmas daisies and pentstemons blooms later in the summer, and yet another, of phlox, Japanese anemones, and spiky lythrums, keeps on blossoming into fall. The two borders zigzag along the walks, filled with lovely pink and mauve flowers edged with silvery-gray leaf plants. The rock garden that meanders along the edges of a stream is full of a charming profusion of flowers from early spring to late autumn. This is a garden artists and color photographers will surely enjoy. It is at its height in early August.

At *Insch*, only a few miles east of here, is *Williamston*, with mixed perennial borders, flowering shrubs, and a woodland garden.

Next, we come to another of the truly great gardens of Scotland, at *Pitmedden House* in *Udney*. This is a reconstructed formal 17th-century garden owned by the National Trust. I hope you can see it in midsummer or even a little later, when it is in its full glory. Stop for a moment at the top of the steps leading down to the garden and study the intricate way some 20,000 small annuals are bedded in old-fashioned patterns, edged in boxwood. One design represents Lord Pitmedden's family crest. The walled garden has raised terraces on two sides, faced with splendid perennial borders. There are pavilions, fountains, and a rose garden. It is not often that historic landscape design is resurrected as effectively as the "Great Garden of Pitmedden." How lucky we are that this is available to the public every day of the week.

Try to see the extraordinary tropical gardens of Inverewe, even though they are far out on the west coast. If you follow the itinerary I have suggested so far, you could, if you pick your dates properly according to the Garden Scheme booklet, see one or more of the private gardens on the beautiful north coast along the way. This will take you up into Banffshire—the county of whisky and good beefsteak—to *Blackhills*, near *Elgin*, a wonderful treat for anyone interested in rhododendrons. Mr. Sylvester Christie, the present owner, inherited the garden from his uncle, who was a tea planter in Ceylon, and became interested in collecting rhododendrons from Yunan, Tibet, Nepal, and Burma (many of the original specimens grew as high as 15,000 feet up in the Himalayas). He brought his collection to Blackhills forty years ago, where they now thrive in a natural Highland glen setting. These are all rhododendron species, not as large in flower as the modern hybrid varieties, but with some of the most glowing deep colors imaginable. They are in bloom from Christmas to August. Be sure to notice the leaves as well as the flowers, for these vary in their white or brown furry backs, and their shapes—slim or round, short or very long. Mr. Christie said he had found one leaf thirty-two inches long. Some of his rhododendrons have won highest awards at recent shows.

From here it is only a short distance to *Cawdor Castle*. Though the gardens here are open only once in May and once in August, I hope that you will be able to see them. When we were there in May they were exceptionally lovely. Lady Cawdor has kept the original design of the gardens intact as much as possible, with formal oval and rectangular beds in the center and winding paths bordered by flowers along the sides. Do notice the edging; some of it, instead of being made of stone, is constructed of blocks of peat, making a charming little wall of hazy purple. The colors of flowers in Scotland always seem especially vivid, and here the for-get-me-nots that edge beds filled with tulips, primulas, and other early flowers, are the bluest I have ever seen.

There is a charming kitchen garden, as well, and by going through a gate in the stone wall you will come to a little hidden water garden with primulas and wildflowers along the brook. It all seems so quiet and peaceful in contrast to the castle's history—for this is where Macbeth is said to have been murdered! There is a delightful story of how the castle came to be on its present site. It seems that the first Earl of Cawdor asked a magician for advice. He was told to load his treasures in a chest onto a donkey, let the beast go, and build his castle at the first tree at which the animal stopped.

This the Earl did; he built his castle tower around the hawthorn tree where the donkey halted. The old tree trunk and treasure chest are still there.

Now for your trip to see *Inverewe* at *Poolewe,* on the northwest coast. This could easily be combined with a visit to the Isle of Skye. You could stay in Kyle of Lochalsh, at the Lochalsh Hotel, a very comfortable modern hostel with steam heat and picture windows looking out over the water, and go by ferry to Skye and back. From here, start driving up to Poolewe, a distance of some fifty-five miles.

Inverewe is a very beautiful garden in an amazing spot. A hundred years ago this little peninsula, which was called "Am Ploc Ard" in Gaelic, or the High Lump, was just that: a high barren lump of ground where only some heather and creeping crowberry could grow on the acid black peat. In 1862, Osgood Mackenzie bought it and started to make his garden. First he had to plant a heavy windbreak of pine and fir trees to make a shelter from the terrible gales that sweep the salt spray over the island. Then good soil had to be brought in baskets for every spot in which something was to be planted. The entire area was fenced in against deer and rabbits. Finally, he began to create the garden itself. Once the winds were kept off, the mild effect of the nearby Gulf Stream made itself felt, and little by little tropical and subtropical plants were introduced and began to thrive. Now you will see in this spot—like an oasis in the center of the wild moors—palms and tree ferns, Mediterranean pines, creepers from Tasmania and Chile, passionflowers, the parrot's bill of New Zealand, a cherry blossom from Japan, and the huge tender forget-me-not, Myosotidium nobile.

Be sure to buy the little guide to the gardens so that you can follow the plan to the sections that would interest you most. There are several fine rock gardens with rare alpine plants, water plants growing around a pond, azalea groves, a rhododendron walk. In one small plot named "America," you can feel at home among the mollis azaleas and some of our fine Oregon lilies. I won't try to lead you through this paradise of a garden; there are so many tempting side paths all along the way that each visitor will certainly want to work out his own route. If you are a warm-blooded and serious-minded horticulturist, perhaps you would want to come here in March to see the fabulous Magnolia Campbellii in bloom and the early rhododendrons and bulbs, but most of us would wait till late spring and summer, for even then the winds are strong and likely to be cold. The finest rock garden and rhododendron displays come in late April or early May. All through June and July there are massed plantings of primroses and meconopsis in flower. The perennial border is at its best in July and August. There is always something colorful in each section throughout the seasons.

Inside the Walled Garden, which has fruit trees, flowers, and vegetables all combined, you will always find shelter. And as you wander in and out among all these flowers and trees from the warmer climates, you will forget entirely that you are up on the northwestern edge of Scotland. If you think you have problems growing some things at home in your own garden, just remember the odds against which Osgood Mackenzie worked (and his daughter after him) to convert this bleak land into a flowering oasis that some fifty thousand tourists roam each year, now that it is part of the National Trust. The restaurant in the gardens is open all day long, for you really need time to see all there is here.

The next group of gardens I have to suggest is much farther south. Driving down at the end of May and early June from Inverness to the Great Glen, you will see wonderful wild rhododendrons in bloom and many spring flowers. If you are an alpine-plant enthusiast, you might stop off to do some hiking up Ben Lawers, taking along the book, *Ben Lawers and Its Alpine Flowers*, published by the National Trust for Scotland. For these next gardens you could use

Glasgow as your center, or perhaps the lovely homelike Ard-may House Hotel at Arrochar, at the northern tip of Dun-bartonshire. Have a tourist office in Scotland help you work out a route, whether you are driving or going by bus, for these gardens are scattered and you will have to know which ferries or bridges to use to cross the lochs and get to the islands where many of the gardens are.

About eight miles south of Arrochar, on Loch Lomond, the little village of *Luss* is worth seeing, for the cottages all along the main street have flower gardens blooming in front and roses twining up their walls. Twelve miles south of Arrochar on the western highway there is a lovely garden, *Glenarn* at *Rhu*, open regularly for the Garden Scheme. You will see over 500 varieties of rhododendrons here, mainly of the original species that we saw at Blackhills farther north. There are flowering shrubs, a fine rock garden, and many of the lovely "candelabra" primulas. At *Dunoon*, a few miles west, there are two attractions for the garden lover. The pri-vate garden of *Eckford* is open daily from April through June, when you will enjoy the rhododendrons, the wild gar-den, and lots of daffodils. Then, seven miles north of Dun-oon, you can visit *Benmore, The Younger Botanic Garden* that is part of the famous one at Edinburgh. Here there are a formal garden, water and rock gardens, and a splendid collection of rhododendrons and old trees including some sequoias. Be sure to walk up to some viewpoint from which you can get a look at the beautiful Holy Loch. This garden is open daily from 10 A.M.

From here you have to head north and west to get around Loch Fyne. You will pass through Inveraray, with its fine castle and quaint old shop windows, to get to *Minard.* Or you could take the Campbeltown bus all the way from Glas-gow, and stop right at the door of the next garden I recom-mend, *Crarae Lodge,* open every day from dawn to dusk between April and October. It is best in May or early June, for that is when the azaleas and rhododendrons are in bloom. These are fine hybrids, but planted in such a natural way all over the banks of the woodland glen that one feels as if nature must have placed them there. Climb up and down the dirt paths along the brook to enjoy one charming view after another, cross little wooden bridges that look down on the tiny waterfalls, to get to the other side, and stop there to absorb the lovely colors as you brush past. There are tall straight pine trees and a great variety of rare trees and shrubs. Beyond the Glen Garden there is an excellent arboretum with unique collections of eucalyptus and conifers. The owner of these gardens, Sir George I. Campbell, and his son, Ilay Campbell, who is a well-known garden writer, are both enthusiastic dendrologists, and have made Crarae Lodge a goal for many tree-loving travelers.

You are now well along the road toward the *Isle of Seil*, so why not cross the "bridge over the Atlantic" (a few yards of arch) to take in *An Cala*, the lovely garden at *Easdale* there? This is open once a week in the afternoons for the Garden Scheme. An Cala is particularly famous for its many flowering cherries, but it is a beautifully planned garden with much to see, so allow plenty of time. It is surrounded on three sides by a steep hillside, down which tumbles a roaring waterfall. The third side has been protected from the bitter Atlantic gales by a high wall of gray brick covered with clematis and other vines. The water from the fall spills into a meandering brook that stops every once in a while to spread into a pool. This has been delightfully planted along the course of its borders with primulas, iris, azaleas, and other bright spots of color. There are several fine rock-garden sections, a rose garden, and a special wild garden, each featuring unusually fine flowers and shrubs. One pool into which the brook flows is accented by a splendid silver-leafed weeping pear (Pyrus salicifolia pendula). Though the gardens are only some thirty years old, everything here has been so carefully arranged that the effect is one of luxuriant natural growth.

If the weather is good you might drive south on the mainland from here to West Loch Tarbert and take a steamer to the *Island of Gigha.* (The Stonefield Castle Hotel, just north of Tarbert, has some very fine rhododendrons.) Or go still farther on to Tayinloan for the ferry to Gigha. (Look up the directions for getting there in the Garden Scheme booklet and check locally as well.) There is a very worthwhile private garden on Gigha called *Achamore,* which is open every day. You will see many tender exotic shrubs and trees here from Chile and New Zealand, as well as choice camellias, rhododendrons, and azaleas. In the spring there are naturalized daffodils, primulas, and flowering cherries. Summer brings the lilies and roses to full height, and later on you can enjoy the splendid fuchsias and hydrangeas. This is an extensive garden, well worth the trip.

On the *Island of Arran,* easily reached from Glasgow, is the wonderful National Trust garden at *Brodick Castle,* considered by many to be one of the best in the British Isles. It is open every weekday afternoon from May to September. While you are looking at the castle itself be sure to notice the many tiny rock plants that flower in the crevices of the red sandstone. The walled formal garden here was begun 250 years ago and contains many rare tender plants, as do the rock gardens and the woodlands. Rhododendrons, for which this garden is famous, bloom in this mild climate from January to August. There are fine hybrid fuchsias, lovely acacias, and a beautiful lily collection that includes the Lilium auratum, blooming from June to August. The Rose Garden is charming, with its arches covered with climbers. If you would like to live with this garden for a few weeks in the summer, you can actually rent an apartment in the castle, and feel like the duchess who formerly owned it and created the lovely surroundings. The National Trust for Scotland makes it available each year. (For details write The National Trust for Scotland, 5 Charlotte Square, Edinburgh 2, Scotland.)

In *Glasgow* itself forty-five acres of the *Botanic Gardens* are open daily, although the greenhouses open only in the afternoons. In one of these you will find a fascinating collection of delicate ferns and a "forest" of tree ferns that are especially fine. Be sure to visit the herb garden, the fine rock gardens, and the woodland garden. What a joy to discover such a place in the smoky city of Glasgow!

Very near the city is another private garden, open only occasionally for the Garden Scheme, which I hope you can visit. This is *Finlaystone,* at *Langbank,* the property of General Sir Gordon MacMillan. The shrub borders here are particularly beautiful, with some vivid low Spanish gorse that makes an excellent trimmed edging, and brilliant banks of azaleas. The lawns are surrounded by massive clipped hedges crenelated like the top of a castle wall. In one corner of the lawn is the famous yew tree under which John Knox served the first Protestant Communion in western Scotland in about 1556. Lady MacMillan told me an amazing story about the moving of this tree. It was already very large around 1900 when an aunt, who liked to sew in a window of the great stone house, complained that it gave too much shade there. Apparently she was used to her wishes being carried out, for the tree was thereupon moved farther away —but it is still flourishing today and now has a fine great trunk.

Be sure to see the large planting of gentians which Lady MacMillan raises for the London market, and the new woodland pool garden with its Japanese primroses and huge Gunnera plants. Lady MacMillan, like so many estate owners in Great Britain, does most of the gardening herself with only the aid of some college-age girl apprentices. She and her daughter are also famous for the beautiful flower arrangements that they make for weddings and large parties. The examples of her art that I saw in the house were exceptionally lovely.

Our last regional garden tour in Scotland will take you right through the country associated with Robert Burns, in Ayrshire. At *Maybole*, you will find *Culzean Castle*, which we Americans regard with particular affection since an apartment there was given to former President Eisenhower for his lifetime use, in recognition of his war services. This is a National Trust property, and the gardens are open daily. Perhaps you will agree with many visitors in thinking that the Fountain Garden in front of the castle is one of the most beautiful in Scotland, with its Old World terraces and overflowing flower borders. You will also see an excellent example of an old Scottish walled garden, and enjoy the fine Rose Garden next to it. Be sure to stop in at the Camellia House when these are in bloom, and take a walk through the woodland gardens to see the many fine exotic trees, including the flame-flowered embothrium that we saw so often in Ireland. There are many interesting semitropical trees and plants everywhere throughout the grounds, and there is something in bloom from the first snowdrops in February through to the last hydrangeas and other late flowers. If you are a garden club member you will especially appreciate the exquisite flower arrangements inside the castle, which are done voluntarily throughout the summer by the women of the Ayr and District Floral Club.

Down near the southernmost tip of Wigtownshire is *Port Logan*, with its deservedly famous *Logan Gardens*. This is another amazing example of a Scottish garden in which the delicate plants from all the tropical and subtropical regions of the world seem to feel at home. In the various walled enclosures you might easily think you were in Italy, looking at the formal pools, the elegant urns, the lush plants and brilliant flowers, all backed by great tall palms and thriving tree ferns. There is a charming rock terrace planted with dwarf rhododendrons from China, while in other places the hybrid varieties have grown to twenty or thirty feet in height. In the spring you will see a veritable carpet of primroses from China and the Himalayas, and later, great masses of choice azaleas. In late summer lovely Chinese hydrangeas reflect themselves in a pool.

Some fifty miles east of here is an interesting place to visit, the *Threave School of Practical Gardening*, at *Castle Douglas*. Having seen so many beautiful places in Scotland that are in such dire need of more gardeners, it is encouraging to learn of the training given here. Besides the two-year gardening course offered to the young people by the National Trust, there are a number of lecture series that can be heard by adults in the vicinity. The property of 1300 acres is open to the public daily all the year around, so you could visit the walled gardens, the rock and peat gardens, the arboretum, and the greenhouses. The naturalized daffodils are particularly lovely there in spring. Perhaps you will see some of the students at work in the gardens.

You may not get to all the gardens that I have mentioned on this tour around Scotland, but I hope that I have tempted you to visit some of the most important ones. Plan your next tour there with the help of the booklets listed below, so that you can tuck into your plans a number of the pretty private gardens along your way, on the days when the owners so generously open them to the public.

USEFUL INFORMATION

The following organizations can be helpful to you in answering questions or furnishing lists of gardens to see in Scotland. Write to them in advance. Lists are free unless specified otherwise.

THE BRITISH TRAVEL ASSOCIATION, 680 Fifth Ave., New York 19, N.Y.: Booklet, *Historic Houses, Castles and Gardens,* issued annually to give up-to-date list of dates and hours when gardens are open.

THE NATIONAL TRUST FOR SCOTLAND, 5 Charlotte Square, Edinburgh 2, Scotland: Annual membership ($2.80) entitles you to receive their monthly bulletins, get free admission to all National Trust properties in Scotland, and join their conferences and exciting boat cruises and bus tours to different gardens each year. It will also help this worthy enterprise that supports many of the fine castles and gardens you will see. Even as a non-member, be sure to send for the booklet, *Seeing Scotland,* which is an annual guide to the castles, houses, and gardens open to the public, with current dates and hours, including a list of those opened for Scotland's Garden Scheme as well as those of the National Trust. (Price 66¢ including postage.)

SCOTLAND'S GARDEN SCHEME, 26 Castle Terrace, Edinburgh 1, Scotland: Information about their special coach tours to houses and gardens in Scotland.

THE SCOTTISH TOURIST BOARD, 2 Rutland Place, West End, Edinburgh 1, Scotland: Touring information, if not available from the first address above.

chapter 10

FRANCE: FORMAL GARDENS
AND ROSES—AND EXOTIC
MONACO

HE French put their gardens together much
as they do their food—with careful atten-
tion to detail, complete concentration on the desired effect,
calculated logic, and an occasional burst of genius. They
trim and shear and ruthlessly cut back trees and shrubs to
formal patterns; they lay out a garden plan with ruler and
compass.

This unemotional approach to gardening is sometimes difficult for the American to understand. We feel closer to the
British, with their love of color and devotion to the develop-
ment of each flower or shrub to its ultimate possibilities. If
we take the right attitude, however, we will find much in the
French gardens to admire and enjoy. You will gain a great
deal if you read something of the history of French gardening before looking at the formal gardens of France (just as
it helps you to study the various periods of painting and the
lives and ideas of the artists, before visiting an art gallery).
If you enjoy weaving or embroidery, you will get real inspiration from the study of these gardens. Look at them as

you would look at a piece of needlepoint or an Oriental rug —designs meant to be admired from above. The scrollwork of the clipped hedges, the contrast of colored sand and occasional flowers, may even inspire you to make sketches to copy in some form of needlework.

The home gardener in France keeps his flowers in neat rows, as a rule—like the vegetables. Most Frenchmen have a passion for roses, and at times for iris, the "fleur-de-lis," which is the symbol of France. The dahlia also has appeal to the Frenchman, probably because of its organized arrangement of petals. You will find some very fine specialized gardens of these flowers. The home gardens in this country, like the homes themselves, are walled in for complete privacy, arranged for the comfort of the family, rarely opened to strangers. The only concession to the passerby is the row of potted plants decorating the space between house and sidewalk in all the villages, and the delightful flower boxes overflowing with color at windows and balconies.

The French Government Tourist Office, like that in Ireland, keeps up an annual contest to inspire the citizens of each town and hamlet to use more flowers on the buildings, in parks, and at roadsides. The admirable booklet sent out to mayors to promote this "Fleurir la France" effort (Make France Flower) could well be translated and sent out all over America. Floral decorations should be concentrated, it states, where citizen and tourist will enjoy them most; they should be planned for unity; should make use naturally of native wildflowers whenever possible. A chart of suitable flowers, their colors, and need for sun or shade, is included. In 1963, the fifth year of the contest, more than 3000 communities participated, including over 80,000 people. Surely you, as a tourist, should see the effects of this great national effort and be grateful for this emphasis on beautifying a whole country with flowers.

Another national effort with great appeal to the flower

lover is the great annual Flower Show, the "Floralies." For a description of this, see the chapter on "Flower Shows in Europe"; for dates of specialized or local flower shows throughout France, and tours to gardens, consult the French Horticultural Society (see "Useful Information," at the end of this chapter).

PARIS

Even if you see little of the rest of France on your travels, you will certainly visit Paris, so let's begin our garden-touring in that enchanting city. Here you will find something to enjoy in three categories: the formal 17th-century garden, the rose garden, and the botanical garden.

The *Luxembourg Gardens* are probably the loveliest example of a great French-style park, with many formal parterre designs, some of foliage plants only, others with gorgeous big-blossomed begonias. There are 62 acres of wonderful tree-shaded paths, benches everywhere to sit on while you watch the children at play, their nursemaids and mothers gossiping nearby. You will find oleanders blooming here in spring, sculptured urns filled with geraniums, formally clipped shrubs and trees in ball shapes, neat, precise patterns. At the *Tuileries* you will see very colorful parterres filled with flowers changed at every season—sometimes red geraniums, yellow marigolds, purple ageratum, and the gray relief of artemisias; other annuals replace them later on. Many of the famous buildings have formal green beds in front, or sometimes flower "embroideries."

At the new Unesco building on the Place de Fonteney you will find something very unusual: a Japanese garden in France. If you are taking your children to the fine *Zoological Garden*, look for some of the colorful flower beds near the buildings. In one of them we saw masses of deep-blue larkspur, geraniums, and cannas in vivid color contrast.

Le Jardin Shakespeare (Shakespeare Garden) at the Pré-Catelan in the Bois de Boulogne is open from April to October, showing flowers mentioned by the dramatist. Also in the Bois de Boulogne is a little Poet's Garden. It features small plots of flowers that famous poets have used as inspiration. Each label quotes an appropriate poem for that plot's contents. I've seen the same idea employed in Japan, and it would be an interesting one to use in your own garden, using your own favorite bits of verse.

If you like flowers, Paris has much to offer you besides. You will certainly want to see the *Flower Market* at Les Halles, if you get up early enough to be there between 5 and 8 A.M. Here they sell potted small trees and shrubs for balconies, as well as cut flowers. You will find other flower markets open later in the day, like the one on the Île de la Cité, at the Quai de Corse, and the Place Louis-Lépine, just a block from Notre Dame. At the *Fleuriste Municipal,* 3, Ave. Porte d'Auteuil, you will see acres of greenhouses——94 in all —that are open daily from 10 to 6. Some 1,200,000 plants are grown here each year for use in the city parks. You will find an arboretum of rare trees, including 140 varieties of camellias; a collection of palms; rock-garden plants of every kind; orchids; cacti; succulents; bromeliads; and almost every imaginable flower. If you are in Paris in April, be sure to see the Azalea Show here; in October-November, the Chrysanthemum Show.

If your passion is roses, there are three gardens in Paris that will be sheer delight. At the *Musée Rodin,* 77 Rue de Varennes, you will be able to enjoy much of the famous sculptor's work in a garden setting of 2000 rosebushes, including 100 varieties.

The *Bagatelle,* on the edge of the Bois de Boulogne, is one of the loveliest gardens in Europe. Be sure to read its delightful and unusual history as told by Peter Coats in *Great Gardens of the Western World* (see chapter on "Suggested

Reading About European Gardens"). The original palace and garden were constructed on a bet by the Comte d'Artois in two months—using 900 workmen day and night—as a gift for his sister-in-law, Queen Marie Antoinette. If you are a flower lover, you will want to go there each month of the year, for you will find Christmas roses in January, crocuses in February and March, thousands of tulips and narcissus in April and May, as well as rhododendrons, magnolias, and many flowering shrubs. By the end of May, the special iris garden is coming into bloom, and then, from June into July, you will revel in the fragrance and color of the spectacular rose garden. This has been beautifully designed for decorative effect, with rectangular and curved beds filled with the choicest of modern roses, surrounded by tall columns of climbers and tree roses like small fountains of bloom. Cone-shaped topiaries give the proper accent here and there. You will see 20,000 rosebushes in all, of 2,650 varieties, many of them new ones being tested for the annual International Rose Competition held here each June. The entire garden of Bagatelle has been planned as a demonstration of the best products of French horticulture. It has also been carefully restored as much as possible in the spirit of its first 18th-century design, with acres of beautiful park, many lakes, a maze, statuary, and some of the charming original buildings. This is a place of beauty until the last asters and chrysanthemums fade in the autumn.

The third great rose garden of Paris is that of the Roseraie de l'Hay, a fascinating living history of the rose, described in the chapter "Follow Your Garden Hobby Abroad."

Another very interesting garden is the *Jardin Albert-Kahn*, at the Quai du Quatre-Septembre near the Bois de Boulogne. It was founded by the well-known banker, Albert Kahn, and is now part of the Paris Park Department. Here you will find a number of separate entities: an orchard of carefully espaliered apples, pears, and peaches; a simulated Vosges mountain forest; a French park area; and an authentic Japanese garden complete with teahouses, red lacquer bridges, stone lanterns, and some 300 "bonsai" trees of great age, in the original pots.

If you are interested in herbs, or alpine plants, don't miss the wonderful collections in the *Jardin des Plantes*, entrances at Place Valhubert or 57, Rue Cuvier. This is open daily. The Alpinum, or "Jardin Alpin," is near the Jussieu station of the Métro, and has rare plants from the Alps, Pyrenees, and Himalayas, and even from the North Pole. In the herb garden you will find some 11,000 unusual herbs and medicinal plants. There is another section with 17,000 desert plants for those interested in cacti and succulents; an exhibit demonstrating the whole history of gardening; and many other botanical collections, all carefully labeled. For those less fascinated with plant study, there is a lovely park area with flower beds of early bulbs, English daisies, wallflowers, and pansies in early spring (other flowers later), and a 17th-century maze.

AROUND PARIS, THE ÎLE DE FRANCE

You will find a number of the finest gardens of France in the area surrounding Paris called Île de France. See our map of this area, which has six suggested excursions by car marked on it, each a round trip starting and ending in Paris. All of these include some gardens, so you can follow the routes and see many picturesque villages, castles, cathedrals, and abbeys along the way as well.

Heading directly north from Paris on Excursion A, you will come to the charming château of *Chantilly*, now a splendid museum. The grounds here were designed by the famous landscape architect—perhaps the greatest of all time—Le Nôtre, so this would be a good time to do some advance reading about this interesting man and his ideas on garden design. You will find many books about him in your library, and discussions of his theories in most books about the history of gardening. For a brief but fascinating summary, I recommend Richardson Wright's book, *The Story of Gardening* (see "Suggested Reading About European Gardens"). Le Nôtre planned all his famous gardens on paper much as an architect designs a house—studying the relationship of spaces and the use of water, trees, sculpture, and buildings. His creations were made for use as outdoor reception rooms, for in the 17th century the gardens of the aristocrats were meant to display the wealth of their owners, to entertain the guests at great fêtes, to serve as a background for the pastel silks and satins of hundreds of people. They even included secluded nooks for flirting. Le Nôtre knew his blasé contemporaries; he sought to make each garden different and to develop novelties that would surprise guests on each estate. He ordered sculpture and small buildings to decorate special spots, much as an English gardener would select flowers and shrubs for contrast and color. Gardens were carefully planned to make a stunning impact upon the arriving guest as he looked down from the first terrace near the house. So, you, also, should stop each time to take in that first impression, look down and study the delicate scroll patterns of the parterres, the contrast of brick dust and white pebbles, the crisp accents of pointed topiaries, and the effective background of trees on each side, seemingly in a natural forest area, but each kept sheared and controlled to serve as the correct background. Then let your eyes sweep off into the distance and try to appreciate the genius that planned those great perspectives, the opening up of view after view, accented by pools, fountains, or statuary.

At Chantilly you will not find such a vast garden design as Le Nôtre created in many other château grounds. But you will be able to study all the essential principles of his art, particularly the elegance of his great, wide staircases leading down to the parterres. Imagine the famous beauties of the day descending these stairs slowly, glancing at the scene beyond to locate their favorite companions, utterly conscious of the stir they themselves were creating as they went down, step by step, into the garden.

When you go on Excursion B, you will find wonderful examples of these period gardens: at *Champs,* where they were designed by a nephew of Le Nôtre, you will see a garden masterpiece embellished with colorful flower parterres; at *Meaux,* you will see the Bishop's Garden, planned by Le Nôtre himself; at *Provins,* you will have a change of pace in a luxuriant rose garden; and the climax is at *Vaux-le-Vicomte* (Maincy), the first garden created by Le Nôtre—to me in some ways even more exciting than that at Versailles. For some unknown reason this great garden is ignored in most of the guidebooks, which is a pity. The park is open only on Saturday and Sunday afternoons from 2 to 6, and on holidays, but it is so near Paris that no garden lover should miss seeing it.

Vaux-le-Vicomte is the place where you can really let your imagination run riot, to recreate the scene as its owner, Nicolas Fouquet, Finance Minister of France, entertained his king, Louis XIV, and hundreds of members of his court and their friends. The fête began in the afternoon and lasted for twelve hours, each bit of entertainment designed to show off some other section of the newly created garden: a play by Molière in one setting, a ballet with orchestra of twenty-four violins, suppers and more light suppers, and a grand finale when a "whale" appeared in the big canal spouting fire and smoke, followed by an overwhelmingly brilliant display of fireworks. Unfortunately for Fouquet, this tremendously ostentatious display, coupled with recurring rumors of graft on a large scale, lost him his job as Finance Minister, and put him in jail. The King, jealous because this great garden far exceeded anything he had, ordered the entire property confiscated, and had much of the statuary and even many of the trees and other plants transferred to his own garden at Versailles.

Just south of Paris, if you take the Métro or start on either Excursion C or D, you will come to the *Château de Sceaux,* where there is a magnificent park designed by Le Nôtre. The atmosphere here is quite eerie, as the château itself is in ruins. Continuing south on Excursion C toward Melun, you will find a lovely rosarium at *Evry-Petit-Bourg.*

When you visit *Fontainebleau,* either by yourself on Excursion C or on a conducted bus tour from Paris, you will see another of Le Nôtre's parterre designs; and again one at Dampierre, if you follow the route of Excursion D. The highway from Paris to Fontainebleau, incidentally, is beautifully planted along its borders with roses, iris, lavender, marigolds, and other flowers. Circling around on Excursion C after Fontainebleau, you come to the *Château de Courances,* famous particularly for its great pools and basins of all sizes and designs. One surprise here is the charming little Japanese garden, a refreshing informal spot unusual in the formally laid out French estates.

You will, of course, be visiting *Versailles.* Le Nôtre's gardens here are considered by many to be his greatest masterpiece. Don't try to look at the gardens when you are on a conducted bus tour, for this allows much too little time after you have looked at the interior of this vast building. Versailles is so close to Paris that you can go there several times by yourself, on a public bus or train. Find out from the Paris Tourist Office when the great fountains will be playing, and when the night illuminations take place. Be sure to look at the fine rose garden, as well as all the more formal areas, with their beautiful sculptured fountains, the Temple of Love in the natural "English" garden, and the flower parterres in front of the Grand Trianon. If you can, allow plenty of time to enjoy this great garden.

If you are driving, you can follow Excursion E, stopping first at Versailles, then at the *Château de Rambouillet,* and then go down to see the great cathedral of *Chartres.* Before leaving this hallowed spot, stop for a moment to rest in the charming little garden in back of the church. Circling around now toward Paris, you will come to the great formal gardens at the *Château de Wideville,* and perhaps end up just before entering the city by admiring the superb "flower mosaics" in the park at *St. Cloud.*

On Excursion F, you will want to stop at Empress Josephine's delightful home of *Malmaison,* with its pretty flower-bordered walk leading up to the front door. In June this is a picture, with tree roses in bloom, forget-me-nots, English daisies, wallflowers, and pansies making patterns below. The *Restaurant Le Coq Hardi,* at Bougival, near here, has a delightful garden as well as excellent food. There is a fine formal garden at the *Château de Rosny,* and if you want to drive just a little farther than the route indicated on the Île de France map, you can visit the home of the painter Claude Monet at *Giverny,* where you will find a charming intimate flower garden with the artist's favorite waterlilies in a small pond.

NORTHERN FRANCE

Just a little farther north you come to the famous city of *Rouen,* where cherry trees bloom around the cathedral in early May. There is an interesting botanical garden here, the *Jardin Botanique,* at 114, Ave. des Martyres de la Résistance. You will find a good collection of alpine plants, and greenhouses with the big Victoria regia waterlily, orchids, insect-eating plants, and other exotic flowers.

At Clères, very near *Rouen* (on route 6), the gardens of the *Château de Clères* feature colorful flower beds that will remind you of England.

If you head west to stay in beautiful old *Caen,* the "city of spires," you could visit a number of gardens from there on a Wheel Tour. In Caen itself there is a fine botanical garden, the *Jardin Botanique,* of the city and university, at 5, Place Blot. This specializes in the flowers of Normandie, and you will also find an interesting rock garden, a section with medicinal plants, and greenhouses with exotics. There are 12½ acres in all. South of Caen, there is a fascinating garden at *Mézidon,* at the *Château de Canon,* which may be seen on request. You can walk around in a beautiful park that offers many canals, a large pool, and statues and temples in the French style. Most interesting of all, you will find here many "Chartreuses," which are walled gardens filled with flowers in the spring.

Immediately north of *Carrouges,* at Saint-Christophe-le-Jajolet, is the *Château de Sassy.* Here you will find an exquisite garden combining three terraces that step down from the house in Renaissance style until they reach long canals. These surround 17th-century scrolled parterres of very intricate design, the edges accented with small conical and domed topiaries. As you look down on these parterres from the upper terrace, you will see a charming summerhouse centered at the far end; go down and reverse the process, looking back up from the summerhouse, and you get a splendid view across the parterres and stairs to the fine château.

A short distance west of Caen, just eleven miles beyond Bayeux, you will come to the *Château de Balleroy,* at the town of the same name. Here you will see another good example of the formal French-style garden, with intricately designed parterres of cut box, surrounded by small trimmed trees in tubs.

A route that would take you north of Paris in a curving line toward Brussels passes through two towns of interest to garden lovers. The first is the *Château de la Bagatelle,* at

Abbeville, which has a fine formal garden. Then in the city of *Lille,* suburb of Douai, near the Belgian border, you will find another *Jardin Botanique,* a botanical garden, at 39 Boulevard Vauban; here there are a rock garden and greenhouses with orchids, succulents, and tuberous begonias.

If you want to drive due east of Paris toward Germany, and see something of Alsace-Lorraine, you could visit some four gardens. The *Jardin Botanique,* at *Metz,* on the Rue de Pont-à-Mousson, has much to appeal to the flower lover, for here you will find roses, dahlias, and spring bulbs, as well as tropical and subtropical plants in the greenhouses. There is another botanical garden at *Nancy,* the *Jardin Botanique,* on Rue Ste. Catherine. This offers a good collection of alpines, tulips, iris, dahlias, and interesting medicinal plants. In the *Parc de la Lignière,* in Nancy, you will also see a charming rose garden. Farther south, at *Lunéville,* stop at the beautiful rose-pink *Château de Lunéville,* to admire the lovely color scheme—the castle reflected in the big pool, surrounded by beds of pink petunias and gray foliage plants, with the sharp cones of sheared topiaries as accents. This garden shows the transition from the formal French design, near the castle, to the "English landscape" type that became so popular later on, which you can find in the surrounding park. Still farther south, at *Epinal,* you might like to see the fine *municipal rose garden.*

FROM ORLÉANS THROUGH THE LOIRE VALLEY AND "CENTRAL FRANCE"

South of the Alsace-Lorraine region, on routes leading into Switzerland, you will find three gardens: At *Dijon,* in Burgundy, a *Jardin Botanique* (botanical garden) at 1, Avenue Albert I, displays many native plants from this area in collections that amount to 6000 different plants in all. Not far east of here you come to *Jallerange,* where the *Château de Jalle-*

range may be visited on request. Here you will see another of the splendid formal gardens designed by the master, Le Nôtre, with some very interesting innovations. The sheared hedges surrounding the parterres are shaped into delightfully prim little porticoes, some arching over open "windows" with small ball-shaped trees between. They make you think of the trim little trees and arbors in the illustrations for the Kate Greenaway children's books. Continuing east again, you arrive in *Besançon,* not far from Berne, Switzerland. In the *Jardin Botanique,* run by the city and the university here, you will find a rose garden, an alpinum, ferns and water plants, medicinal plants, and the Victoria regia among other exotics in a greenhouse that features 2000 varieties of plants.

Northwest of Dijon, there is a large formal garden at the *Château de Bussy-Rabutin,* in *Montbard.* The owner of the castle had angered King Louis XIV and was banished to this domain. In retaliation, he had the gardens of Versailles copied for his own property. You will find it interesting to compare the two.

Going from Orléans through the Loire Valley, you will find many charming formal gardens at the famous châteaux. At *Orléans* itself a real treat awaits the flower enthusiast. Besides the Municipal Rose Garden, you will find a new *Parc Floral d'Exposition Permanente* (Permanent Floral Exposition), opened in the summer of 1964, which is unique in France. This is located in the Parc de la Source. You will be able to follow special road markers saying "Parc Floral," to find it in the southeast section of the city. The park includes the source of the river Loiret, which has always been a tourist attraction. In this new Floral Park you will find a tremendous display of flower gardens, put together by the best growers in France. Among the displays are a rhododendron walk, a rose garden, special gardens of iris and dahlias, and everywhere, along the many walks throughout the extensive grounds, decorative beds overflowing with seasonal bloom. The rose garden alone contains 25,000 shrubs; there are 25,000 perennials, some 100,000 annuals. This is a feast for the eyes, a refreshing change from the all-green formal gardens of France. All the national horticultural societies and commercial nursery organizations have joined in this new venture, which should stimulate much more interest in flower growing among the French people. You can spend a whole day here if you wish, for there is a restaurant on the grounds (and a playground for children as well).

East of Orléans there are two interesting places to see. On the road from Orléans to *Montargis*, at Bellegarde-du-Loiret, there is an especially fine rose garden. Then going south of *Montargis* about ten miles, you arrive at Nogent-sur-Vernisson, and just a bit further south, the *Arboretum des Barres*. This is a splendid place for tree enthusiasts, with 700 acres of old and unusual trees. There are magnificent conifers, many from the Orient; several California redwoods over a century old and 120 feet tall; a large collection of magnolias, fruit trees, and flowering shrubs, some 3000 varieties in all.

Fourteen miles due south of Orléans you come on *La Ferté-Saint-Aubin*, and the château of the same name. There is a lovely rose garden, and the grounds are floodlit in the evenings.

Turn west from here into the valley of the Loire, and you reach the fascinating "château country." We stopped there in Amboise, and stayed at the Hôtel Le Choiseul, which serves some of the best food in France.

Among the châteaux in the area that have particularly interesting gardens, I would mention the one at *Ménars*, which includes flowers; the gardens around the chapel of St. Gilles, at *Montoire; Chenonceaux*, with its fine formal design along the canal, where you will see roses and other flowers. The *Château de Langeais* has a beautiful geometric parterre garden with a crown and fleur-de-lis made of flowers. *Ussé* is the castle that inspired Perrault to write "Sleeping Beauty"; here you can dream of fairy-tale princesses in grounds appropriately ornamented with roses.

Most interesting of all, from a garden standpoint, is *Villandry*. The fascinating parterres and kitchen garden here, first planted in the 16th century, have been beautifully restored. You are not allowed to walk in the garden itself, since the paths are kept raked in geometric patterns; but you will be able to look down from the terrace above and enjoy the details at your leisure. The formal parterre nearest you from this aspect is of sheared boxwood, each square in a different design. Our guide explained the meaning of these designs to us (which we have never heard mentioned by other guides or seen described in books). The four squares symbolize the different kinds of love. One is designed as daggers and knives, meaning dangerous love. Another has fans and butterflies, for frivolous love; yet another features hearts, wings, and arrows, for passionate love; and the fourth represents foolish love with a maze. The rest of the parterre has other geometrical hedge designs. All are filled with flowers throughout the seasons—forget-me-nots and pink tulips when we were there in early spring, other annuals later on. The hedges along the paths are broken at intervals by yew topiaries clipped in precise spirals. Fountains and basins reminiscent of Spain punctuate the paths from time to time. Above the parterre on each side are orange trees, carefully sheared and planted in tubs. Now look beyond this formal garden and study the design of the equally interesting kitchen garden. This, too, has been laid out for beauty, the dark bronze of beet leaves carefully planned at intervals to contrast with lighter green lettuce or carrots. The plan of this garden is also formal, brightened at the corners with delicate rose arbors. What a lesson for our home vegetable plantings!

Château de Villandry, France (*Photo J. Boulas*)

West of here you will find the *Château d'Angers,* at *Angers,* where you will want to see the famous collection of old tapestries. Almost as beautiful are the patterned flower beds in the garden outside. Still farther west, on the lower reaches of the Loire, you will come to *Nantes,* where there is another flower-filled *Jardin Botanique,* on the Rue Stanislas Baudry. Here you will find a wonderful collection of roses; 240 varieties of magnificent camellias; orchids and cacti in the greenhouse.

South of the Loire Valley region lies *Poitiers,* a very charming small town with much to see. Look for the fine *rock garden* on the ramparts.

SOUTH FROM VICHY

At Effiat, near *Lapalisse,* northeast of Vichy, you will find another fine garden designed by Le Nôtre with great terraces, canals and grottoes, at the *Château d'Effiat.* Continuing toward Lyon, you will arrive at *Roanne,* where there is an interesting arboretum of conifers, plane trees, and other varieties at the *Parc Grands Murcins.* You have already heard me describe the delightful rose garden and extensive alpine collection of the *Parc de la Tête d'Or,* at *Lyon,* in the chapter "Follow Your Garden Hobby Abroad." This same park, in its *Jardin Botanique,* also has some 1200 flowering shrubs, an arboretum, subtropical and tropical plants of many varieties, including orchids and succulents, and the Victoria regia waterlily in some of its many greenhouses. This is a very large garden that you can drive through, open from May to October.

Northeast of Lyon, near the Swiss border, is another fine alpine garden high in the mountains, the botanical garden and alpinum *"La Jaysinia"* near *Samoëns.* Farther south, at the Col du Lautaret, there is the *Station Biologique et*

Alpinum. Both are described in "Follow Your Garden Hobby Abroad."

Southwest of Lyon, an interesting "hub" for a Wheel Tour would be the delightful hilly pilgrimage town of Le Puy, completely off the beaten tourist track. Stay at the Hôtel du Cygne, in the center of this little cobblestoned bit of old France, and ask the proprietor, M. Roger Pestre, to tell you about the surrounding châteaux and gardens. In Le Puy itself there is the private garden of *Henri Vinay*. The garden at the *School for the Deaf and Dumb*, (Et. Horticole Institution de Sourds-Muets) has strange bottle-shaped topiaries and rows of flowers and vegetables cultivated by the students.

You will find this whole region rich in reminders of the Marquis de Lafayette, especially the *Château de Chavaniac*, at *Chavaniac-Lafayette*, where he was born and spent his youth. Below the entrance courtyard you will see a fine formal rose garden, very well kept. The vast sloping lawn to one side is flanked by broad, colorful annual borders. The woodsy area beyond contains a brook and cascades.

At *Lavoûte-sur-Loire* is one of the *Châteaux de Polignac* (the other is a ruin and has no garden). There is a nice formal parterre garden in the courtyard, and the views are splendid. You will find more formal gardens at the *Château de Cluzel* at *St. Eble* near Langeac and at the *Château de Monistrol* at the place of that name.

Southwest of Le Puy north of *Figeac* you will come to the *Château de Loubressac*. Here you enter the formal gardens from a pretty covered terrace and suddenly look out on a glorious expanse of distant valleys. Continuing north of Lascaux, you will find *Hautefort*, with magnificent parterres of flowers set in fine lawns, at the *Château de Hautefort*. There is also a lovely iris garden planted by the French Iris Society. South of *Lascaux* on the Dordogne River lies the *Château de Marqueyssac* at Roque-Gageac, with magnificent terraced gardens.

If you should drive through *Brantôme,* look at the charming gardens in the 18th century *Benedictine Abbey.* Going still farther west, at Saint-Porchaire near *Saintes,* you will find the *Château de la Roche-Courbon.* This has a vast formal garden with terraces, conical topiaries, and a beautiful reflection of the castle in the great pool, further decorated with swans and ducks. Here also you will see iris cared for by the French Iris Society.

Some 25 miles south of *Bordeaux* lies Preignac, where there are fine Italianate gardens with terraces and statues at the *Château de Malle.* We drove south from here to the coast of France and the famed Riviera. If you stop at *Albi* (40 miles northeast of Toulouse) to see the great collection of Toulouse-Lautrec paintings in the *Palais de la Berbie,* be sure to look down from a balcony at the beautiful scroll parterres in the garden below; they are much like designs for an Oriental rug.

If you are a real plant enthusiast, and continue going south, don't miss the fine *Jardin Botanique* of the university at *Montpellier.* This is an extensive garden with a number of greenhouses, where you can enjoy the orchids from January to March. The native wildflowers and herbs there bloom in the limestone rock garden at the end of May, but there are other blossoms throughout the grounds all summer. You will find many interesting trees in the arboretum, particularly the pretty Chinese balsam (Populus Simonii) with an almost-white trunk like a birch. The lotus pond is so filled with this plant that one does not see the water—only the myriad shell-pink blooms, or the strange round seed pods. There are a whole section of cacti and succulents and a splendid cypress walk. For those who want to identify every plant and learn more about it, the labels used here are particularly interesting, as each one gives not only the Latin and common name, but also the original homeland marked on a map. This is the sixth-oldest botanical garden in the world, founded in 1594, and has become the largest center for botanical research in France.

Heading east from here, you come to *Nîmes*, where there is a formal garden, the *Jardin de la Fontaine*, of special historical interest. You will find few plants here, but a succession of great staircases, sculptures, urns, and impressive terraces. The garden was built here to take advantage of an unusually fine spring of water that assured the designer, Maréschal, of a good supply for great basins and canals. Actually these are on the site of an early Roman Temple of Diana, whose baths you can still see. Look down at the whole design from the highest terrace and see how, in spite of the careful balancing of statues, steps, and pools, great variety has been introduced. The only flowering bit is a fantastic "crocodile" bed made of begonias and chained to an ivy-covered palm. A few miles north of Nîmes lies Générargues, (before you reach *Alés*,) where you will find *Les Jardins au Domaine de Prafrance*. This is an arboretum of great variety, with a famous collection of 32 different bamboos, as well as giant sequoias, magnolias, rhododendrons, azaleas, and many kinds of trees.

At *Ansouis*, you will find another formal garden of intricate arabesques of box, with a long pool and cascades, at the *Château d'Ansouis*. In *Marseille*, the famous bustling port also boasts a *Jardin Botanique*, the Parc Borély, at 52, Ave. Clôt-Bey. The pride of this garden is its rosarium, with 2500 plants of 230 different varieties.

If you have followed my suggested tour plans, you soon reach the warmth of the blue Mediterranean, where every town you pass through will be overflowing with palms, bougainvillea, poinsettias, and other flowers. There is a new national park on the island of *Port Cros*, almost opposite *Le Lavandou*, which has the luxuriant growth of a tropical paradise. Around Le Lavandou, you will enjoy the fragrance of wild lavender everywhere. At *La Napoule*, the late American sculptor Henry Clewes lovingly restored the 14th-century *Château de La Napoule,* and embellished its garden with a fountain and his own statues. Between *Grasse* and *Cannes* are the scented gardens raised for blossoms that will be made into perfume. You can drive through a forest of mimosa trees here; see the fields of roses, hyacinths, heliotrope, jasmine, and violets and the orchards of orange blossoms, all spreading their fragrances on the air at various seasons. You can also take a conducted bus tour from Cannes to see the people at work in the fields and watch the whole process of conversion into perfume in a factory. Just for an example, it takes 220 pounds of rose petals to make 50 grams of "absolute"—the final essence. A little over two pounds of this "absolute" will make from 400 to 500 bottles of scent.

If you are on the Riviera in February you can enjoy the Mimosa Festival while these flowers are in bloom. *Antibes* is the rose-growing center, for both the perfume industry and the commercial florists. Here also you will find a botanical garden at *Villa Thuret,* with luxuriant bloom especially from April to June, in a setting of palms, eucalyptus, and a fine arboretum of Mediterranean and subtropical trees. Many were first planted by the artist-diplomat Gustave Adolphe Thuret after he bought the place in 1860 and have grown to great height. At *Nice* you will see a particularly vivid flower market on the Rue Saint-François-de-Paule, and a fine rose garden in *Retiro Park.* The Battle of Flowers along the Promenade des Anglais during Carnival time is a joyous occasion to watch.

Do stop in *St.-Jean-Cap-Ferrat* to visit the *Musée Île-de-France* on the Avenue Denis-Séméria. The museum is surrounded by magnificent tropical gardens of about twelve acres, including a sunken Spanish Garden, an Italian Garden, an Exotic Garden, and a French Garden. There is a series of small statues along the waterfront here that is most amusing; one looks like Napoleon playing a bass fiddle, another like a howling coyote. At *Menton,* you will find an extensive collection of subtropical plants at the *Serre de la Madone,* particularly colorful in April, June, or July. At *Eze,* there is *Lou Sueil,* a garden specializing in fascinating succulents, as well as flowers. On the peninsula of *Cap Martin,* near Monaco, you will enjoy the wonderful garden of *Villa Roquebrune* with its extensive collections of ornamental plants brought together by an Englishwoman, Mrs. G. Warre. This is on a precipice several hundred feet over the blue Mediterranean. In spring you will see many early bulbs, mimosas, lavender, and South African asters. There are masses of cacti, succulents, and pelargoniums. Be sure to look for the scabiosa plant from Sicily (Scabiosa cretica), a rare blue-flowered shrub that grows four feet tall. There are many fine trumpet vine varieties, and on the patio you will find Chinese ground orchids (Bletilla striata) grown in terra-cotta pots. The height of bloom here is in April, July, and August, but the garden is always lovely.

THE PRINCIPALITY OF MONACO

In this little country the streets are lined with palms and foliage plants, the atmosphere is hot and sunny, and everything grows luxuriantly—always up, never sideways, for there is so little room. As you go about in *Monte Carlo* you will be either climbing or descending a steep hill. Up on one of these is the wonderful *Jardin Exotique,* an extraordinary garden of giant-size cacti and succulents. The paths wind back and forth along the steep slope, and you will find huge cucumber-like cacti arching overhead, great plate shapes bristling with long spines on either side of you, brilliant spots of color everywhere in the yellow, orange, pink, and white blossoms —a veritable desert landscape in bloom, but all crowded into a small space. At each turn you get another glimpse of the deep-blue Mediterranean below, framed by waving palm branches, prickly cactus stems, and the fleshy petals of the many varieties of succulents. Some of the cacti look like long green snakes winding about among the white rocks or twining around a tree trunk. Others resemble huge bristly hassocks, and the palm trunks thrust their way through in strange fat bottle shapes. This is a weird garden of fantastic forms and gaudy colors. If you can stand the sudden change in temperature, go into the shivering-cold grottoes on the lower level to gaze at the stalactites there, and then try to remember how hot you were in the sun among the prickly cacti.

Whether or not you gamble yourself, you will probably visit the *Casino,* and see the beautifully kept gardens around it, full of crotons, coleus, cannas—a reminder of home to those from Florida—and in December, magnificent beds of cyclamen. These are among the oldest subtropical gardens of the Riviera, containing many fine trees. The sunken garden is always full of flowers.

USEFUL INFORMATION

FRANCE

THE FRENCH GOVERNMENT TOURIST OFFICE, 610 Fifth Ave., New York 20, N.Y.: The supply is too limited to give to individuals, but if you are with a group such as a club, going especially to see gardens, this office will give you a free copy of the book *French Castles Revisited,* an exquisitely illustrated guide to the châteaux open to the public. It gives visiting hours, directions for finding châteaux, etc. They will send to individuals, free, an excellent little guide called "Paris, Where, What, When, How," which gives much useful garden information.

LA MAISON RUSTIQUE, Rue Jacob (Île de la Cité), Paris VI, France, is a wonderful bookshop specializing entirely in books in many languages about gardening, horticulture, botany, agriculture.

SOCIÉTÉ NATIONALE DE HORTICULTURE DE FRANCE, 84, Rue de Grenelle, Paris VII, France: This is the French Horticultural Society. Ask for Madame Beaupere (an Englishwoman) if you have any questions about gardens; or better still, join the Society ($3.60 a year) so that you can participate in her delightful two- and three-day tours to gardens of France. She also conducts a number of garden tours to other countries of Europe. As a member, you will also receive the Society's monthly magazine (in French), giving dates of the many specialized flower shows all over France, as well as interesting articles on gardening.

MONACO

PRINCIPALITY OF MONACO INFORMATION CENTER, 630 Fifth Ave., New York 20, N.Y.: for all tourist information.

chapter 11

*HOLLAND: SPRING AND
SUMMER BLOOM*

URELY no garden lover going to Europe in
spring would want to miss seeing the tulips
at *Keukenhof,* near *Lisse,* less than a half hour from Amsterdam. Bus tours from many points and regular bus service
from the railroad stations at Leyden and Haarlem make it
easy to be among the 800,000 annual visitors to this famous
garden.

Keukenhof is not merely the showcase for Holland's great
bulb-growing business, but is a beautifully designed park
covering sixty-five acres, with blossoming cherry trees and
small ponds and brooks that reflect the flowers planted along
their banks. Since each group of flowers is carefully labeled,
you will see many home gardeners there making notes of
varieties they would like to plant that fall in their own gardens. The masses of bright color are arranged with such
artistry, however, that many go there simply to enjoy the
scene or to take color photographs. Holland's Queen, having
bought her own ticket at the gate, is often seen among the
crowds, wandering happily about, just like the rest of the
tourists.

Included in the seven million bulbs you can see blooming

here—in addition to the great carpets of tulips—are the finest crocuses, daffodils, and hyacinths. There are a pavilion where you may take lessons in flower arranging and terraces and teahouses for an occasional rest. Keukenhof is open all day long from late March into mid-May.

Be sure to visit *Linnaeushof* gardens nearby also. These were once the trial gardens of the great eighteenth century botanist Linnaeus. There is a beautiful display of tulips here in May.

During this time you will never get far away from tulips. Cars have garlands of the blossoms on their hoods. Many of the front yards and squares feature bright mosaic designs made entirely of the flower petals—a labor of love on which the citizens, including many children, spend long hours. Ask the V.V.V. Tourist Office of whatever city you are staying in to tell you where to see these.

Not far from Lisse you could stop for lunch at the *Restaurant Treslong,* in *Hillegom,* which is famous for its early spring garden. Great parts of the provinces of North and South Holland are gardens in themselves, for this is the area where acres of tulips and other flowers abound on the commercial bulb farms. Even the barges piled with tulip heads for disposal are a colorful picture on the canals at the end of spring. This season in the Netherlands is a feast for the eyes.

Few people realize, however, that Holland is also overflowing with bloom all summer long. Roses, perennials, and annuals decorate every park, home, and place of business. Large wooden tubs of pink geraniums or purple heliotrope stand outside of public buildings, on street corners, and on trolley islands. Flower boxes decorate the houses everywhere, and you will see baskets of colorful plants suspended over some of the shopping streets. Many towns have elaborate annual flower shows and parades of floats.

The city of *The Hague* is spilling over with roses from June to fall. There are special rosariums in the *Josef Israel-*

splein and in the *Zuiderpark;* the latter is also famous for its unusual trees of over 1000 varieties. Beside the *Peace Palace* there is a large rose garden surrounded by borders of early-blooming azaleas and rhododendrons, followed later by brightly hued perennials. Gayest of all is *Westbroekpark,* where you may wander at will over fine lawns to admire the large mixed borders, the rock garden, and the choice roses, especially those entered in the International Rose Competition. Here commercial growers set out beds of their newest varieties for a three-year testing period to vie for the coveted Hague Gold Medal. There are more than 20,000 shrubs of 345 varieties in the entire rose garden, sent in from twelve countries.

The *Linnaeushof,* at *Lisse,* is transformed in summer into a fine perennial garden backed by flowering shrubs. Driving there from The Hague, in July, you will pass fields of fragrant freesias and the fine front-yard gardens that well-to-do Hollanders living in *Bennebroek* cultivate.

If you explore other parts of Holland, you might stop in Rotterdam to admire the flower-bed patterns from high up on the Euromast—a viewing tower 365 feet tall; or eat at the *Prinsenkelder Restaurant,* in *Delft,* and see its quaint old garden with flower beds surrounded by miniature hedges. The daily wholesale flower auction at *Aalsmeer* is a delight both for color and for fragrance, as are the many flower markets throughout the country.

A visit to *Delden,* near Hengelo, up near the German border, is well worth any amount of travel. Here Baroness van Heeckeren at her *Kasteel Twickel* has made what is surely the loveliest garden in Holland. You will see a charming French-style garden with flower beds, topiaries, and orange trees in tubs lining the walk. Then wander through the large perennial garden and rockery by the lake. Still farther, at some distance from the castle, you will come to a large rose garden. You will see splendid old trees through-

Kasteel Twickel, Holland (*Nationaal Fotopersbureau*)

out the grounds, as well as some excellent dwarf Japanese varieties in pots. If you go to Kasteel Twickel in May you will marvel at the superb rhododendron walk leading into the gardens, and many other fine specimens here and there. But there is bloom enough to delight any garden lover from spring to fall.

The Baroness, who is now eighty-five, still superintends every bit of work throughout the gardens personally, making some changes each year to improve the color schemes, the gradations of heights, or the general aspect of the flower beds. She designed the gardens herself, and could certainly hold her own with any professional landscape architect. We were fortunate enough to have her as our guide when we visited the gardens. I am known to be a rather brisk walker myself, but it was all I could do to keep up with this wonderfully spry little lady.

The gardens are open to the public only on Wednesday and Friday from 1:40 to 4:30, when a gardener will lead each group for an hour-and-a-quarter tour.

Not too far from Delden is another small castle, *De Geldersche Toren*, at *Spankeren* (near Rheden in Gelderland). Neither the castle nor its perennial garden is ever open to the public, but you could attend a two-day festival here on either the last weekend in July or the first in August. Then you will see expert flower arrangers who come from all over Holland to show their skill in an exhibit, while the band plays to lend gaiety to the occasion.

An interesting way to see the sights of Holland, and, incidentally, to look at the many private gardens behind the houses, which can only be seen in this way, is to hire a cabin cruiser as we did one spring. With four to six passengers sleeping on board, getting most meals in the galley, this is a surprisingly inexpensive way to travel. The captain who came with the boat did all the navigating and the dishwashing as well. We particularly enjoyed seeing the beautiful homes and gardens from the canals in Breukelen (ancestor of our Brooklyn). Another very rewarding boat trip goes along the River De Vecht, running from Utrecht into the former Zuidersea, at Muiden, near Amsterdam. Here you will see the gardens of many lovely 18th-century mansions, as at Nieuwersluis, Sterreschans, Rupelmonde, and Vreedenhof. South of the village of Loenen, there are some mansions with small teahouses in the gardens on the east bank of the river, as well as some in the northern part of the village on the west bank. Be sure to notice the fine old wrought-iron gates of these gardens. Actually you could reach any of the gardens I have mentioned in this chapter from the canals, provided you had plenty of time. Write to The Netherlands National Tourist Office, 605 Fifth Ave., New York 17, N.Y., for information about cabin cruisers.

If you want to see something in Holland that most tourists miss, go to one of the cities that have elaborate flower shows and parades of flower-decorated floats during July and on into September. These are called "Bloemencorsos" and are a great source of civic pride. Some dates for these are indicated in the "Key to Gardens." (See also "Useful Information" at end of this chapter.) In *Zundert*, near the Belgian border, there is so much excitement over the contest for dahlia floats that each one is decorated secretly under a temporary shelter to keep the product a great surprise. The festival in *Lottum*, near Venlo, in July, specializes in roses. A number of towns feature contests and flower parades for children, for in Holland the love of gardening is instilled in the young, many schools having their own plots for children to plant. No wonder that the whole country is abloom from early spring to fall!

There are also quite a number of fine arboretums in the Netherlands, which will interest the tree lover, and some excellent botanical gardens. These are listed and described in the "Key to Gardens," as are a good many historical gardens attached to manor houses and castles not usually visited by tourists. The Royal Netherlands Horticultural Society was kind enough to prepare a special list of these for me, which has never before been published. Be sure to look these up in the Key to Gardens if you are interested in the history of landscape architecture in Holland.

USEFUL INFORMATION

Send for the following before you start planning your garden tour of Holland:

THE NETHERLANDS NATIONAL TOURIST OFFICE, 605 Fifth Ave., New York 17, N.Y.: List, "Holland Coming Events," which is issued annually and includes dates of flower festivals (called "Bloemencorsos") in many towns. They can also give you last-minute information about the height of the tulip season for each year, and special ship and plane tours, also bus tours, to take in the tulip festivals.

While you are in Holland, stop at the tourist offices, *V.V.V.* (pronounced vay-vay-vay), or the National Tourist Office, A.N.V.V., in Amsterdam or The Hague, and ask for the lists of the flower markets, flower auctions, and regions where flowers are grown commercially. These are mimeographed in Dutch, but your hotel porter will be glad to translate what you cannot guess at yourself.

NOTE: The Dutch word for "garden" is "tuin," pronounced very sharp and short as "tine." The Dutch are so fussy about pronunciation, however, that it is always safest to write out the places you want to see and show the paper when asking directions.

chapter 12

GERMANY: FLOWER-FILLED
PARKS AND GARDENS

s soon as you start traveling around Germany you will discover that this is a nation of flower lovers. Everywhere, especially in medieval towns such as Rothenburg, you will see gay window boxes. Modern picture windows are filled with carefully arranged house plants to delight the passerby even more than the owner, for often curtains are drawn behind the flowerpots to make a background. When you arrive or depart by train or plane, German friends present you with bouquets. When you pay a call or go to dinner in a home, be sure to take flowers as a gift, and offer them without their wrappings, as is the local custom. College students who must take such courtesy gifts, but have little money to pay for them, have named the inexpensive carnation "The Student's Flower." When you ride in a private car or a taxi, you will often see vases in them filled with fresh flowers.

The bookshops, so plentiful in every German city or hamlet, have shelves full of how-to-do-its for the home gardener, and many magazines as well. There are garden clubs all over the country, made up mainly of men, who enjoy exchanging advice and hearing lectures or taking excursions to the German Flower Shows or famous parks.

Because most city-dwellers live in apartments, you won't see many front-yard gardens. But go into the outskirts some Saturday or Sunday, and watch the thousands of families busily at work in their small patches of community gardens (Kleingärten), row after row of them, each with its own arbor or neat little weekend house. These patches of land are rented from the city government for very small sums. Competition is keen, as each plot-owner tries for the neatest and most productive garden in his section, and for the golden Harvest Crown, awarded in inter-city contests. On Sunday evenings you will find the roads and trolley-cars full of families laden with vegetables or flowers that they are bringing home from these rented plots.

When not working in their own gardens, the Germans go to the nearest park or botanical garden. There they study the labels, make notes about new flowers that they would like to buy, or just sit on a bench or in the ever-handy open-air restaurant having a glass of beer among the trees and blossoms. One of the joys of traveling in Germany is that you can eat every meal outdoors in season if you wish. Breakfast on your own hotel balcony edged with boxes of geraniums or petunias; lunch on a garden terrace in a park; dine under a grape arbor or beside a flower-bordered lake, at the pleasant times of year. If you visit any of the health resorts, you will find the large grounds around the mineral baths carefully planted with flowers, blossoming shrubs, and splendid old trees wherever you walk. In the Black Forest area, even the little bridges over the canals and streams are colorful with flower boxes.

You will find a selection of some of the most interesting public gardens of Germany in the "Key to Gardens" at the back of this book. Out of this list I have selected a few of the most outstanding ones to describe here. In order to make

your tour planning easier, these are divided geographically
into the gardens of Northern, Central, and Southern Germany.

NORTHERN GERMANY

In *Hamburg* you will find one of the finest parks in Europe, called *Planten un Blomen,* which means, in north-
German dialect, plants and flowers. The great 1963 International Horticultural Exhibition was held here, and because
of this the park is now more extensive and beautiful than
ever before. You will see practically every flower native to
Europe and many others from tropical climates. In early
spring there are some 250,000 narcissi, tulips, and hyacinths
of about 200 varieties, as well as primulas, anemones, and
the wild Alpine rose (a form of low rhododendron).

In late spring don't miss the iris garden, with 1200 varieties, the largest assortment to be seen in Europe. You can
look down upon this colorful garden from the terrace of the
Restaurant Seeterrassen. The rose garden displays 60,000
shrubs of over 300 varieties, including many new ones shown
each year by leading European growers. You will find a very
attractive planting of roses on an embankment, which is a
fine example of what can be done in a hilly garden. The
Restaurant Rosenhof is surrounded by roses, and is a fragrant
place for a snack or a meal. There are many lilies, including
a great assortment of hemerocallis, and large plantings of
perennials throughout the grounds. One interesting feature
of the perennial beds is the display showing older and newer
varieties of the same flower.

If you are interested in rock gardens (Steingärten), you
can study the plants used in four different types; there are
gardens built around slate, chalk, colored rocks, and rough
stones. The garden of medicinal plants (Apothekergarten)
is arranged in an interesting manner, with plants that heal

different parts of the human body grouped in categories. You will find many ponds, lakes, and brooks with water-loving reeds and flowers, including some warmed basins for tropical waterlilies and papyrus; others may be found in the tropical greenhouse. The large meadow devoted to sports tournaments, fireworks, and similar events has a splendid planting of rhododendrons around it. Special flower shows are often held in the exhibition houses near the main entrance. If you want to get a bird's-eye view of this great park, take the elevator in the glass shaft to the top of the observation tower (the Philipsturm).

You will see a spectacular playing of the fountains every two hours from May to early October, beginning at 2 P.M. on weekdays, from 10 A.M. on Sundays and holidays. There are more than 400 of these sprays, and almost as many colored underwater lights. The most exciting fountain display each day takes place at 9:30 P.M. and lasts for 25 minutes, when the water is illuminated in varying colors and the play of the fountains is synchronized to music. There are other band and orchestra concerts every afternoon and evening during the week and in the mornings on Sundays and holidays. You will always find plenty of comfortable chairs, including deck chairs, to relax in while you enjoy the colorful scene around you and listen to fine music. This wonderful garden is open all day long.

For the rhododendron enthusiast, the outskirts of *Bremen*, along the Autobahn, offers a mecca, the *Rhododendronpark*. This beautifully landscaped park is internationally famous. Here you can study hundreds of varieties of rhododendrons from many different countries, which have been planted there by the City Garden Department and the German Rhododendron Society. Go at the end of May, or in June, when the blossoms are at their height.

The park is now part of the *Botanical Garden* of Bremen (Botanischer Garten), which is designed specifically to help both the amateur and the professional gardener. Here are demonstration flower and vegetable gardens; sections with medicinal and commercial plants; alpines native to northern Germany; plantings that profit from shade; and a large collection of annual flowers. Others are arranged by geographical areas or biological interest. There are about 6500 varieties in all.

While in this neighborhood, if you are driving, you might enjoy seeing the *Schlosspark* and *Rhododendron Garden* (Rhododendronanpflanzung) in *Oldenburg*, and the homes and farms around *Bad Zwischenahn* and *Rastede,* all of which boast beautiful rhododendrons. And if you like smoked eel, the local inns in this region will delight you.

Just a few miles northwest of here, at *Wiesmoor*, an interesting two-hour tour goes on. Ask the Tourist Office in Bremen for information. The earliest vegetables and strawberries to be offered in the markets of Bremen and Hamburg come from here, also many of the best vegetable and flower seeds. On the tour you will visit greenhouses, fields of flowers, and farmhouses on the moors.

South of Wiesmoor you will find a unique garden at *Aschendorf.* This is a private garden at *Haus Altenkamp,* belonging to Herr Dr. Behnes. Ask your hotel porter to telephone for an appointment to see it. This is a baroque garden surrounded by fantastic topiary hedges of clipped yew. They are shaped into 86 "posts," each 18 feet high, at regular intervals, topping a hedge over seven feet high and nine feet deep. Here and there along the hedge you will see further topiary fancies, small towers, arches, grottoes, and the like. The yew is thought to be over 200 years old.

From here you can go south to *Hannover,* a city famous for its commercial fairs, but also for the most beautiful baroque garden in Germany, *Herrenhausen.* This royal garden of the Hannoverian kings was designed in 1680, and is fully as lovely today as it was then. It is not only perfectly kept, but, unlike any other garden in Europe, is filled with actors in the silks, satins, and powdered wigs of a period past, whenever a play or ballet is being presented in the outdoor theater or in the garden. Instead of just imagining the gay fêtes of the past, you feel yourself moving back in time, as you watch these pastel figures gently swaying through the flower-decked scrolls of the elaborate parterres.

You approach this garden through a "Grand Allee," over a mile long, bordered by some 1300 great lime trees planted in 1727. After entering the gilded wrought-iron gate, you pass the Gallery Building, where opera performances are given, and come to the garden itself. Actually, this is designed as a whole series of units. In it you will find small gardens of statuary surrounded by high hedges, an elaborate maze, and an old-fashioned flower garden with topiaries in animal shapes. You will also discover a Renaissance Knot Garden of small flower patterns, copied from one designed for the castle at Heidelberg in 1620, a French baroque garden designed with colored gravel within boxwood hedges, and an old "Secret" rose garden. Don't miss the unusual "Island Garden," in the center of a formal pool, where tubs of agapanthus and statuary surround a scroll parterre of box hedges within the water. There are a great many delicate small fountains in addition to the "Bell Fountain," with 167 sprays, and the "Great Fountain," created in 1720, the tallest in all Germany, which turns to liquid gold when the gardens are illuminated on certain summer nights. The background and wings of The Garden Theatre, planted toward the end of the 17th century, are made of clipped hedges, accented with gilded Dutch sculptures. Their seats for 800 people are greatly in demand for matinee and evening concerts, plays, and ballets. Ask the German Tourist Information Office (see address at the end of this chapter) for a list of dates of performances, and arrange for your tickets well in advance.

The *Berggarten*, adjacent to Herrenhausen, is a botanical

Herrenhausen, Hannover, Germany (*Foto Heinz Koberg*)

garden designed for scientific purposes, but it is delightfully landscaped and of much interest to the amateur. The first greenhouse, established here in 1666, featured tobacco and mulberry plants that were cultivated and exported. Here the first anthurium, Victoria regia, and usambara violets came to flower in Europe. There are demonstration perennial borders showing what to plant for sun or shade and for bloom at different seasons. There are palms, ginger plants, orchids, African violets of types first developed in these gardens and greenhouses. If you like heathers, be sure to see their collection. Both the Berggarten and Herrenhausen are open all day, from 8 A.M. to dusk.

South of Hannover, you will find a very interesting climbing rose at Hildesheim. This is said to be 1000 years old. In 1945 when the whole town was aflame from bombs, the rose was charred and buried under rubble. New shoots came up, and the next summer it bloomed again. It is now 30 feet high and climbing the apses of the cathedral. It is a simple wild rose (Rosa canina).

If you are flying into *West Berlin,* be sure to allow enough time there to see some of the fine gardens that have been restored since the war. The most important of these is the *Zoo Garden* (Grosser Tiergarten), which is really a great park. This wonderful garden area was almost completely destroyed in World War II, not only by bombings, but by being used for planting much-needed potatoes and cabbages. Even the benches were burned by citizens as fuel, and small gardens of vegetables were developed in the rubble. The final disaster came in the hard winter of 1946-47 when the desperate Berliners came to get every trunk, branch, and twig, and even the roots of the very last trees, to use for cooking and for warmth. The restoration of the gardens was begun in 1949, when many German cities made donations for it. Bremen, for example, although itself almost totally destroyed, sent 30,000 young trees.

Today you will see here in West Berlin's Zoo Garden a wood with 3000 rhododendrons in bloom from May to middle of July. A garden at the Reiterbruecke displays thousands of summer flowers, including a fine show of dahlias. There are patterned beds at the goldfish pond, edged with English lavender and blue grasses, and an English Garden, whose plants are mainly gifts from England, in which small flower shows are held at regular intervals. There is even a reading room where the ardent gardener may look up some unknown plant or sit and enjoy a book on his favorite flowers.

The castle garden at *Schlosspark Charlottenburg* has also been restored to its former beauty, the Great Parterre being kept full of flowers from tulip season on. You will see lovely waterlilies blooming in the pond in June and July. The terrace of the palace itself is kept bright with pots of tall fuchsias, myrtle, lantanas and other annuals. If you should walk to the moat near the Mausoleum you will find a swamp cypress 140 years old.

The *Botanical Garden* (Botanischer Garten), covering some ninety acres in the Dahlem section of Berlin, is the largest in Germany, and one of the largest on the Continent. It is beautifully landscaped, so I am sure you will enjoy walking around the extensive grounds to see the world-famous garden, divided by geographical origins. There is no other alpine garden in the world, according to many experts, to compare with this in extent, and in the way in which the geographical characteristics of each mountain range have been reproduced. Here, in a comparatively small area, you can see how the wildflowers grow in the Alps, the Carpathian mountains, and those of the Balkans, the Near East, and the Caucasus, to the Himalayas and West China. A large space is devoted to the representation of the mountains of Japan and the Rocky Mountains of North America. In another part of the gardens you will find the moist area for water and swamp-loving plants.

The arboretum fortunately escaped war damage, and is of great interest to the student of trees, as it is arranged according to plant families, although it appears to be merely a well-designed park. There is an Italianate garden in front of the greenhouses. These are exceptionally interesting. One large house is entirely filled with palms, another is devoted to the huge royal waterlily (Victoria regia), and others are bright with tropical and sub-tropical plants, cacti, and succulents. This garden is open weekdays from ten to dusk, when a small admission is charged. On Saturdays, Sundays and holidays it is open free from 1 P.M. to dusk.

Two gardens that you can see in West Berlin are connected with the famous Swedish botanist, Linnaeus. One is that on the Peacock Island (*Pfaueninsel*), near Potsdam, where there are still many trees he planted. The other is the *Glienicke Park* (Volkspark Glienicke), in Berlin-Wannsee, which is a landscape garden designed and supervised by Linnaeus until his death in 1866. In the *Lietzenseepark* you will find a number of gay perennial gardens, and if you like roses, don't miss seeing the *Humboldthain,* where you will find 18,000 roses of 75 varieties, including a collection of superb wild roses.

CENTRAL GERMANY

The most interesting gardens in this area are all in cities along the big super-highway, the Autobahn, so they are easy to see if you are driving, but they are also connected by frequent fast train service.

If you are coming from northern Germany, your first stop would be at the Ruhr District industrial city of *Dortmund.* This is a smoky place full of steel mills and coal mines, so the city government has made a special effort to compensate with parks and flower gardens that workers can enjoy in their leisure hours. The most beautiful of these is the *Westfalen-park*, which was greatly extended and improved by having the big German Flower Show (Bundesgartenschau) there in 1959. (See chapter on "Flower Shows in Europe.") It is open daily for a small admission fee. All the shrubs, trees and flowers are well labeled so that the German home gardener can learn about plants he would like in his own grounds. The landscaping has been so deftly done, however, that you can forget the educational aspects and just wander about admiring the beauties of the different areas. You will see an exquisite Japanese garden with a tea-house brought from Japan; a fascinating heather slope with broom shrubs in unusual colors; special gardens for roses, water plants, summer flowers, and dahlias. If you get there early enough in the spring you will find glorious beds of tulips. One interesting demonstration shows all the different kinds of groundcovers; another has samples of the many ways of making garden paths; while still another educational feature is the compost-making exhibit. When you get tired from so much walking, sit down in the small stadium and watch the great fountains playing in harmony with selections on the organ.

Very close by is the *Botanical Garden and Aviary* (Botanischer Garten), which is also treated as a recreational park, and includes greenhouses full of orchids and palms, and a valley of naturalized primroses and tulips for early spring. Later on you can enjoy rhododendrons, roses and summer flowers.

South of Dortmund you come to another industrial city, *Essen*. The *Gruga Park* here is one of the largest and finest in Germany. A walk through all of it will take you about three hours, but you can see much of it by riding around in the miniature railway. This park was made on the bombrubble of World War I, and was later enlarged by the German Flower Shows of 1938 and 1952. You go up and down gentle hills here, see a valley full of rhododendrons, a water garden, and quantities of flowers from tulip-time on. There is a fascinating section devoted to sample home gardens of different types, one of them a "Green Garden," which has aroused much interest. But the most exciting display of all in this park comes in late summer when the Dahlia Arena is completely filled with colorful bloom. This is a circular valley devoted entirely to this one flower, making a picture from above which you will never forget. If you should be in Essen in August, don't fail to visit the *Botanical Garden* here as well, to see the carpet of gentians in bloom, and the famous collection of alpine plants.

From here you can move south again to the cathedral city of *Cologne* (Koeln), where you will find the last garden created by Linnaeus before his death. It is called simply *Flora*. This is a landscaped park which was combined with a botanical garden. It contains a lovely rockery, and many fine azaleas. The particular attraction here, however, is the large number of greenhouses, said to be the most modern in Europe. These are filled with cacti, succulents, palms, ferns, tropical flowers, and in one there is a pond which is half inside the glass for warm water plants, such as the Victoria regia, and half outdoors.

In the *Rheinpark,* in Cologne, you can take a cable-car to look down from above on the flowers grouped in many specialized gardens: spring bulbs, iris, water plants, roses, and others. On Sundays and holidays you can also ride around here in a miniature railway.

Not far from Cologne, is the interesting baroque palace of *Bruehl,* with a large formal garden of French style, designed by a pupil of Le Nôtre. This, like all gardens of its type, was planned for outdoor fêtes and you must fill it in your imagination with silk-clad, white-wigged ladies and gentlemen. Down the center you will see a series of formal pools with fountains, surrounded by low boxwood parterres. There are fine old trees around the garden, also trim orange trees, bay trees, pomegranates, and blue Agapanthus in tubs. When the Queen Mother of Greece visited here some years ago, the entire geometric design of the parterres was outlined at night with wax candles. What a picture that must have made! Before you leave here, be sure to step into the little flower garden at the side, where you will see thousands of purple heliotrope in the summer.

We went next to the bustling modern city of *Frankfurt*. You could land at the big airport there in the first place, and make your tour of garden cities in direct reversal of our pattern. Be sure to allow plenty of time for the gardens in Frankfurt itself, for the city fathers are justly proud of their many green areas. Instead of staying at any of the noisy hotels downtown, we always take a room in the little Hotel Pension Palmengarten (Palmengartenstrasse 7), which is just opposite the entrance to the *Palmengarten,* perhaps the most famous and beloved park in Germany. This enables us to go there early in the morning for a walk before my husband starts on his business appointments, and again in the evening when we very often have dinner on the terrace. You won't see many tourists there, but always Germans, for many of them seem almost to live in the park. You will see university students sitting in a corner doing their homework; children playing in the paths or on the playground while their mothers knit and gossip; young couples walking arm-in-arm along the lake, listening to the afternoon band concert; and always some ardent gardener making notes on unusual flowers or plants. This is actually a botanical garden, and everything here is lovingly labeled.

When you have walked through all the ornamental plantings, seen the glorious display of roses, and the waterlily pond, lost yourself in the wild meadow garden, you can go to the section where all these flowers are raised in experimental beds and study each variety separately. Even then you will only have begun your explorations, for you must not miss the world-renowned greenhouses. Among their displays are lush tropical ferns and palms; a house full of cacti and succulents; and one brilliant house devoted to gloxinia. The orchid collection boasts 1500 varieties; the begonia house has over 150 kinds; then there is a greenhouse where the flowers are changed each month. Fortunately the park has been laid out not only for walking, but for sitting and resting as well, so you will find benches or metal chairs everywhere in which you can relax and try to absorb the beauty. Even the music selected for the afternoon and evening concerts will often be related to flowers. At the Rose Festival, in late June this past year, the theme of all orchestral and vocal selections was the rose; you could listen and see the Rose Show at the same time.

Another interesting, but rather small flower garden in Frankfurt is the *Bethmannpark*. This was designed as a demonstration for the home gardener, and there is always someone here to answer any horticultural question you may have. The citizens of the entire city know the Plant Doctor here, who is ever ready to look over an ailing house plant, suggest treatment for it, or even to keep it for awhile and nurse it back to health in his "Plant Hospital," all without charge.

Frankfurt is an excellent place in which to observe the apartment dwellers at work in their small community plots, the *"Kleingaerten."* There are 14,000 of these within and around the city, in 220 different locations. The people who work these small gardens for a nominal rental fee have organized themselves into a large club, which at times has been able to exert enough pressure on over-eager developers to save these areas from suddenly being converted into skyscraper settlements. There are also many gardens connected with schools, where the children learn how to raise their own vegetables and flowers. For information and directions for reaching all such gardens, inquire at the City Garden Office (Gartendirektion), Glauburgstrasse 95.

Frankfurt, though it is an ultra-modern businessman's city, is as eager for a beautiful facade as any of the quaint medieval towns in other sections of Germany, and sponsors an annual contest with prizes for the best window-boxes on the house-fronts. There is also a society whose purpose is to prevent the destruction of fine old trees, even in private gardens.

SOUTHERN GERMANY

From Frankfurt, you can drive south on the Autobahn to the upper part of the Black Forest. The little garden at *Rastatt,* which I would like to mention first cannot really be rated as one of the most important gardens in Germany. But it is very charming at all times, and since it was my own discovery, and is not mentioned in the German Garden Clubs' listings or in any guidebook, I cannot resist telling you about it. The garden is at the *Pagodenburg,* directly on Route #3. Here you will enter through a lawn covered in early spring with narcissus, leading up to an old chapel. Just beyond this is the garden, filled with tulips and other spring bulbs as the weather begins to warm up, later on a riot of roses, perennials and annuals. The garden, although modern, was laid out in the old style with terraces descending from an upper wall, ornamental statuary here and there. The focal point of the garden, and what gives it a very special charm, is the lovely little baroque palace, a miniature of those you will see at Nymphenburg in Munich. This was built in 1722 as a play-house by the archduchess for her grandchildren. There is a refreshment terrace and small zoo just below this, where families with children like to go. But if I were a child, I would keep pressing my nose to the windows of the little palace and imagine myself playing house there.

Not far from here, west of Karlsruhe, there is an exceptionally fine *Rose Garten* (Rosengarten), at *Zweibruecken*. This is open from dawn to dusk, and contains 60,000 bushes of 700 rose varieties. You will also see a special collection of French roses. The newest introductions from all countries are displayed here. The time to go is mid-June to early July.

Heading west a few more miles we come to *Saarbruecken* where you will find a heart-warming example of postwar friendship of the traditional enemies, France and Germany. In 1960 citizens from both sides of the border created a great *Garden of German-French Cooperation* (Deutsch-Franzoesischer Park) which is still today a thing of great beauty, cared for by garden enthusiasts of both nationalities. It is so large that you can ride through it in a miniature railroad or get a bird's eye view from a cable car if you wish. There is a fine Valley of the Flowers; demonstrations of gardens in the shade; a garden of ornamental grasses, another of evergreens and still another of heathers. The terraced parterre of annuals is strikingly colorful, and you must be sure to look for the French dahlia and gladioli garden. What a transformation has been made here on the site of a former battleground! The city also boasts a splendid perennial garden, baroque flower parterres and a rose garden at the palace, and flower beds in many of its lovely parks.

The city of *Stuttgart*, east of Karlsruhe, is justly proud of its *Hoehenpark Killesberg*. This park is situated on the slopes of one of the mountains which hold the city as if it were in a cup, so you will have fine views from many spots in the gardens. Two German Flower Shows have been held here, each adding to the permanent collections of bloom. You will see fine displays of tulips and primroses early in the year; then the roses and perennials, finally the dahlias and begonias.

Just a few miles north lies the *Schlosspark*, of the palace at *Ludwigsburg*, with its famous flower parterres and hedged rose gardens, called "Baroque in Bloom (Bluehendes Barock)." Perhaps you will agree with me, however, that the really startling garden here is the Perennial Garden, farther off at one side of the palace. Follow the signs to the "Staudenwiese" (pronounced Shtah-oo-den-vee-zay). When you walk these winding paths edged with colorful flower borders, you will think you are in a typical English country-house garden. Whether you go in May, when 50,000 tulips and hyacinths spread bright carpets all around, or whether you go in late June, as I did, to see the hybrid lilies, the tall spikes of delphinium, orange-yellow Eremurus, and deep red Pentstemon, you will have your fill of color. Don't miss the big bed of astilbes at one side, in all the shades from white through pink to deep wine-red, or the special rock-garden path higher up, where you will see many a choice alpine flower. Perhaps you will do as we did, stop for a cooling drink at the terrace restaurant, then walk through the gardens slowly all over again. If you tour the palace interior, you will see from a window an authentic copy of an old baroque parterre design laid out in colored gravels.

If you are touring Germany, you will surely go to *Munich,* and out to the beautiful 17th century pavilions and palace at *Nymphenburg,* with their 18th century gardens after the French style. Here, you will see the remnants of a former grandiose garden design, with long geometrical pools and canals stretching off into the distance. One of the charming pavilions, called Marly, was built as a dressing-room for actors who performed in an outdoor, hedge-backed theatre, like the one we saw in Hannover.

Allow enough time after seeing all these delightful buildings, to roam around in the Jewel Court (Schmuckhof), just inside the entrance to Nymphenburg, for this is one of the most interesting and beautiful *Botanical Gardens* in Germany. It is open daily from 9 to 7. On top of the walls surrounding the garden, you will see strange and colorful big birds made of the famous Nymphenburg porcelain. You will find an alpine garden, rhododendrons, a grotto of ferns, a beautiful heather garden, and many colorful flower-beds. The greenhouses contain fine collections of orchids, ferns, cacti and succulents, and one of the best examples of the great water-lily, Victoria regia, to be seen in Germany.

In the center of Munich itself, be sure to see the lovely flowers in the park which was originally the botanical garden. You can see another good example of the French parterre gardens at the castle of *Schleissheim.*

Whatever gardens you visit in Germany, don't miss seeing the *Island of Mainau* (named for the little wild Mayflower), in Lake Constance, one of the most beautiful gardens in all Europe.

Whether you reach the island by the connecting causeway on foot (no cars are allowed on the island), from the city of Constance, or whether you arrive by boat from one of the beautiful lakeside towns, you will want to allow plenty of time for a complete tour of the gardens. The shortest boat trip, about 25 minutes long, starts at Meersburg, where you can explore the oldest castle in Germany.

The lake is bordered not only by Germany, but also by the shores of Switzerland and Austria, but strangely enough the Island of Mainau is owned by Count Lennart Bernadotte, nephew of the King of Sweden. He inherited it from the Princess of Baden who later became Queen of Sweden. When the Count began developing this island paradise with its mild climate, he found a rather formal garden and many exotic old trees which the former owner, Grand Duke Frederick of Baden, had obtained from Kew Gardens in England and many other parts of the world. These are now over 200 years old and are one of the great attractions of the grounds; here you will see cedars of Lebanon, Paulownias from Japan, tremendous pines from the Himalayas and Siberia, trees from every continent, all carefully labeled. One section is com-

Island of Mainau, Germany (*Foto Siegfried Lauterwasser*)

pletely tropical with bamboos, fig trees, oranges, bananas, which are covered in winter with temporary greenhouses.

Count Bernadotte is an expert landscape architect as well as an outstanding horticulturist, and has, in the last forty years, converted the whole island into a natural park overflowing with flowers. You would enjoy it early in the spring, for this part of Europe begins to get comfortably warm very soon. You will see great carpets of naturalized bulbs, beginning with the species tulips in April, on into the other tulip varieties through May, and including narcissus, hyacinths, scillas and grape hyacinths—some 600,000 bulbs in all.

Some of the roses also begin blooming in May, rising to a great climax in June, with many of them continuing on into the late fall. There is a total of 25,000 rose bushes in the formal Rose Garden and all the additional areas given over to this favorite flower, intermingled with tree-form heliotropes.

If you are a rose fancier you will probably never get beyond these gardens, but do try to explore some of the other paths along the shore and see the perennial borders, the small rock gardens, and enjoy the far views of beautiful Lake Constance. If the dahlia is your specialty, you should certainly visit Mainau in September, when you can admire some 18,000 plants, grouped in masses of one hundred of each variety.

In this chapter I have described only a few of the gardens listed in the "Key to Gardens" at the back, and there you will find also suggested "Wheel Tours" for visiting many in neighboring towns.

USEFUL INFORMATION

SOME GERMAN WORDS YOU MIGHT NEED: The word for "garden" is "Garten"; perennials are "Stauden": pronounced Shta-ooden; dahlias are "Dahlien"; Botanical garden is "Botanischer

Garten." You will find most Germans speak some English, however.

GERMAN GARDEN SOCIETY (address them as Deutsche Gartenbau-Gesellschaft e. V.), Koelnerstrasse 142-148, 532 Bad Godesberg, Germany; The secretary, Frl. Elizabeth Goering, speaks English and will gladly answer questions.

GERMAN TOURIST INFORMATION OFFICE, 500 Fifth Ave., New York, N.Y. 10036: Very helpful with leaflets about all regions and other touring information.

NOTE: If you read German, when you are in Germany buy the book *Gartenwunder am Reisewege*, published in 1960 by the German Garden Society through the Energie-Verlag, Heidelberg. This lists and describes many more gardens in Germany and includes photographs of almost every garden. It can be bought in bookstores in Germany, for about $4.50.

chapter 13

ITALY: HILLSIDE GARDENS

IF you are interested in Italian history or in formal landscape design, in architecture and sculpture, you will find enough in the gardens on this peninsula to keep you happy for years. Each one that is open to the public has a story to tell that can carry you back many centuries.

Some of the gardens will also appeal to flower lovers, but these are the exceptions. Most of the flowers you see in Italy are spilling out of the terra-cotta pots that stand on parade in front of the humblest homes, or hang on the walls, or overflow with blossoms from balcony railings and rooftops. Even when the houses hang on a cliff, edged only by street and sidewalk, you will see flowerpots abloom on every windowsill. For the feast of Corpus Christi, in places like Genzano, for example, you can watch the citizens filling whole street pavements with intricate designs made from flower petals. But the average Italian is more susceptible to fragrance, it seems, than to color. Often, you will notice someone riding a bicycle who stops to break off a twig of laurel from a nearby garden, crushes it in his fingers, and sniffs it appreciatively while he continues on his way. Space is at a premium in the towns, so there is little room for a garden for the average person; in the country districts, life is hard, and energies must be spent on the vineyards, the fruit and olive trees, and the vegetable patches, rather than on flowers.

The more well-to-do homes in Italy today are adding many of the modern features that we enjoy in America—terraces for reading and relaxing, bathing pools, eating areas, even when these must be carefully designed in separate sections so as not to disturb the formal, historically treasured gardens of these old villas.

Strangely enough, one must go back to the letter of Pliny the Younger, written to his friend Gallus about A.D. 100, to get a picture of an Italian garden similar to those we have in the United States. Pliny's country house was located about seventeen miles from Rome, and he tells of his delight in the beauty of his garden, its quiet, its careful planning for his needs. He describes the fine view of the garden that he has from the window of the room where he eats; how he likes to walk out, barefoot, on the wandering path edged with boxwood and rosemary, to his small vineyard; how he goes from there to his flower beds that scent the air with the perfume of violets. He outlines in detail the design and purpose of a long, covered walk-way with windows that give shelter from the strong winds, the location so planned that it is shaded in the hottest part of the day. At the end of this walk he had an open summerhouse where he liked to take sunbaths, and from which he could revel in his colorful flower beds on one side, the blue Mediterranean on the other. Adjacent to this was his bedroom, with an open wall for the enjoyment of the garden, but with shades to pull down for complete quiet and seclusion when he wanted it. He spoke of this home and garden as a refuge from the noisy saturnalias of his country neighbors, a place where he could work and sleep.

When you read the histories of the later Italian villa gardens, especially those constructed from the 16th to the 18th century, you will find an entirely different approach, a purpose diametrically opposed to that of Pliny. In the days of Italy's grandeur, in the period of great wealth and ostentation on the part of its ruling classes, the garden was designed as a show place, as a status symbol, and as a space in which great entertainments could be given.

These gardens were constructed, more than they were planted, for they are filled with stone, marble, and concrete, tremendous staircases, great bulky fountains of intricate water play, and sculpture and more sculpture everywhere; the formal pools, cascades, and waterfalls demanded the ultimate in ingenuity from hydraulic engineers.

In contrast to the French gardens of Le Nôtre, which were leveled off as much as possible to get distant views, the Italian landscape architects retained and used their hilly locations to great advantage, planning the progress from terrace to terrace with balustrades and statuary, with vistas always looking downward or back up to the crowning building at the top. What level spaces there are were designed as areas for plays, operas, concerts, and the gatherings of a large and fashionable multitude. For additional diversion, they designed elaborate mazes, grotesque statues, and "surprise" fountains, which suddenly drenched the unwary visitor—a favorite pastime throughout Europe at one time. There were even hydraulic organs, and artificial singing birds.

To frame and accent all this architecture and elegance, to lend the garden dignity and even solemnity at times, the great dark trees of Italy were the ideal material. The sharp spears of the almost-black cypresses, the great brooding spread of the umbrella pine, the weeping evergreens, the prim box and yew that could be clipped into formality— these were the ingredients that characterize the old Italian gardens, as we see them even today. Large trees and shrubs were needed to give shade from the heat of summer, shelter from the disagreeable winds. These gardens have little appeal to the color photographer; they are essentially studies in black and white, in dark trees and shrubs relieved by white statuary and staircases. To the student of landscape architecture, they are a never-ending casebook on the use of balance, symmetry, and proportion, and the bending of nature's whims into man's controlled plan.

You may find some of these gardens today rather untidy and ill-kept. One English friend who toured Italy said that she constantly had to resist the urge to kneel down and start weeding. The shortage of labor and lack of money combined have left many a place overgrown and fuzzy on the edges. Yet even this, for some travelers, has its own charm. If you are the kind of person, for example, who likes a cemetery that is neatly manicured, the stones clean and shiny as if recently scrubbed and polished, you would probably prefer the great formal gardens of France, which are always well swept and tidy, even when the palaces are not. But if you like your graveyards old and enjoy poking about the mossy, tumbled-down grave markers and dreaming about the days gone by, when the ghosts of this place were alive and gay, then you will like the ancient Italian gardens, too. Delve into the books about Italian history, steep yourself in the life of the various centuries, from the 15th to today—then let your imagination run loose as you roam through the gardens of Italy.

There are so many of these typical old villa gardens that it would be impossible to list them all. In the "Key to Gardens" you will find some of the most famous ones, those that are regularly open to the public or for which it is not too difficult to get permission for a viewing. The best method for seeing gardens in Italy is to take a local guide, who can often obtain admission to some that you would not see otherwise and tell you about the historical background of each one. In Florence, you will find the Garden Tours of great interest, as these are scheduled so often that you can see different places each time.

Even though most of these formal gardens attached to villas lack flowers and color, you will find some, not as well publicized as the old villa gardens, that have flower beds and are vivid with tropical plants. Because these are unusual in Italy, I have described a number of them below.

NORTHERN ITALY

Let's suppose that you are driving to Italy from the south coast of France. Stop first in *Ventimiglia,* to see the superb garden at Villa Hanbury, called *La Mortola.* This will remind you in many ways of some of the finest gardens of England, for its plan includes many small hedged gardens—one of them devoted to fragrant flowers. There are a great many exotic trees and shrubs from other parts of the world here, also. But the garden's English tradition is well-founded, for it is actually the result of much planning and dreaming on the part of Sir Thomas Hanbury, who purchased the 100-acre property in 1867, upon his return to Europe after many years in China. From then on, he spent all his time importing plant specimens, to develop one of the largest and most varied collections in Europe. In some ways it became a botanical garden, and for years there was an exchange of students of horticulture between La Mortola and Kew Gardens in England.

The scented garden in front of the 14th-century villa is backed by a brick wall covered with a tremendous rosemary plant, with bright-blue Mediterranean campanulas (Trachelium caeruleum) perched in the crevices. The lemon verbena is another fragrant plant in this garden. A long pergola is covered with brilliantly flowered vines from Mexico, Brazil, Peru, and other warm countries. There is a lovely collection of mimosas, some of which begin blooming in January, with others still pouring out their golden showers in midsummer. If you should be there in April, be sure to look for the Sacred-Flower-of-the-Incas from Peru (Cantua buxifolia), with its purplish-red drooping blossoms. Whenever you visit here you will see flowers and color contrast ranging from the silver-gray of the olive trees to the brilliance of the camellias. Most of the plants are labeled, so that you will be able to browse and investigate any that are unfamiliar. Far from being a geometrically arranged botanical garden, this has been planned for beauty of design as well, with a small temple, ornamental fountains, and careful planning of colors, sizes, and textures of plants for the loveliest effect. Whether you are driving or are seeing Italy by train or bus, it will be a simple matter for you to see this garden, as you can reach Ventimiglia by train, and then the San Remo bus will take you there.

If you stop in San Remo, go to the Flower Show in season, and be sure to take a look at the Villa Municipale, with its balconies festooned with roses and bougainvillea and its pots of geraniums.

There are many other interesting gardens north of here, including two unusual alpine gardens described in the chapter "Follow Your Garden Hobby Abroad." These also are listed in the "Key to Gardens."

Certainly no one going to Italy should fail to visit the beautiful northern lakes, where you will also find some of the country's loveliest gardens.

You could see some of the most interesting gardens of Italy and some of its most beautiful scenery just by staying a week at *Lake Maggiore.* Allow at least half a day to see the grounds of *Villa Taranto,* at Verbania-Pallanza. This lies on the north shore of the lake, between Pallanza and Intra, about half an hour from Locarno, or an hour by car from Milan. The gardens are open daily from April through October, with the height of bloom in April, May, July, and

August. You will find guides there who speak many languages; be sure to take one on your tour of the garden.

The garden of Villa Taranto covers 100 acres and was created, beginning in 1930, by a Scotsman, Captain Neil McEacharn. Upon his death in 1964 it became the property of the state. Partly laid out on a promontory 300 feet above the lake, with a view of the snow-covered Swiss Alps, it was designed to display a great collection of botanical specimens, its beauty being only a happy by-product. It is certainly the finest modern garden in Italy, and one of the greatest gardens in the world. If you can plan your tour of Italian gardens in such a way that you see Villa Taranto last, it would be the fitting climax; everything you see elsewhere will suffer by comparison if you see it first.

It would be impossible to give a detailed description of all there is to see in a garden of this size and scope in the space available here, but I do hope that you will read the beautiful descriptions in the three books mentioned in the chapter, "Suggested Reading About European Gardens."

I will mention only some of the glories there, starting with the magnificent magnolia collection that bursts into bloom beginning in March, and the valley that it took more than a hundred men two years to dig, now covered with daffodils, lilies, hostas, and particularly azaleas. There are five large rock gardens harboring delicate alpines from many lands, a pool completely filled with glorious lotus blossoms, and a heather garden with almost every variety you could name. There are old and unusual trees throughout the grounds, including many of the lovely Paulownias with their fragrant lavender blossoms; Japanese cryptomerias; and a whole series of rare specimens planted by Spanish royalty in years past, and, more recently, by Princess Margaret of England. Many of the beautiful plants you will see here have progeny in gardens all over the world, for the Villa Taranto Seed Catalogue, which is available to garden experts and botanical gardens, now lists 4000 varieties. To the thousands of Italian visitors who flock here every year perhaps the most interesting thing of all is the great expanse of beautiful lawn, a bit of the British Isles rarely found in Italy.

There are a number of island gardens in Lake Maggiore that have great appeal. On *Isola Madre,* the largest of the four owned by Prince Borromeo, there is an arboretum containing many unusual trees that have grown to great size in this mild climate. There are several California redwoods over 100 feet high; a beautiful weeping Himalayan cypress nearly 100 feet tall, with branches like silvery lace; a pine from Mexico, a myrtle from Chile, and trees from many parts of South America, including a giant palm (Jubaea spectabilis) now over 100 years old. The magnolias, camellias, and azaleas have grown to great size, and there are rhododendrons with trunks nearly a foot in diameter. The garden is well landscaped into many levels, with winding paths and some lovely views of the lake.

The other island garden belonging to Prince Borromeo, *Isola Bella,* is quite different, as it is laid out in baroque design, with many formal terraces, statuary, and fountains. As you approach the island by boat it looks like an elaborate stepped Egyptian pyramid, with pointed spires and statues relieving the edges, all reflected in the blue water of the lake. If you see it in May, your lasting impression will probably be a picture of the green "theater" contrasting with white azaleas and white peacocks that preen themselves in the warm sunshine. There are many espaliered fruit trees— oranges, lemons, and apricots; oleanders, fig trees, mimosas, coco and camphor trees. This is a romantic garden of great beauty, with many flowers blooming especially in April and September, but lovely at any time.

There is another island garden in Lake Maggiore, perhaps less well known or publicized than the others, that you should not miss—the island of *Brissago,* now the property of the Swiss nation. The garden here has had a strange history. Some eighty years ago, a very wealthy Russian lady of the Imperial court, the Countess St. Leger, saw the island and decided that she must own it and create a garden there. In order to accomplish her purpose, she had to build a harbor at Porto Ronco, from which boats could bring loads of good soil to the island. Then she sent out letters from her own post office to friends throughout the world, asking for young plants and seeds. Soon she received date palms from the Canary Islands, cedars from Lebanon, lotus and papyrus from Egypt, bamboos from China—exotic treasures from the whole world. In spite of some setbacks, most of these plants grew, and soon the island became a tropical paradise.

Unfortunately, the Countess was also an inveterate gambler, and little by little her fortune disappeared. She ended her days completely destitute, having lived in the poorhouse at Intragna for twenty years before she died. The island garden of Brissago passed through various hands, until one day it was rumored that some financiers were about to buy it and turn it into a gambling casino. The Swiss people were so outraged at the idea of losing such a beauty spot, that they took up a collection throughout their little country and managed to purchase the island, turning it into a Swiss Botanical Garden. The place had deteriorated into an overgrown jungle, and it was some time before order was brought out of chaos.

Opened to the public in 1950, it is now a research station for the testing of plants for their needs as to climate and soil and for the study of their flowers and fruits and their decorative uses. Many of the trees that the Countess planted—the date palms, the bamboos, the camellias—have grown to great size. There are pomegranates, azaleas, cacti and succulents, a great variety of plants, now growing in a more controlled setting but still with the luxuriance of a tropical jungle. Strange to think of this exotic island as being a part of Switzerland!

You can easily move on from here to the vicinity of *Lake Lugano*, to see the *Villa Cicogna* garden, at Bisuschio. This is a superb example of a typical Italian villa garden of the 16th century. Here you will see a beautiful water-staircase, the water running in a little sloping canal between the steps. Below it a terrace leads to the sunken garden with its parterres on one side, the terraced garden on the other toward the lake. One of the most interesting features is the subterranean passage, designed for cool walks in the heat of the day, refreshing with its delicate clusters of maidenhair fern in the rustic stone. You may also tour the inside of the villa to admire the splendid Renaissance furnishings, for this is one of the few Italian private houses open to the public.

Lake Como is justly one of the most popular regions for tourists, and here you will find many beautiful gardens. If you stay at the famous *Villa d'Este Hotel* at Cernobbio, you can enjoy the views of the old garden with its long flights of stone stairs, through the glass walls of the dining room. Or you may walk down to the edge of the lake, where a wisteria vine droops its lavender blossoms on a pergola beside the blue water.

From here you can make a number of excursions to various gardens. Ask at the Tourist Office in Bellagio which ones may be seen, and on what days. One garden that is open regularly is at Cadenabbia, at the *Villa Carlotta*. The former property of a German prince, it now belongs to the Italian government. The garden is laid out on a steep hillside with terraces on many levels, from which you will see the snow-capped mountains above and a riot of flowers below, with the deep blue of the lake as a ribbon in between. Here, there are many little "secret gardens," great clipped hedges twenty-five feet high, and the fragrance of lemon blossoms or the yellow of the fruit itself. It is a place of delight to the flower lover and plant student alike, for you can see trees and shrubs from Australia, Asia, Africa, India, and South America. Buy the booklet at the gate that lists everything of botanical interest. There are large specimens of the giant sequoia, the Japanese cryptomeria, tall palms, fine-leaved bamboos. You will find orchids from the Himalayas, Brazil, and Mexico, and a collection of 15 kinds of clematis. But the greatest attraction of all, which draws tourists by the thousands in April and May, is the massive—almost overwhelming—planting of azaleas and rhododendrons, in a blaze of color along the water.

Another garden on Lake Como that has a beautiful hillside of azaleas is that of the *Villa Melzi*. This is the home of Duke Tommaso Gallarati-Scotti, former Italian ambassador to Great Britain, who has introduced many new varieties of azaleas, rhododendrons, and camellias that he imported from there. You walk through this garden along a lakeside path under a roofing of plane trees, with lawns sloping down to the water on one side and a view of the azaleas up above on the other side. Returning by an upper path you will see a charming Japanese water garden, a surprise in this Italian setting, with wisteria over a bamboo bridge, and iris and lotus along the edges of the pool.

There are so many gardens near Bellagio that it would take you weeks to get permissions and see them all. Start your tour here at the *Grand Hotel Serbelloni*, which has a fine modern garden of its own. Not far from it is the *Villa Serbelloni*, which like so many of these lakeside properties has sloping ground developed into a series of garden terraces. These are formal in design, accented with conical clipped yews, and colorful with annuals and perennials, roses, and flowering shrubs. Here and there you will come to a bench where you can sit and rest and admire the views, and you will need to, for this is an extensive garden. The steps down to the lower level are very steep, but the colorful flower beds awaiting you below make the descent well worth while. This garden is a great contrast to the typical green hillside ones of which we spoke earlier, for there are no great stone staircases, no statuary, only a delightful combination of formality and informality, with a profusion of bloom—dahlias, zinnias, calliopsis, stock, all the flowers you love in your own garden at home.

There are other lovely gardens in the Lake Como region listed in the "Key to Gardens," and you will find more by asking questions at the local tourist offices. If you should continue your tour to *Lake Garda,* you would see the famous rock garden there, at Gardone Riviera, called *Villa Hruska,* which is described in the chapter "Follow Your Garden Hobby Abroad." At Garda itself there is the delightful *Idania,* one of the most beautiful modern gardens in Italy. The owner, Mrs. Ida Noble Borletti, is kind enough to allow foreign visitors to come if they are really interested in gardening and will telephone or write for an appointment. Originally designed by Mr. A. Edwards and then developed by the eminent Henry Cocker, both Englishmen, this is a truly British garden with its wide lawns and fine mixed flower borders. Its setting is completely Italian, however, with superb views of the lake and large olive groves and vineyards forming the background. The two parts of the garden are linked by a very lovely rockery, made of native limestone, and there are stone steps and dry walls in many places, all sprouting little alpines, dwarf annuals, and small bulbs. In spite of the very alkaline soil it has been possible to grow many fine azaleas, rhododendrons, and camellias. In the wide border along one side of the lawn there are many of my favorites, such as hemerocallis, pentstemon, monarda, and two members of our familiar milkweed family, Asclepias incarnata, which is our common roadside variety, and the brilliant-orange butterfly weed that has been seeding itself into my American garden from surrounding meadows. You will also see a fine rose garden with bloom continuing into December.

Follow the long pergola-covered path to the workshops and classrooms, where a number of boy apprentices are being trained as gardeners. In another section you will come on the horse paddocks. If your tour should take you on to *Milan*, don't fail to follow your visit to Idania by stopping at Mrs. Borletti's florist shop, *La Fiorera*, where you will find cut flowers, pot plants, and an excellent selection of books on gardening. (If you should be staying for any length of time, you could take a course in flower arranging taught by a representative of the London School of Floristry, or one in the art of Ikebana flower arranging that leads to a diploma recognized in Japan.)

In the "Key to Gardens" you will find a suggested Wheel Tour based on *Vicenza*, an area extraordinarily rich in gardens. If you need further information about any of these, ask for the Marchese Giuseppe Roi, president of the regional tourist office (Ente Provinciale per il Turismo, at Piazza Duomo 5 in Vicenza), as he knows the gardens well. Near there you will see the oldest botanical garden in the world, the *Orto Botanico* at *Padua*, founded in 1545 and still on its original site. Architecturally, it is unique among the botanical gardens of Europe. The original garden of four acres is encircled by a 16th-century wall, fifteen feet high, decorated on top with balustrades and busts of former directors and curators. The gates are topped with iron yucca plants in urns. The gardens, though not designed for beauty, have a certain charm in the regularity of their square plots surrounding occasional fountains. You will find a number of historically interesting trees: a chaste tree (Vitex agnus castus) planted in 1550; a famous palm (Chamaerops humilis arborescens) planted in 1585, which inspired the German poet Goethe to write a book on plant research; an Oriental plane tree of 1680, a ginkgo from 1750. This garden was the source of many plant introductions to European gardens, for the lilac was first introduced here in 1565, the sunflower in 1568, the potato in 1590. Other novelties first grown in Europe here were rhubarb, cyclamen, and the tree of heaven (Ailanthus). Among the flowers you will see particularly lovely iris, asters, and allium. There are about 6000 varieties of plants for you to study, many of them in the greenhouses.

IN AND AROUND FLORENCE

You will surely want to stay in *Florence* as long as possible to savor its Old World charm and its many interesting historical and architectural treasures. This city is a delightful center for one of our Wheel Tours, for there are innumerable lovely gardens to see—in the city itself, in nearby Settignano and Fiesole, and in the towns of Lucca, Caserta, and Collodi. Many of these are listed in the "Key to Gardens," and you will find more if you inquire at the Tourist Office in Florence. Ask at the American Express or Cook's offices for an up-to-date booklet about the many garden tours that will take you to some you would not be able to see by yourself. Or you could hire a local guide who can get the permissions you need to see gardens not regularly open. An excellent guide who knows the gardens is Miss Maria Christina Poccianti (address: Villa il Platano, Scandicci, Florence, Italy).

If you are in Florence at the end of April or in May, don't miss the superb *Iris Garden* (Giardino dell' Iris), on the Piazzale Michelangelo. This was founded in 1955 by Mrs. Flaminia G. Specht, who also brought the Italian Iris Society into being. You will be amazed to see what she has accomplished in this short time, for this is now a world-famous iris garden with over 1000 varieties from many different countries. When Mrs. Specht heard of the historical iris collection at the Presby Gardens in Montclair, New Jersey, which has specimens grown as early as the 16th century, she wrote to ask if she might obtain some of these rhizomes. These were sent to her, and now the whole series of iris from five centuries are blooming in Florence as well. Each year an international iris contest is held here for the new introductions; the prizes are medals that are replicas of old Italian florins, which were decorated with an iris design.

Another garden with American connections is that of the *Villa I Tatti* in *Settignano* outside of Florence, the former home of Bernard Berenson. It was left in his will to Harvard University, to serve as an institute for the study of Mediterranean art. The garden has a quiet, dignified charm, with geometrically clipped box hedges, pebble mosaic paths, and rows of lemon trees in terra-cotta pots. Though modern, it is typical of the old Italian villa gardens.

Also in *Settignano* is the world-famous garden of the *Villa Gamberaia*. This is a truly historical place, first laid out in 1610, and though it is small, it offers everything that the larger Italian villa gardens have. Ask at the cottage for permission to see the garden. From the house you will walk on a long lawn, unusual in Italy, passing at times beside great hedges, towering cypresses, and high white garden walls topped with marble statues or urns, until you come to a shady, cool green grotto. In the center a large fountain is bright with sparkling water, surrounded by sculptures and pebble mosaics. At one side you will step into a small green garden with clipped box hedges and lemon trees. But the large flower-embroidered parterre is perhaps the loveliest spot of all, gay with tulips in early spring, bright with other blossoms later on, all reflecting in the long formal pools, or vying for attention with the exquisite lotus blossoms that stretch up out of the water at the pool's far end. The design and proportions of this garden are worth careful study. The paths are in the form of the usual long cross, flanked on either side by rectangular pools, with a circular basin and fountain where the walks meet. At the end is a semicircular pool backed by hedges clipped into tall arches like those we see in Spain. One long side consists of a great clipped cypress hedge, the other of carefully spaced shrubs. The severity of this underlying plan, however, is delightfully softened by the carefully spaced bushes, pointed cypresses, topiaries, flower beds, and low hedges; this is truly one of the loveliest gardens in Italy. As if this were not enough, the Villa Gamberaia is placed high on a hill with a superb view of the surrounding countryside.

Another garden that you should not miss seeing, because of its great beauty as well as its historical interest, is that of the *Villa Reale de Marlia* at Fraga, near *Lucca*. This was created in the 17th century for the Orsetti family and then for Elisa Baciocchi, sister of Napoleon, who used the garden almost as a series of elegant rooms, for the lavish entertainment of her aristocratic guests.

You start touring at the formal garden near the house, where there is a bright "embroidery" design of ageratum, geranium, and coleus. From here you pass through oaks and laurel to one of the smaller garden "rooms," the delightful Lemon Garden, gay with bright fruit, a splashing fountain, the play of sunlight and shadow on the statuary and flower-filled vases. This so enchanted the American painter, J. S. Sargent, that he captured its spirit in one of two watercolors he made at Marlia late in the 19th century. During the presidency of John F. Kennedy, these paintings were lent to Mrs. Kennedy by the Boston Museum of Fine Arts, and hung in the White House. At one end of this garden is another vivid spot where potted bougainvilleas, trimmed like great carmine parasols, line the walk leading to a decorated pool.

Now you will come to the most exciting feature of this great garden, the Green Theater, circular in shape, with its high walls, backdrop, wings, even the little shades for candle footlights, all made of clipped yews. You will see a platform for the conductor, a prompter's box, all cut from the living green. You can sit in one of the yew "boxes" and peer out at an imaginary performance through the small opening; or take your place on one of the stone benches and gaze at the marble statues of Harlequin, Columbine, and Pulcinella, startlingly white against the dark yew, until they seem to step forward to dance and speak on the stage before you.

As you wander farther you will find a number of newer gardens with wide lawns and flower borders, the formal old water garden, and the large lake with its splendid trees and natural surroundings. Everywhere you will enjoy beautiful old statues of Carrara marble (some of these were sold and can now be seen at Chatsworth, in England). The present owners of Marlia have added a lovely Spanish Garden, a swimming pool, and other modern amenities for their many guests. These are so well designed and carefully placed that they do not disturb the magical atmosphere of the old grounds, but only enhance it. This is a garden to charm everyone—landscape architect, historian, or just flower lover.

While you are in Florence you will surely want to see many of the other gardens listed in the "Key to Gardens," and you will spend much of your time walking through the famous Boboli Gardens to admire the splendid big trees and the many terrace gardens with their fountains—a place of endless variety and quiet charm.

CENTRAL ITALY

If you go to *Rome* around Easter time, you will be there for the spectacular display of azaleas, massed in color group-ings, along the *Spanish Steps*, all the way up to Santa Trinita. There are other flowers arranged there at various times of the year, also, but this is perhaps the most colorful display. You will have to go very early in the morning if you want to take pictures without having thousands of tourists milling around for the same purpose. Be sure to notice the great variety of terra-cotta pots holding the plants. You will find them on sale in innumerable shops. Only a very strong-minded tourist, if he or she has a garden at home, can resist shipping some of these back to America.

Another colorful place for the flower lover who visits Rome in May is the *Municipal Rose Garden* (Il Roseto all' Aventino). After the original rose garden was destroyed in World War II, this new one was started in its present location, with one half devoted to a charming rosarium for popular enjoyment, the other to the growing of new varieties competing for the annual international Gold Medal and for testing various roses as to suitability for this warm, dry climate. Both gardens are in the shape of an ancient amphitheater. In the ornamental rosarium you will see 781 different varieties of roses, among them 149 climbers, and 144 botanical specimens, showing the history of this flower for the last 150 years. The beauty of this garden is further enhanced by beds of iris, which bloom at the same time. If you are in Rome in September you will enjoy the second bloom of the roses.

In October, the gardens of the *Villa Doria Pamphilj* are open to the public for ten days. This features a gorgeous display of chrysanthemums and a lovely perennial rock garden in which all the plants are labeled, as well as an extensive formal park. In the garden of the *Villa Sciarra* or *Wurts*, now a fine public park, you will also find special flower displays at various times of the year. The gardens of the *Villa Borghese*, which are always open, have brilliant masses of azaleas and cinerarias in spring, as well as some lovely flower parterres in both arabesques and geometric designs. Many of the fine trees here are labeled. You will also see colorful flower parterres accented with conical and round topiaries in the handsome *Vatican Gardens.*

I am only mentioning a few spots in Rome where you can enjoy flowers. There are a great many fine gardens to see, some of which are listed in the "Key to Gardens," and others for which a local guide or perhaps a friend can obtain admission. Don't fail to see the garden of the *Villa Lante di Bagnaia,* at *Viterbo,* one of the best designed of the really old gardens of Italy, which is being well restored.

Whatever tour you take in and around Rome, you will certainly see the garden of *Villa d'Este,* at *Tivoli.* You may not consider this a "garden" at all, though it has many fine trees, for its principal features are the gigantic stone sculptures, staircases, and pools which are the framework of its famous and elaborate water display. The great force, height, and number of the fountains are stunning. Your senses will be almost overcome by the roaring of the waters, the sight of this vast complex of stone ornamentation, the fragrance of wet earth and foliage. The men in your party will be fascinated by the complicated hydraulic engineering that went into the building of this display. Be sure to get the pamphlet sold here that details the history of the Tivoli Garden's creation, and offers a plan that you can follow to explore the grounds.

SOUTHERN ITALY

You will find another water garden of a very different sort if you travel south to *Caserta,* near Naples. The *Royal Palace* here was the headquarters of the Allied High Command in World War II and was the scene of the unconditional surrender of the Germans in 1945. The 18th-century garden was laid out on the grand scale. To see it you walk about two miles along a continuing series of cascades, stone terraces, and long rectangular pools. The water disappears underground at intervals to appear again soon after in another series of small waterfalls and great basins, all gracefully ornamented with stone balustrades, statues, and urns. At one point you can walk behind a solid sheet of water

Villa d'Este, Lake Como, Italy (*Photo "ENIT" Ital. State Tourist Off.*)

falling over a stone wall, and stand, surrounded by small wet ferns, listening to the roar overhead.

Finally you come to the end of the Water Garden and turn right to enter a different world—an English Garden created in the 19th century, with curving beds of annuals, dense shrubbery, and exotic trees. The first camellias to be introduced in Europe from Asia are said to have been planted in this garden, and here you see many old specimens; there are also cedars of Lebanon and palms from other lands. Walk farther until you come to a little lake of waterlilies, then along the brook, and on to another pool lovely with pink lotus blossoms. Going back toward the palace, you pass a small garden of cacti and succulents and come to greenhouses full of lovely orchids, ferns, and palms. If you have children with you, don't fail to ask directions to the Children's Woods, where you will find a fantastic miniature castle, built to delight the royal children, complete with its own moat and drawbridge.

Also near Naples you will find the *Palazzo Rufolo*, at *Ravello*. When you enter the grounds, you will think you have suddenly stepped into a Spanish palace, for confronting you in a profusion of Moorish ornament is a charming patio garden with tall papyrus growing in a small pool. This is an unusual example of a private medieval garden full of tropical color. It is said that these gardens inspired Richard Wagner with the idea for his "Home of the Flower Maidens," in the opera *Parsifal*.

If you go to see the ruined city of *Pompeii*, be sure to ask your guide to take you to some of the restored home gardens there. They are fascinating, for here you can see what such a garden must have looked like before the eruption of Mt. Vesuvius in A.D. 79. Only plants that were mentioned by Pliny or other contemporary writers have been used in the reconstruction.

At *Palermo*, on the island of Sicily, you will find a very

beautiful place, the *Botanical Garden of the University* (Orto Botanico dell' Università). The lush tropical and sub-tropical growth on these 75 acres is astonishing. You will see a whole jungle of rubber trees, tropical vines, avenues of palms, and groves of bamboo. Follow the path straight ahead, crossing the avenue of date palms (surrounded by almost every other kind of palm in the world); on the right you will see spiky succulents in front of an Abyssinian straw hut, beyond which there is a pond and bamboo jungle. Following straight on, however, you will encounter an amazing pagoda rubber tree (Ficus magnolioides), its branches spreading out nearly 60 feet into a great roof, many of them supported by roots that come down from these to form supporting columns. In another section of the garden you will find medicinal and commercial plants and an orchard of bananas and citrus fruits. The strange trees with trunks covered with thorns are the false kapok (Chorisia insignis), which have fruits like long cucumbers filled with fine threads. This is a paradise for the botanist interested in unusual trees from all over the world. For the flower lover, there are perennials ranged in rows of pots on top of the walls. The gardens are perhaps most beautiful between April and September.

USEFUL INFORMATION

For General Touring Information while You Are in Italy: *American Express, Cook's,* or the *CIT* (*Compania Italiana Turismo*), or the *Enit* (*Italian Tourist Bureau*), for information as to which gardens are open and when, and how to get special permissions. A guide can often get such permissions for private gardens.

For Information Before You Leave the United States: *Italian State Tourist Office,* 626 Fifth Ave., New York 20, N.Y.

Note: The Italian word for "garden" is "giardino," pronounced "djar-dee-no," and the phrase for "botanical garden" is "orto botanico."

chapter 14

SPAIN: SUNNY SKIES AND
SHADY RETREATS

*T*HE gardens of Spain, whether planned for kings or commoners, are places of retreat: retreat from the noisy bustle of life to the quiet family circle; retreat, particularly, from the heat and glare of the sun to cool green shade and the refreshing sound of fountains.

With long months of high temperatures, dust, and drought to contend with, Spain sustains few blossoming flower gardens as we think of them, though there are occasional exceptions. Instead, as you tour the Iberian Peninsula, you see tall avenues of cypresses or other trees designed for shade, small irrigation canals, cascades, and fountains everywhere. The popular "glorieta," seen in many gardens, is a tiny private "glory," an arbor of living green or stonework where one may sit to talk or eat in cool privacy.

In most Spanish houses you will not see a patch of ground adjacent to the house reserved for flower gardens, such as you find in England or France. Instead, you come on small spots of hanging gardens—flowers and greenery dripping down from wall-bracketed pots or balcony railings in the patios that form the vital center of every house. Often the green of plants and the white house walls are relieved only by the colorful tiles of the patio floor, a bench, or an ornamented alcove.

You will find many ideas for your own grounds in Spain—not in the choice of flowers, but rather in garden ornamentation—the lovely shapes of small pools, the use of potted plants on pool edge or wall, the variety of garden seats of stone or tile, the use of irrigation canals, and especially the decoration of patios and terraces.

If you are fond of coleus, cacti and succulents, you will find many fine specimens, especially in the botanical gardens.

You could start your tour, as we did, at the eastern end of the south coast of Spain, entering by car from France. This permits you to stop off and enjoy the lovely beaches of the Costa Brava. You might like the Park Hotel in *Blanes,* which we enjoyed so much, and you can see a number of gardens from there.

The first is the botanical garden (Jardín Botánico) of *Marimurtra,* under the direction of the Carlos Faust Foundation. Karl Faust was a German who came to Spain and created at Blanes a private botanical garden for the use of botanists and the enjoyment of the general public. Since his death in 1952 the foundation has been caring for the grounds and developing them still further.

Located on the side of the San Juan mountain, with magnificent views of the blue Mediterranean and the resort city of Blanes along the shores below, this is a garden planned for beauty as well as for scientific investigation. The paths wander up and down and around along the slope of the mountain, well marked with numbers to follow so that you will be sure to see every part of the grounds without getting lost. A wall of clipped hedges frames a stair leading you to the particularly lovely small "Temple of Linnaeus," set on a point of land, framed by dark cypresses, and backed by deep-blue surf beyond. At another place along your path a plaque offers you the famous lines from the opera *Mignon*

Marimurtra, Blanes, Spain (*Photo by James L. McFadden*)

in German, Spanish, and Catalonian, "Oh, know you the land where the lemon trees bloom?" This is set against a stone wall edged with geraniums in pots, a semicircular pool below holding waterlilies and reeds. The tall cypress avenue is another dramatic spot as it leads you on down the slope toward the sea beyond.

The plant material consists mainly of exotic cacti, succulents, the striking "red-hot poker" plants (Kniphofia or Tritoma), enormous agaves, and many subtropical foliage plants. Among the many Kalanchoës—which we use as house plants at home—is one named Kalanchoë Faustii, after the garden's creator. The long pool with its surrounding tropical planting is especially beautiful when the delicate pink lotus is in flower. If you see the cacti blooming in the spring you will find the garden particularly colorful, and all through the summer you encounter bright spots of zinnias and cannas here. Everything is labeled, so you can browse without a guide and learn much about plants for use in hot, dry locations.

Another garden to see in Blanes, if you are interested in cacti, is *Pinya de Rosa,* the private garden of an industrialist, Don Fernando Rivière-Caralt. Mr. Rivière is most gracious in permitting cactus specialists to make visits to this mecca, if you telephone in advance. This is a working garden, where you will see the cultivation of every conceivable variety of cactus and succulent from the tiny seedlings in their own plots to the great masses of older giants in rows. There are 650 species of Mesembryanthemum alone, and a tremendous collection of Opuntias. If you are a cactologist—delightful word!—this is a paradise for you.

Just a few miles north of Blanes, towards Lloret de Mar, is *Santa Clotilde.* This is a private estate owned by the Marquéses of Santa Clotilde, but they allow visitors to view the park. This is unique, as it consists entirely of cypresses, thousands of them of every size and shape, planted on terraces and alleys through which you can occasionally see the blue of the Mediterranean below.

Barcelona is not far south of Blanes, but the traffic is so congested that I would suggest you stay in the city itself to see the gardens there, rather than try to go back and forth from Blanes. In Barcelona, you will want to see Gaudi's waterfall and the flower beds in the *Parque de la Ciudadela;* the morning flower market along the *Rambla de San José,* part of the great main street lined with plane trees; and the *Plaza de Cataluña,* with its gardens and cascades. The large formal garden on the side of the mountain, the *Parque de Montjuich,* is well worth exploring, to see its many terraces, stairs, and statues, and especially the Great Fountain in front of the palace, whose numerous sprays and waterfalls are illuminated at night. You might like to eat dinner near there at the *Restaurant Miramar,* which has its own lovely gardens. Also near here is the rather new *botanical garden* of some fifteen acres, specializing in plants from the Balearic Islands, Africa, and Morocco. Barcelona is a modern, commercial city of great activity, but it is justly proud of its fine park department and many green areas.

You could make a flying visit to the island of *Majorca,* from either Barcelona or Valencia; the plane trip is just under an hour from either city. There are two first-class hotels there with especially nice gardens—The *Hotel Formentor,* on the northeast tip of the island, in the town of the same name; and the *Hotel Bahia Palace,* in Palma. The best way to see some of the other gardens open to the public is on one of the many bus tours run by Cook's or other travel agencies, or you can rent a car and visit them by yourself, but inquire at the travel office about hours of admission. At *Raxa,* you will see a garden terraced at eight levels, with beautiful 17th-century stairs leading down from one to the other. There is also an impressive long promenade under tall arches of clipped cypress. In the garden of *Alfabia* at Buñola you will follow meandering paths under a living roof of green. Enter the one made of pebble mosaic, between octagonal stone columns covered with vines, and stop to see all the little fountains in the intervals, spouting from stone vases, until you come to the large round fountain at the end. These are typical Moorish gardens meant for quiet contemplation and the refreshment of shade and running water. At the 14th-century convent in *Valldemosa,* where Chopin and Georges Sand stayed one winter, you will see many small courtyards, one opening out from each cell, and every one decorated with a small basin or fountain and fragrant lemon or orange trees, and occasional flowers.

Now, if you drive on south along the coast from Barcelona, you can stop in the sleepy little town of Benicarló for a meal, or stay overnight at the delightful Albergue de Carretera, one of the government-run motels of Spain.

As you continue on the highway towards Valencia, be sure to notice the effective border plantings of oleanders, roses, and deep-blue morning-glories, which brighten the otherwise rather bleak landscape.

Valencia likes to call itself the "City of Flowers." You would appreciate this description during one of the great festivals, such as the Cruz de Maio in May, when religious crosses throughout the city are beautifully decorated with flowers; the Corpus Christi processions, when fountains and altars receive garlands, and bouquets; and most exciting of all, the Battle of Flowers in July, when you see elaborate floral floats parade through the streets amid showers of blossoms tossed by participants and onlookers alike. Ask the Spanish Tourist Office for dates.

Go to the *Jardínes del Real* (or *Viveros,* since the gardens go by both names), the loveliest park in Valencia, and have lunch in the patio of the Viveros Restaurant, famous for its fine food. Then stroll about in the trellised rose gardens,

down the shady paths, past pools and fountains, and—finally—
you can find a beautiful tiled bench on which to relax.

If you are interested in the history of landscaping, don't
fail to see the garden of *Monforte*. This mid-19th-century
garden has been declared a National Property of importance,
but for some reason no effort is made to help the public in
finding it. Take a taxi to ♯1 Llano de Real, and ring the bell
at the door, which has no plaque or sign of any kind to
identify it. The caretakers will be delighted to welcome you
and let you view the garden by yourself. The first unit is a
formal one that you approach by a short stair. It is filled with
intricate geometric hedges and marble statues and busts that
seem startlingly white against the dark yews and myrtle. At
one side there is a long shady arbor. Beyond, you will find
a natural wild garden, with paths that turn sharply or climb
up and down. Monforte has a rather eerie quality, it is so
quiet, so quaint, like a little old lady in prim dark skirts and
a tiny bonnet. Perhaps it is just as well that it is not publicized too much, so that you can enjoy its air of peaceful
seclusion by yourself.

Valencia has many lovely parks set among its bustling,
modern streets. Whenever you get tired of sightseeing in a
Spanish city, you will always find a park or cloister garden
with benches, palm trees, a pool where the tinkling fountain
will rest you with its rhythmic music. There is a Botanical
Garden in Valencia, too, but it is a sad affair, not well-kept,
with little of interest to the plant lover. If you like flowers,
go to the *Huerta* with its many small plots, where you may
even buy a gay bouquet to brighten your hotel room. Or go
to the *Restaurant Terraza Jardín Rialto* some time for a meal
and a walk through the famous rose garden.

Following the coastal road south, you will travel about
120 miles to get to *Elche*, which is located away from the
shore and is reputedly one of the hottest areas in Spain. We
were there in July, however, and did not find the tempera-

ture any less bearable than elsewhere. Certainly famous *El Palmeral* (Palm Grove), unique in Europe, should not be missed. Try to go there very early in the morning before the sun gets hot, and take a guide so that you will find the most interesting trees. There are more than 170,000 of these date palms. Some are about 60 to 80 feet tall; occasional specimens reach a height of 130 feet. The largest, called the "Palmeria Imperial," has seven side trunks and is 200 years old; also see the "Romeo y Julieta" and the "Villa Carmen," which has a view-platform. The dates (inferior to those of the Sahara Desert) are harvested from November to spring, each tree producing about 75 pounds of fruit every other year. Below the palms are plantings of pomegranates, vegetables, and cattle crops. After April, some of the palm leaves are bound together for bleaching and then distributed all over Spain for Palm Sunday. They are blessed by the priests and are often tied to balconies to guard the homes against lightning.

Another garden to see in Elche is the *Huerto del Cura* (Curate's Garden), an extensive green garden whose main feature is another strange palm with seven trunks all equally thick.

There is another charming government hostel, the Albergue, at Puerto Lumbreras, which is an excellent place for meals or staying overnight. The drive along the coastal hairpin curves after that, between Murcia and Motril, is one I should not care to repeat. I recommend it only for those with very steady nerves. Perhaps the solution for the nondriver is to keep his eyes on the glorious scenery instead of worrying about the continual succession of blind turns. It took us almost three hours to do the 66 miles.

Beyond that, you can relax again and enjoy the trip to *Málaga*. We liked the Miramar Hotel here very much; it is centrally located near the cathedral, and only a short walk away from the charming series of small gardens along the waterfront. Though the delightful open carriages take you by this long park (*Parque de Puerta Oscura*), it is much better to walk through it to see the colors of the tropical leaf plants, the palms and plane trees, the vivid tiles of the benches and pools. At one side you will see the high hill with the ruined *Alcazaba*. Take a stroll through the small formal park on the street level below this, looking at the geometric clipped hedges and flower beds. Then climb up the zigzag path of the hill, with its terraced gardens, to get a view of the same park from above and admire its intricate patterns. From here you will also get an excellent bird's-eye view of the harbor, the Mediterranean, and the bullring close by.

A very interesting side trip from Málaga would be up to the picturesque city of *Ronda,* one of the oldest and most interesting in Spain. Here you could also visit the garden of the *Marqués de Salvatierre,* which he very kindly opens to visitors. It is surrounded by tall columns ornamented with strangely carved sinuous creatures, and a wall deeply scalloped to allow one to see the breathtaking panorama of mountain scenery in the distance.

From Málaga, you will certainly want to go north to the inland city of *Granada,* high in the mountains, the mecca of all who are interested in Moorish architecture and gardens. Be sure to make a reservation far in advance to stay at the fabulous *Parador de San Francisco,* a government-run hostel within the Alhambra itself. This is an ancient convent, now modernized inside for every comfort, but retaining its Old World charm. Notice the interesting contrast at the entrance: on one side a spruce tree with cones, on the other an orange tree with blossoms or fruit. When you go up to your room, you will be able to look down through the wooden grill into a typical Spanish patio with flowers in pots, a wall fountain, and beautiful designs in the pebble mosaic floor. Through the windows you see magnificent views of the

Alhambra, the Generalife, and the Sierra Nevada range of mountains.

When you go up to the Alhambra, you pass through the *Alhambra Park*, which is famous for its ancient elms planted by Wellington and its glorious nightingales. At the *Alhambra*, you pay an admission fee, and can join a guided tour through the building that will give you more details on the history and beauty of ornamentation of this wonderful structure than you will perhaps be able to absorb. Before you go to Granada, be sure to reread Washington Irving's book, *The Alhambra*, which he wrote while living in one of the rooms there, and also some of the books mentioned in the chapter "Suggested Reading About European Gardens," which will give you some preparation for the breathtaking beauties of the two palaces, the Alhambra and the Generalife.

The buildings, both built by the Moorish kings in the 14th century, are quite different. The Alhambra, true to its Arabic name "Medinat al-hamrâ" (the red town), is of red stone. The Generalife, which was the summer palace, high on the hill, is white. Both have enough beauty of Oriental architectural detail and ornamentation to keep an art student fascinated for months. The courtyards of the Alhambra have great charm; but it is the gardens of the Generalife that will most attract readers of this book.

When you visit the *Generalife*, (pronounced hen-eh-ra-lee-fay) try to detach yourself from the guided tour—many people do—so that you can absorb the delightful colors, fragrances, and ornamentation of the gardens at your leisure. According to etymological authorities, "Generalife" means "Sublime Garden." In its exquisite beauty, this place lives up to its name.

You enter through an avenue of cypresses festooned with yellow Banksia roses, and then there is a small modern garden that has been beautifully designed in the spirit of the older parts. A straight canal down the center is almost filled with large white Arum lilies, and the edges of the pool are lined with pots of pale lavender and pink geraniums. Beyond this, on each side, are rows of tree roses, backed by high clipped yew hedges, and at the far end two very tall cypresses give emphasis and a sharp accent.

As you pass through one garden after another, you find an infinite variety of combinations and designs using the same basic elements: clipped hedges, some in tall narrow arches; walks of pebble mosaic in black, white, and shades of soft brick color; plantings of shrubs and flowers in delicate pastel shades, the blue of delphinium and larkspur, the garden pinks and roses, carnations, geraniums, and oleanders in all shades from coral to lavender. Everywhere you see pools and fountains and hear the murmur of running water, the tinkle of drops from delicate sprays into the canals and basins. In the fountains of the first courtyard you find ornamentation of two Oriental types, both drawn from the lotus blossom, one showing the bud, the other the open flower. If you have seen the Taj Mahal, or the gardens of Kashmir, Lahore, or Iran, you will have seen these same lotus-bud fountains playing from the sides of the pools. The Patio de la Riadh is perhaps the most beautiful of all, with its long canal bordered by these fine curving jets of water.

Before leaving Granada, walk around in the residential quarters and peer into the courtyards and the famous villa gardens called "carmenes." If you are an earnest gardener, really interested in plants and landscape design, the owners will often invite you in for a closer look.

There are a number of lovely gardens to see in *Córdoba*. The first is in the *Alcázar*, a beautifully designed series of terraces on various levels reached by broad white stairways. You will see long rectangular pools edged with red roses and accented with tall cypresses; the delicate lavender of plumbago pouring down the walls; tall topiaries like rounded columns, some with flat tops; and low flower-filled clipped hedges with ball-shaped corners. The gardens are flood-lighted at night. At the *Museo Provincial de Bellas Artes* (Fine Arts Museum), be sure to notice the beautiful pebble mosaic paths in the patio garden. The *Museo Arqueológico Provincial* (Archaeological Museum) in Calle Comedias has a charming flower-filled patio. Not far from the Alcázar are the *Sementales Barracks,* where you can look over the highly bred Arabian horses, and enjoy at the same time an avenue of rose trees and a long open promenade with a view of the river. An especially interesting place is the famous *Casa de Don Gome* on the Calle de Santa Isabel. There are fourteen very beautiful patios in this house, filled with jasmine and roses climbing around the trunks of fig trees; carnations, geraniums, fragrant sweet basil, and espaliered heliotrope; oleanders, dahlias, and hollyhocks in season. There are charming fountains, wells, and statuary, with many small birds and white doves flitting about. If you visit the *Museo Romero de Torres,* ask permission there to see the formal Renaissance garden with its subtropical plantings. An interesting place to stay, just outside of Córdoba, is the *Parador la Arruzafa,* which has fine gardens of palms and orange trees and superb views of the city from its terraces. Not far from here are the Hermitages, *Las Ermitas.* Here are elegant buildings of Arabian architecture, surrounded by lovely gardens full of tree roses, magnolias, ornamental fountains, and cypresses, orange trees, and boxwood.

When you get to *Sevilla,* you have two first-class hotels to choose from, both former palaces, which have fine gardens. One is the *Andalucía Palace Hotel,* near the tobacco factory which was Bizet's model for the setting of the opera *Carmen.* The other the *Madrid Hotel,* has an even more romantic story—it seems that a lover walking by this palace asked for a rose from the garden for his lady; when it was refused, he simply bought the whole palace with its roses included. You will enjoy the exotic patio here.

In Sevilla, there is the very interesting royal garden of Charles V, at the *Alcázar*. This is a continuous series of units surrounded by high walls covered with bougainvillea and passionflowers. Follow the brick paths to see the many courts within courts, the tiled fountains and baths and benches, the hedges of myrtle and others of tall cypress trimmed into tall narrow arches, all on different levels. This is a veritable museum for studying the use of tiles in a garden. For a flower lover it is interesting to see how many of the old Arabian designs and symbols on such tiles, adopted by Spain, are based on flowers. Look for these whose meaning was changed to fit Christian beliefs: the glowing rose typifying the fire of missionary zeal; the blue iris for heavenly contemplation; white iris, the flower of hope, light, and power, sacred to the Madonna. Even the lotus in its flower pot, worshipped by Orientals as the flame of life, was changed to a lily in a similar pot. The star-shaped tiled fountains in the Alcázar have been much copied in modern Spain.

If you should be in Sevilla in March, you would see many almond trees in bloom. In June, you will find the gardens gay and fragrant with jasmine, agapanthus, cannas, plumbago, and magnolias.

Be sure to visit the *Duke of Alba's Garden*, which is open to the public. This is a charming, intimate family garden, rather unusual for Spain, for it is full of flowers. You will see delphinium, larkspur, lemon trees, and geraniums espaliered on the wall to reach the second floor.

The Maria Luisa Park is a typical Spanish garden, with a continuous series of enclosures centered with tiled fountains, potted geraniums, and palms reflecting in the water. At one point you will find yourself in a small rose garden. On the Plaza de America you will see a large formal pool with waterlilies, surrounded by a balustrade of the same red stone as the interesting Palacio Central from the Ibero-American Exposition of 1929–30. There is a charming quiet patio garden in the Palace of the Dueñas, and one in the cathedral that features the contrast of dark cypresses against white oleanders.

If you have chosen to use the coastal route from Málaga to Gibraltar and Sevilla, you will have a chance to stay at the *Hotel Reina Cristina,* in *Algeciras,* which is not only very modern and luxurious with excellent food, but has a large garden full of a riot of annuals and perennials: petunias, geraniums, pentstemons, coreopsis, daisies, oleanders. Though definitely not planned for good color combinations, the garden is refreshing and cheerful.

From here you can head north to Madrid. A good stopping-off place is the new Parador (inn) at Merida, which has a fascinating garden of cypresses clipped into columns with pediments and arches.

In *Madrid,* be sure to go to *El Retiro Park,* to see the rose garden. This is rather small, not extensive enough to include the best in modern roses, but it is so attractive with its flowering arches and pools that it is well worth a visit. In the West Park (*Parque del Oeste*) you will find a much larger rose garden only ten years old. It is designed in two long rectangles with half-circular beds at the ends. The narrow beds are filled with roses to be judged in the annual International Rose Competitions. There are two lovely fountains and a background pergola completely covered with the deep red of Paul's Scarlet Climber roses. Tree roses, climbers, and shrub varieties—some 30,000 specimens in all—make this one of the prettiest spots in the city.

If you have time, see the *Botanical Garden* on the Plaza Murillo, near the Prado. It is not very large, but contains many plants from Central and South America, arranged for botanical study. The dahlia was first introduced to Europe from this garden in 1789. The *Jardín Real* (Royal Garden), which is a public park, has many clipped maze-form hedges, like those of formal French gardens, surrounded by statues of the Spanish Kings of the 8th and 9th centuries. The *Estrela Park* also has some beautiful hedges clipped in scrolls. And there are good public gardens surrounding University City.

Madrid could be used as the "hub" of a Wheel Tour, so that you drive by car in each direction to see various famous gardens. About thirty miles south of Madrid is *Aranjuez,* where you will find one of the loveliest of the royal gardens of Spain. The surrounding area has unusually rich soil and is known for its fine crops of strawberries and asparagus. The Royal Garden, too, is a lush oasis in an otherwise bleak, dry area, and is spoken of by Spaniards as a little paradise on earth. Philip II, husband of Mary Tudor, who apparently admired the English elms when he went to meet his bride, had some sent to his gardens in Aranjuez. You will find these elms throughout the town as well as on the palace grounds.

At the entrance of the garden you will see vast numbers of red roses around a huge fountain and an interesting parterre, the Spanish coat of arms, cut in miniature box hedges. The island garden, Jardín de la Isla, is particularly lovely, surrounded by the Tagus River, planted with more great elms and an avenue of plane trees. The gardens are in the formal Italian style throughout, with stepped, clipped hedges and many fountains and geometric flower beds, and were used by the court for elaborate festivals and secret trysting places.

Some thirty miles northwest of Madrid is the great palace of *San Lorenzo,* at *El Escorial,* with its adjoining monastery. This is a fabulous place to see—enormous buildings, beautifully furnished and decorated, with a whole series of great gardens that include 88 fountains, clipped boxwood hedges, roses, and flowering shrubs.

Just north of here, about seven miles from Segovia, is another garden at *La Granja* (pronounced gran-ha), one of the finest in Spain. This is at an altitude of 3795 feet, with a glorious panoramic view of the surrounding mountains. The gardens are designed in the formal French manner, with a large sunken parterre near the entrance, many ornamental fountains, and waterfalls. There is even a fountain in the central dining room, which was fed by a canal conducted through the palace itself. Go on a Thursday at 5 P.M. or on a special festival day (consult a tourist office in Madrid or Segovia) when the fountains are turned on. The highest jet, La Fama, is 115 feet tall. The long stepped cascade, faced with an alternating design of circles and squares, is particularly interesting. Just beyond this is a parterre of round and long flower beds. You will see square pools, circular basins, white sculptured urns and statuary, and bright spots of annual flowers everywhere. There are 350 acres of gardens here, so much to see that you should allow plenty of time.

One excursion that every flower lover should make from Madrid is a trip to the *Canary Islands.* Planes fly daily, taking less than two hours to Las Palmas on Gran Canaria. The islands have an extraordinary variety of plant life, ranging from the profusion of tropical flowers at sea level, through pine forests, to Alpine flowers on the fringes of snow-capped mountains. The wooden balconies on the flat roofs of the houses are covered with climbing roses and flowering vines. You will see streets edged with flowering trees, walls draped with bougainvillea and morning-glory, and everywhere great splashes of geraniums. Some geraniums along the roadsides are four feet wide and a yard high. Even the center space on the dual highways is filled with geraniums, one color to every half mile.

On the island of *Tenerife,* in the little town of *Icod de los Vinos* you will find the most famous of the islands' dragon trees (Dracaena draco), said to be 3000 years old. This odd mushroom shape with its bristly top is, strangely enough, related to the lily family. You will see others almost as ancient here and there as you travel about. On Tenerife you will find the greatest variety of colorful plants: miles of road-sides lined with the Mexican poinsettia, the stained-glass colors of red and purple cinerarias, the pale lavender of plumbago, and the jacaranda trees. The home gardens are filled with bougainvilleas, hibiscus, oleanders, the flame trees with their scarlet orchid-like blossoms, and splendid clumps of amaryllis. Wherever there might be a bare spot, it is filled with creeping pink geraniums or the orange and yellow of nasturtiums.

Near *Oratava* you will find the famous *Botanical Gardens,* Jardín de Aclimatacion de la Oretava. This has been used as a sort of way-station for plants, to accustom those from the hottest climates to a slightly more moderate zone, before introducing them to other parts of Europe. You will see 220 varieties from some 80 plant families, including 30 different kinds of palms. Wandering around here is like taking a trip through the tropical areas of the world.

When you fly back to Madrid, if you should want to explore the northern coast of Spain, which is much greener and more fertile than the south, you might stop in *La Coruña* in the very northwest corner, to see the beautiful garden of *San Carlos* and the Flower Clock in the town itself. Otherwise you will probably go directly from Madrid to Lisbon, to visit some of the lovely gardens of Portugal.

USEFUL INFORMATION

The Spanish word for "garden" is "jardín," pronounced "har-deen."

You will find very little information about gardens in the leaflets put out by the Spanish Tourist Office. Do get the following guidebooks, however, for each city you visit: *City Guides for Spain,* published by Editorial Noguer, available in every book-shop or souvenir store there. Excellent descriptions, history, and pictures. The one on Córdoba particularly mentions gardens.

chapter 15

PORTUGAL: GAY, SOPHISTICATED GARDENS

*I*F you come up into Portugal from southern Spain in the heat of midsummer, as we did, the contrast is startling. After passing through sunburned barren mountains and dry riverbeds, you suddenly find yourself actually drinking in the green lushness of the Portuguese landscape like a longed-for glass of cold well water. The houses, too, change character, from the monotony of golden-yellow with red roofs in Spain, to the rather garish but delightful lemon yellows and bluing-blues so beloved by the Portuguese, interspersed with pink, lavender, and an occasional white. As you explore the gardens of this friendly little country, you will find more of this added color, not only in the abundance of flowers, but also in the gay, elegant sophistication of the yellow and blue tiles and pottery jars.

The great difference in climate is due to the fact that the breezes of Portugal come off the water, while those in Spain dry up crossing great expanses of mountain and dusty plain. Around Lisbon, the weather is much like that of the west of England, damp and never very hot or very cold. Yet it is almost tropical in its flowering seasons; you will find the fluffy yellow mimosa balls spreading their fragrance on the

February air, tree ferns of tremendous age and size, palm trees everywhere. Camellias live for several hundred years here, and develop great trunks and strong branches. Camellia blossoms, however, are always picked without stems, for the florist and flower market, and wired, as the twigs of these plants grow very slowly, even in this favorable situation.

During the days of royalty, especially in the reign of the last king and queen, who were greatly interested in horticulture, there were many beautifully kept public gardens throughout Portugal. These were mainly historic places, tended with loving care and unchanged for hundreds of years. But with the advent of the republic the stress on gardens suddenly vanished, great (and much needed) housing developments swept away many a historic green space, and no funds were allotted to care for those that were left. Fortunately, the Federation of Landscape Architects is tackling the problem today, attempting to save some of the old gardens from destruction and to restore and care for those that have survived. Within a few years, these efforts will certainly be evident to the tourist seeking out gardens of national character. Even today there is much to see.

Let's begin in the delightful modern city of *Lisbon,* with its fine wide boulevards and many green parks. If you take a bus tour of the city, you will stop at the most unusual garden of all, the *Estufa Fria* (Cool Oven), which is an outdoor conservatory, roofed and walled with openwork slats. Here, with just enough protection from the hottest sun or cold winds, is a lovely tropical jungle arranged for the delight of man—paths lined with huge palms, whole groves of tree ferns, rampant vines clinging to trunks and branches, and a ground cover below of mosses and delicate ferns. Here and there you will find the bright blossoms of cinerarias and begonias, or an occasional white statue or bust set off by a dark green tree. There are moist grottoes and a brook with rustic bridges—a place of cool green that forms a well-loved oasis in this bustling city.

The Royal Botanical Garden of Ajuda is in two parts. *The Royal Park of Ajuda,* which is 300 years old, is an arboretum to delight the tree enthusiast. You will see a splendid specimen here of the dragon tree (Dracaena draco)—native to the Canary Islands—that is nearly forty feet across and over two centuries old. The other part of the Royal Botanical Garden is the *Tapada da Ajuda,* on the outskirts of the city, with an agricultural research station and a garden that is being gradually transformed with decorative flowers. Another botanical garden, the *Jardim Botanico da Faculdade de Ciências,* on the Rua da Escola Politecnia, in the heart of Lisbon, is a beautifully kept park of exotic trees, ferns, shrubs, and orchids, every plant well labeled for study. The *Zoological Garden* is interesting not only for the animals you will see there, but also for a charming rose garden and grounds prettily ornamented with a lake and bridges.

Very near the *Jardim da Estrela,* one of the prettiest flower-filled parks in Lisbon, you will see a gate to the *English Cemetery.* Ring the bell for admission, and browse around in this peaceful spot. You will see an avenue of tall cypresses, with their trunks encircled by climbing geraniums, and many lovely flowering shrubs and trees. Here are the graves of Henry Fielding, who wrote *Tom Jones,* and Philip Doddridge, author of many well-known hymns.

At *Bemfica,* a suburb of Lisbon, you will find what is probably the most beautiful and unusual garden in Portugal, at the Quinta de Fronteira, property of the Marquis de Fronteira. It dates from the 17th century. Ask the tourist office or American Express to telephone requesting permission to visit. Just beyond the entrance courtyard is a very large parterre of clipped box hedges, hundreds of years old, arranged to form sixteen squares. This rather severe design is amusingly relieved by odd shrubs here and there and occasional flowers. Beyond this at one side is the great rectangular pool that is the unique feature of this garden. It is backed by a tiled wall of blue and white depicting famous knights on horseback; on each side are staircases, their balustrades punctuated with urns of geraniums, leading up to two towers with pointed roofs. These are connected by a long gallery from which one can look down into the pool and garden on one side, or admire the rows of busts of the ancient kings of Portugal in alcoves along the back. The walls along the gallery, and those supporting the stairs, are also faced with magnificent blue and white tiles. The color effect with the red of the geranium accents is breathtaking.

The tiles themselves offer hours of fascinating study. In one spot they show classical musicians playing various instruments; while on a curved bench of tile in the informal garden beyond, you will find a humorous series labeled "I am a teacher of music," showing a cat instructing a group of monkeys.

The so-called "English Garden" is a natural area of great trees and occasional flower beds, on a higher level again, so that you can look down from there upon the hedge parterre and the great tiled pool façade. In one corner you will find a small circular Garden of Venus with a scrolled baroque pool at its center and a background doorway elaborately decorated with shells and more tile work. There is a sparkling brilliance to this wonderfully preserved garden, a gaiety and love of color that is purely Portuguese. Don't miss this one, even if you cannot see any other garden in this charming country.

There is an interesting place at *Belem,* outside of Lisbon, the *Jardim Coloniale do Ultramar* (Botanical Garden for the Colonies). California tourists will enjoy walking through a long avenue of 60-foot fan palms from their native state. You will find an attractive water garden near the entrance, a conservatory for tropical plants, including an African breadfruit tree, and an arboretum. The rest of the garden is dedicated to research on crops for the colonies, such as rice, sugarcane, coffee, and cotton, while one whole department is planted with bamboos being tested for Macao.

There are a number of excursions to towns in the vicinity of Lisbon where you will see fine gardens. Twenty-five miles south of the city on the road to Setubal, you will find the *Quinta da Bacalhoa,* near the village of *Villa Fresca de Azeitao.* This is owned by Mrs. Herbert Scoville, an American, who is happy to welcome visitors to her garden if they will write to her in advance at Quinta da Bacalhoa, Villa Fresca de Azeitao, Portugal. When she bought this 15th-century royal palace in 1936, even the building itself was in ruins. She has lovingly restored it and brought the gardens back to their original charming design. You will find a garden of boxwood centered by a fountain, the clipped hedges shaped like stars, and other interesting Moorish designs. From here you follow a wide path edged with tiled flower boxes, leading to a pavilion with three pointed towers, containing a loggia completely covered with tiles, most of them from the 16th century. Facing this is a very large pool fed by a wall fountain. To get another fine view of the garden from above, go to the vine-covered loggia, near the house, from which you can look down.

Another beautiful palace garden is that at *Queluz,* not far west of Lisbon, on the road to Sintra. The pink stucco 18th-century palace has been beautifully restored and is still used for official receptions. When we saw the gardens in July, they were overflowing with pastel pink and white petunias that blended into the low building. You will see clipped hedges confining the flowers in formal patterns, white sculptures, urns and fountains in profusion. Don't miss the long canal, completely lined with beautiful tiles. You can visit Queluz on a bus tour if you wish, or take a meal at the excellent restaurant.

Palace of Queluz, Portugal (*Photo by James L. McFadden*)

From here you will certainly want to go on to *Sintra,* the lovely home of so many English writers and artists, called "that glorious Eden" by the poet Byron. Sintra is situated high among hills that are blanketed with magnolias, camellias, and other flowers. In the parks here you will find some 3000 different kinds of vegetation, from all climates, ranging from the African and Asian ferns and trees to the firs and spruces of the north. If you wish, you can hire an open carriage to visit the great parks.

To get up the steep hill to the *Palácio da Pena* you will probably want to take a car, unless you have plenty of time for a carriage trip. Here you will be able to wander in a park that has more than 400 species of trees and shrubs, especially lovely in spring when the camellias, rhododendrons, and azaleas are in bloom. Around the castle itself are attractive patios and a sunken garden.

Back on more level ground, you could stop in the small *Parque de Dr. Oliveira Salazar* and climb up the hill to look down on the flowers and tree ferns. Farther on you will come to *Monserrate,* a wonderful park of subtropical trees unequalled anywhere in Europe. There are no guiding signs, so you will have to keep your sense of direction as you follow the paths up and down the hills and ravines over some 75 acres. This park was developed about a century ago by Sir Francis Cook, and contains an amazing forest of tree ferns, a palm grove, and 120-foot-high pines from the Norfolk Islands, arbutus, jasmine, and bamboos. The forest is so still that you will feel you are all alone on some tropical island.

There are a number of places to interest a garden lover north of Lisbon. If you take the route leading through Santarem, and continue a few miles, you come to *Torres Novas,* where you will want to stop and see the *Municipal Garden.* You will find many lovely flower beds and trees in the central squares of Portuguese towns, but this one is an exceptionally fine example. It is actually on the edge of the town in an area seemingly scooped out of the side of the mountain, making a level space for a very large formal garden. Here you will find clipped hedges in scroll designs, roses, and charming fountains, dramatic cypresses, and pines.

Continuing northeastward, you come to *Castelo Branco*, where there is a lovely garden at the *Belvedere of S. Gens*. The famous attraction here, however, is the fantastic garden of the *Episcopal Palace*. In one area you will see a veritable crowd of topiary forms—low hedges, tall cubes-on-cubes—surrounding intricately shaped pools, with statues and pots of flowers everywhere. Be sure to study another large pool with its unusual planting design of patterned troughs that make an elaborate scrollwork in the water, all planted with flowers, so that there is a garden-within-the-pool. The most dramatic spot, however, is the long flight of stairs and the tiled walk along another basin, lined on both sides with statues of the Kings of Portugal. The garden is on a high piece of land and affords striking views of the surrounding valleys and mountains.

Now you will want to head west again toward the coast, to the interesting university town of *Coimbra.* Plan to spend as much time as you can spare here, for there is much to see. The Children's Portugal (*Portugal dos Penqueninos*) is a most unusual spot, planned to care for the small children of working mothers. All the buildings of this miniature town are child-size small-scale models of typical Portuguese houses, churches, and even the university itself. This is not just a showpiece to admire, however (as is the famous Madurodam in Holland). These small structures, with landscaping carefully scaled to go with them, provide garden plots for young citizens of the area to cultivate themselves. In another section you can find small houses, modeled after those in Portuguese colonies, surrounded by plants from those distant lands.

Castelo Branco, Portugal (*Photo from Casa de Portugal*)

Another place of interest to plant lovers is the large *Jardim Botânico,* adjoining the university, the oldest and largest botanical garden in Portugal. This is a hilly garden, much of it planted on steep slopes and in deep valleys. On the upper levels are flowers and shrubs in neat formal boxwood hedges and many palms and conifers. Below, there are a large grove of bamboos, and trees from many parts of the world. Near the conservatory you will see a sunken garden of Italianate design, covering about two acres. The Portuguese influence is evident, however, in the fine tiled panels set into the surrounding walls. Boxwood hedges border the beds, with flowering cherries and fine roses to lend color, a stately fig tree about 60 feet tall on one side, an attractive fountain in the center. This garden of some fifty acres has much to offer the tree enthusiast, with specimens from Japan, Mexico, the Canary Islands, South Africa, and South America, to mention only a few homelands represented here.

About 40 miles northeast of Coimbra on the side of a mountain is the wonderful National Monument, the *Forest of Bussaco.* This is a preserve of several thousand acres, planted in the 18th century by Carmelite monks who first founded a monastery there in 1268. The entrance at Penacova will be the nearest as you come from Coimbra, or if you should be approaching it from the north, ask for the one at Luso. (At Penacova, be sure to look at the fine formal municipal garden, with its circular flower beds, balustrades, a pergola, and tall cypress arches.)

To enjoy the forest thoroughly, you should stay for several days—perhaps at the deluxe *Palace Hotel,* a former royal palace that includes the remains of the old monastery. The camellia garden and the formal Italianate garden here are in themselves worth a long visit. Don't fail to see the great pergola with its wisteria vine over 100 feet long, and the large historical scenes made out of tiles, in the hotel itself.

In the old days, the monks lived in cells here and there

throughout the forest, some of which you will still see. At one time a papal bull forbade women to enter the preserve, but today it is open, free, to everyone.

As you walk or drive through this beautiful forest, you see many of the Portuguese cypresses (Cupressus lusitanica) that were brought to Portugal from Mexico in the 16th century. Some of them are now 100 feet high. You will also find plane trees, Montezuma pines, holly oaks, and cork oaks. Don't miss seeing the lovely valley of tree ferns (some 20 feet high), azaleas, hydrangeas, rhododendrons, and camellias. Near the northern entrance of the forest you come upon a formal rock garden with a great staircase leading to it, where you can walk about among fountains and pools with swans, and enjoy the rhododendrons and azaleas, the roses, and many other flowers. The forest is a wonderful place for relaxation, a great change from the pressure of sightseeing on city streets.

From here, head north again to the fascinating city of *Oporto* (sometimes called Porto). This commercial city is proud of its gardens, and is said to grow the best roses and camellias in all Portugal. There are many English residents here, and they and the Portuguese have all developed lovely gardens around their houses. One of these is *Quinta da Meio*, owned by Miss M. R. Tait, who is glad to allow garden lovers to visit if they will write ahead for an appointment. (Address her at 219 Rua Entre Quintas, Oporto, Portugal.) This is a typically British garden with lovely mixed flower borders, a wonderful collection of iris, and green lawns and terraces that look out over an estuary and the Atlantic Ocean. The garden was first planted by Miss Tait's Scottish grandfather nearly a century ago. If you come in the spring you will find a wonderful display of the native Portuguese narcissi. Later on you will see splendid camellias, some 80 years old and over 20 feet tall. A tremendous tulip tree, 22 feet in circumference, is said to be the largest in Europe, and has been declared a National Monument. On the villa itself you will see a wisteria vine covering an entire wall. There is an acacia tree from Australia with a deep-red blossom; a jasmine from Paraguay that has purple buds and lavender flowers fading to white; and the only grapefruit trees in Portugal, grown from California seed sent by Luther Burbank.

If you visit this garden in late spring or summer you will think you are in England as you wander about among the delphiniums, columbines, and other favorites. There is also a small brook where ferns and bog plants thrive. It is amazing what hard work and loving care will do to keep such a garden in bloom in this climate, so different from the homelands of most of these flowers.

Not far from this garden you will find the *Crystal Palace*, with a park of fine trees, and a spectacular rose garden. This is planted on a steep hillside overlooking the Douro River, so you can get a wonderful view of the roses, first from the park above, then go down to admire the glorious color and size of the blossoms.

Another beautiful private garden, which you may be able to visit if you write ahead asking for permission, is *Villa Nova de Gaya* (write to the owner, the Count of Campo Bello: Conde Campo Bello, Villa Nova de Gaya, Oporto, Portugal). Here you will find the oldest Camellia japonica trees to be found in Europe, three of them having been planted in the middle of the 16th century. They are nearly two feet in diameter at the base, and about 30 feet tall. They bloom in February and March and sometimes longer. You will also see a splendid hedge of the "Mathotiana" variety of camellia, which has flowers five inches across. Other camellia varieties keep the garden in bloom over a 9-month period. Elsewhere in the grounds, you will find very old specimens of tulip trees and horse chestnuts.

You will want to see the *Jardim Botânico* here, which is

the youngest botanical garden in Portugal. It covers 30 acres and includes a charming formal garden of sheared boxwood hedges, tulips, many roses, perennials and annuals, surrounded by a 20-foot camellia hedge. There are other fine trees, specimen camellias, rhododendrons, and many palms. One great white wisteria tree is a spectacular sight when it is in bloom.

In the "Key to Gardens" for Portugal, you will find many other historic gardens listed that will be of interest to students of landscape design. For permission to visit them inquire at the nearest tourist office.

USEFUL INFORMATION

"Garden" in Portuguese is "jardim," pronounced with a soft "j": "jer-dung."

Be sure to obtain a copy of the *Tourist Guide,* a blue folder of 22 pages, which has a special listing of gardens of Lisbon on page 6, with addresses and key to their locations on the map. You can send for this in advance from the tourist office: Casa de Portugal, 447 Madison Ave., New York 22, N.Y.

KEY TO GARDENS:

Annotated listings for 18 countries

Here you will find over 840 gardens, their addresses, hours when open, best seasons, and special features, listed by countries and towns and also by names of gardens. Page numbers refer the reader to longer descriptions in the front of the book.

Wheel Tour maps follow this "Key to Gardens" section.

KEY TO GARDENS

• = especially fine garden	g = greenhouse
a = alpines, rock garden	h = herb garden
ar = arboretum, unusual trees	i = iris
b = botanical garden	r = rose garden
c = cacti and succulents	t = topiaries
f = flowers	w = water plants

AUSTRIA

In Austria you will find particularly fine Alpine Gardens and collections of alpines in the Botanical Gardens (Botanischer Garten.)

ALPINE GARDENS: See Frohnleiten, Innsbruck, Rannach, Sarstein, Traunkirchen.

BOTANICAL GARDENS: See Graz, Innsbruck, Klagenfurt, Linz, Vienna.
BURGGARTEN: See Vienna.

For explanation of symbols and abbreviations, see inside back cover.

 233

DONAUPARK: See Vienna.

FROHNLEITEN: (near Graz) *Mayr Melnhof'scher Alpengarten* (a, b, f, •), best May–July. One of biggest alpine collections in Europe; about 6000 varieties, many saxifrages.

GARDEN FOR THE BLIND: See Vienna.

GRAZ: *Botanical Garden* (a, b, f), Schubertstr. 51. Apr.–Oct.; closed Sun. and hol. afternoons. Best May–June. Alpines. *Schlossberg* (f), Bastion Flower Garden; color schemes changed every few weeks.

HELLBRUNN: See Salzburg.

INNSBRUCK: On Patscherkofel Mountain, *Alpine Garden* (a, b, f) Take cable car from Igls. Open all day Mon.–Fri., otherwise by asking permission. Best mid-May–end Aug. Many lovely alpines. *Botanical Garden* (a, b, f, g, w) in city, Sternwartestr. 15 in Hoetting. Fine alpine collection, water plants, greenhouse.

KLAGENFURT: *Botanical Garden* (a, b, f), Kinkstr. Open 9–3:30. Best in summer. Alpines of S Alps.

LINZ: *Botanical Garden* (a, b, c, f, g, w, •) Center is beautiful rock garden; alpines best Apr.–June, local wildflowers best May–July. Bog and water plants; greenhouses with 1200 varieties cacti, 300 succulents, orchids.

MIRABELL GARDENS: See Salzburg.

RANNACH: (near Graz) *Alpine Garden* (a, b, f) Take train to St. Veit, then bus. Best mid-Mar.–Mid-June. Alpines of E and W Alps.

SALZBURG: *Hellbrunn Lustschloss* (Pleasure Castle) (f), just outside Salzburg. Gardens designed for a bishop's hilarious parties, with surprise fountains to drench guests, others that operate mechanical figures; still others balance balls in air, etc. Small flower garden at one side. *Mirabell Gardens* (f), formal baroque palace garden, small outdoor theater.

SARSTEIN: At Bad Aussee. *Alpine Garden* (a, b, f) Apr. through Oct.; best May–July. Asiatic and American alpines. Also see wild narcissus in area mid-May–mid-June.

SCHOENBRUNN PALACE: See Vienna.

TRAUNKIRCHEN: *Alpine Garden* (a, b, f) Apr. through Sept.; best Apr.–June. Alpines from all over world.

VIENNA: *Belvedere Botanical Gardens* (a, ar, b, f, •), Prinz-Eugen-Str. 27.; best May–Aug. Oldest alpine garden in Europe; 6000 varieties from all continents; 200-year-old pear tree. Austrian flower garden, terraces. *Burggarten* (f, g), fine park with greenhouse (Palmenhaus). *Donaupark* (a, f, g, i, r, •), large new park created 1964 for Internatl. Garden Show; 250 acres. Special sections for summer flowers, miniature gardens, dahlias, rhododendrons and azaleas, iris, roses, alpines, heathers, unique Tower Greenhouse with plants on moving belt. *Schoenbrunn Palace Garden* (b, f, g, •), Fr.-style formal baroque garden combined with botanical collection, more than a million plants. Flower parterres changed monthly. Beyond small zoo toward the Hietzinger Gate is Palm House with exotics. *University Botanical Garden* (a, b, c, g), Rennweg 14; Apr.–Oct. Greenhouse with orchids, succulents. *Volksgarten* (r), public park with lovely rose garden. *Wertheimstein*

Park (**a, f**), interesting Garden for the Blind, labels in Braille, plants to smell and touch, singing acoustic cymbal fountain. Rock garden in park.

Wels: *Volksgarten* (**c**), large cactus collection in greenhouse.

WHEEL TOUR

Graz as Hub: Frohnleiten, Rannach.

BELGIUM

Belgium is a land of flowers, in window boxes, parks, even on railroad platforms. Near Zandvliet you will find vast tulip fields in bloom in April, reminding you of Holland. The region around Ghent is filled with greenhouses, fields of azaleas in spring, begonias in summer.

Annevoie: *Château d'Annevoie* (**●**), formal garden with many pools, cascades, fountains, all kept flowing by force of three springs, no machinery, as devised by 18th-cent. owner after seeing Versailles and Villa d'Este. Included are many water jokes to surprise guests. Night illumination.

Arboretum Géographique de Tervueren: See Brussels.

Arboretum Kalmthout: See Kalmthout.

Ath: *Château d'Attre* (**f, g, w, ●**), 6 miles south of Ath. May–Oct., Sat. and Sun.; other days ask concierge for permission. A working manor. Fr. formal garden of clipped privet and hemlock, geometric design. Behind castle, flower gardens, greenhouses with grapes, orchids. Orangerie. Brook garden of naturalized bulbs and primulas; bamboos. A curious grotto.

Antwerp: *Middelheim Park,* on SE edge of city, formal setting for exhibit of sculpture. *Provincial Domein Rivierenhof* (**a, ar, f, r**), Turnhoutsebaan 246, Deurne. Best May–Oct. On road from Antwerp to Turnhout. Rose garden, alpinum, arboretum. *Rubens' House* (**f, ●**), Rubenstraat 9. A very original formal garden designed by Rubens about 1630, full of flowers. A famous painting of this garden is in the Pinakothek in Munich. *Zoological Garden* (**ar, b, c, f, g, w, ●**) Wonderful annual flowers changed three times a year; Mexican Garden of agaves, cacti, etc. Greenhouses with flowers from Mexico and Congo. Arboretum with a Paulownia 120 years old. Brook garden, bamboos, waterlilies.

Bellecourt: (Hainaut) *Le Pachy* (**r**), on route 5 going from Anderlues to Mariemont. One of largest rose gardens in the world, old and new varieties. Best June–Sept.

Bokrijk: (Limburg) Near Hasselt, 50 mi. S of Brussels. *Provincial*

For explanation of symbols and abbreviations, see inside back cover.

Domein, 1300 acres including gardens and outdoor museum.

BOTANICAL GARDENS: See Brussels, Ghent, Liége, Louvain.

BRUSSELS: *Arboretum Géographique de Tervueren* (**ar**), Drève du Duc, 106. Trees from N regions. *Château de Beloeil* (**ar, f, r, •**) on road from Mons to Leuze. Apr.– Oct., 9–8. Finest park in Belgium; 300 acres, including Great Neptune Pool covering 15 acres. Magnif. formal 18th-cent. garden in Le Nôtre tradition, fountains, clipped trees and hornbeam hedges, sheared arches surround one pool. Immense copper beeches. Also rose garden of 10,000 shrubs, including 3000 old varieties from Bengali. *Botanical Garden* (**ar, b, c, g, w, •**) at Meise (new location, 225 acres; can also see some of old one in city). Many greenhouses with special sections for plants of Africa, Asia, America, Australia. Aquatic section with mangrove swamp, Victoria regia. Many plants from Congo. Arboretum. *Château de Chimay* (**f**), flower parterres, intricate designs. Near Beloeil. *Château de Gaesbeek* (**f**), magnif. flower parterres. *Flower Market,* daily in Grand Palace. *L'Abbaye de la Cambre,* 18th-cent. terr. garden. *Parc de Bruxelles* (**ar**), wonderful park, interesting clipped lindens espaliered on wires. *Parc de Tervueren* (**f, t**), at Tervueren in outskirts; topiaries, formal garden, peacocks. *Parc Josaphat* (**f**), in Schaarbeek. Wonderful flowers, colored floodlights at night. *Royal Palace Park* (**ar, f, w**) at Laeken, lovely flowers, miles of paths with borders of geraniums, rhododendrons with trunks sheared to make them into trees, big pool with tropical plants. Chinese Pavilion, Japanese Tower. Special flower displays in April for Internatl. Spring Fair. Royal Greenhouses very occasionally open to public.

CHÂTEAU D'ATTRE: See Ath.

CHÂTEAU DE BELOEIL: See Brussels.

CHÂTEAU DE CHIMAY: See Brussels.

CHÂTEAU DE FREYR: See Freyr.

CHÂTEAU DE GAESBEEK: See Brussels.

CHÂTEAU DE ROEULX: See Soignies.

CITADEL PARK: See Ghent.

FREYR: (Namur) In Meuse Valley. *Château de Freyr* (**f**) Elegant Fr.-style parterre garden, 18th-cent; look down on it first from other side of river to see design. Fountains, flower borders, hedges clipped like walls with windows. Pools edged with orange trees in tubs, perhaps first introduced to Belgium.

GHENT: *Botanical Gardens* (Plantentuin de Rijksuniversiteit Gent) (**a, b, c, f, g, w**), Ledeganckstraat 33. Sun. 9–12, Thurs. 2–5.; best May– Oct. On route #1 from Brussels to Ostend. Orangerie and greenhouses, native and exotic plants, Victoria regia, orchids, begonias, cacti, alpinum. *Citadel Park* (**f, r**), fine rose garden; see p. 26. Magnif. alpine garden. Floralia Palace is scene of Ghent Floralia every five years (one in 1965). See p. 26. *Flower Parade* (**f**) of floats takes place first Sun. of Sept. annually. *School-Museum M. Thiery* includes an educational garden.

GROENENDAAL: (Brabant) *Groenendaal Arboretum,* about 8 mi. S of Brussels; 26 acres, especially conifers.

KALMTHOUT: *Arboretum Kalmthout* (**ar, f, r**), 20 mi. N of Antwerp, on main road to Holland. Wed. and Sun., or ask owner, Mr. Robert de Belder, for permission. Finest private arboretum in Belgium. Many trees 100 years old. Many plants from Japan. 20 acres. Rhododendrons, witch hazels, plum, crabs, roses, conifers.

L'ABBAYE DE LA CAMBRE: See Brussels.

LEEUWERGEN: (E Flanders) *Château de Leeuwergen*, near Alost. Beautiful Fr.-style park, long pool, canal bordered by fine trees, and a "green theater" with 1000 seats, said to have been designed by Le Nôtre.

LE PACHY: See Bellecourt.

LIÉGE: *Botanical Garden* (**b, f, g**), 3 Rue Fusch. Greenhouse, bromeliads, begonias.

LOUVAIN: (Brabant) *Botanical Garden* (**b**), Voer de Capucins 34.

MALINES: *Provincial Domein Vrijbroek* (**r**), Hombeeksesteenweg 262. On road from Brussels to Antwerp. Best May–Oct. Rosarium.

MIDDELHEIM PARK: See Antwerp.

OSTEND: (W Flanders) (**f**) Floral clock in park.

PARC DE TERVUEREN: See Brussels.

PARC JOSAPHAT: See Brussels.

PROVINCIAL DOMEIN: See Antwerp, Bokrijk, Malines.

RUBENS' HOUSE: See Antwerp.

SCHOOL-MUSEUM M. THIERY: See Ghent.

SOIGNIES: (Hainaut) *Château Roeulx* (**r**) Apr. through Oct., 10–6; closed Tues.; best June–Sept. Rosarium; Rose Competitions.

ZOOLOGICAL GARDEN: See Antwerp.

DENMARK

BANDHOLM: *Knuthenborg Park* (**ar, c, f, g, ●**), private, but open to public. Fine trees, especially Japanese cherries, fruit trees being tested for climate. Daffodils, flower beds, shrubs, rhododendrons. Greenhouse with large collection cacti.

BOTANICAL GARDENS: See Copenhagen, Vordingborg.

BREGENTVED CASTLE: See Køge.

CLAUSHOLM: See Randers.

COPENHAGEN: *Botanical Garden* (**a, ar, b, c, f, g**), Gothersgade 130. Best May–Sept. Alpinum. Greenhouses with cacti, succulents, orchids from Thailand. Arboretum, fruit trees. *Rosenborg Castle,* called "Kongens Have." The King's garden: includes rose garden. *The Royal Library* (**f, r**), formal garden, clipped hedges, roses. *Tivoli Gardens* (**r**), May 1 to mid-Sept., 9 A.M. to midnight. A beautiful amusement park (**f**), flowers everywhere: see it by day and by night. *Valby Park* (**r, ●**), fine rose garden, see p. 14.

DJURSLAND: In Jutland, *Rosenholm Castle,* open daily to dusk. Park and gardens.

EGESKOV CASTLE: See Kvaerndrup.

FREDENSBORG: *Fredensborg Palace,* surrounding park always open; private "marble garden" only in July, 10–6.

FREDERIKSBORG CASTLE: See Hillerød.

FUNEN: *Langesø,* private estate open to public.

GAVNØ MANOR: See Naestved.

HAVE: *Gisselfeld Cloister* (ar, f, g), best June–July. Arboretum; greenhouse with trop., subtrop. plants, including orchids.

HILLERØD: *Frederiksborg Castle,* fine park in Fr. style; box hedges, terr. May–Oct. 11, 9:30–5.; Apr. and Oct., 11–4.

KNUTHENBORG PARK: See Bandholm.

KØGE: (Zealand) *Bregentved Castle* (•), open Wed. and Sat. Magnif. gardens. *Vemmetofte Castle,* a flower-filled park.

KVAERNDRUP: (Funen) *Egeskov Castle* (f), gardens open 7 A.M. to 9 P.M. Immense beech hedges.

LANGESØ: See Funen.

LEAREBORG: See Zealand.

LERCHENBORG: See Zealand.

NAESTVED: (Zealand) *Gavnø Manor* (f, •) Large park; in May 100,000 tulips, hyacinths, and narcissus.

NYSØ: See Zealand.

ODENSE: *Hans Christian Andersen's home* (f), charming courtyard garden, tulips in spring.

RANDERS: (Jutland) *Clausholm,* manor house; beautiful grounds with terr., cascades.

ROSENBORG CASTLE: See Copenhagen.

ROSENHOLM CASTLE: See Djursland.

TIVOLI GARDENS: See Copenhagen.

VALBY PARK: See Copenhagen.

VEMMETOFTE CASTLE: See Køge.

VORDINGBORG: (Zealand) *Botanical Garden* (b), around ruins of castle.

ZEALAND: Private estates open to the public, with gardens: *Leareborg, Lerchenborg, Nysø.*

ENGLAND

For tips on finding current days and hours of admission, see the booklet *Historic Houses, Castles and Gardens* and that issued by the National Gardens Scheme, mentioned in "Useful Information," end of chapter on "England." In listings that follow, "regular days" means open some days each week; "special days only" means gardens are only open a few days a year for the Garden Scheme; letters "G.S." mean see Garden Scheme listing. Counties are in parentheses.

Membership of National Trust (see end of chapter on "England") admits you free to their gardens. All admission fees are nominal, anyway, 14¢ to 28¢.

ALBURY PARK: See Guildford.

ALCESTER: (pron. oll-ster) (War.) Map B. *Ragley Hall* (**r**), reg. days. Large formal rose garden.

ALNWICK: (Northumb.) Map I. *Howick Gardens* (**f**), reg. days. Bulbs, flowering trees and shrubs, rhododendrons.

AMMERDOWN PARK: See Radstock.

ANNE HATHAWAY'S COTTAGE: See Stratford-on-Avon.

ARBORETUM, THE: See Derby.

ASCOTT: See Wing.

ASHFORD: (Kent) *Godington Park* (**f, t**), reg. days. Formal gardens, Ital. Garden, flower borders, topiary. *Wye College* (**a, f, h, i, t, w**) Foreign visitors phone Gardens Supt. for permission, Wye 401; also G. S. Everything labeled, fine flower borders, herb garden, iris, moraine bed, sunken garden, alp., lavenders, topiaries.

ATHELHAMPTON HALL: See Puddletown.

AVEBURY MANOR: See Marlborough.

AVERY HILL WINTER GARDEN: See Eltham.

AYLESFORD: (Kent) Map C. *The Friars* (**r**), daily. Roses.

AYLSHAM: (pron. ale-shum) (Norf.) *Blickling Hall* (**f, t**), reg. days. Natl. Trust. Formal parterres, flower borders, topiaries, rhododendrons, azaleas.

BAKEWELL: (Derb.) Map E. *Chatsworth* (**a, f, r, ●**), reg. days; grand 17th-cent.; cascades, rock garden, modern roses, flower borders, see p. 98. *Haddon Hall* (**a, f, r**), reg. days; formal Elizabethan, with terraces, clematis, roses, and flower borders.

BALLIOL COLLEGE: See Oxford.

BANBURY: (Oxf.) Map B. *Broughton Castle* (**f, w**), reg. days, flower borders, waterlilies. *Compton Wynyates* (**f, t**), reg. days, delightful topiaries of ladies with ruffs, a cat chasing a mouse, etc. Flower borders. *Sulgrave Manor* (**f**), 8 mi. N at Sulgrave, reg. days; garden as in Shakespeare's time; home of George Washington's ancestors. *Upton House* (**f, i, w**), at Edgehill, reg. days, Natl. Trust. Formal gardens, flower borders, rock garden, water garden, iris, lupines.

BARNWELL MANOR: See Oundle.

BARRINGTON COURT: See Ilminster.

BATEMAN'S: See Burwash.

BATH: (Som.) Map B. *Claverton Manor* (**f, r**), reg. days; copy of part of George Washington's gardens at Mt. Vernon, U.S.A.; roses, flower borders. *Botanical Gardens* (**b, f**).

BAWTRY: (Yorks.) *Serlby Hall* (**a, f, r**), Sun., May and Sept.; Thurs. and Sun., June through Aug. Extensive gardens, old roses, rock garden, flower borders.

BEAULIEU: (pron. bew-lee) (Hants.) Map B. *Beaulieu Abbey and Palace House* (**f**), bulbs, flowers.

BEAUMONT HALL BOTANIC GARDENS: See Leicester.

BEDGEBURY NATIONAL PINETUM: See Goudhurst.

BEECHES FARM: See Uckfield.

BERKELEY: (Glos.) Map B. *Berkeley Castle* (**f, w**), regular days, gardens, lily pond.

BERRINGTON HALL: See Leominster.

BICTON GARDENS: See East Budleigh.

BIRMINGHAM: (War.) Map B. *Birmingham Botanical Gardens* (**a, b,** c, f, g, r), Westbourne Rd. Best in May. Rock garden, rose garden, greenhouses with cacti and succulents, begonias. Fragrant *Garden for the Blind* (f, h).

BLENHEIM PALACE: See Woodstock.

BLICKLING HALL: See Aylsham.

BLITHEFIELD HALL: See Rugeley.

BODMIN: (Corn.) *Lanhydrock House* (f, r, t), reg. days; Natl. Trust. Cent.-old garden, rose garden, topiaries, rhododendrons, magnolias.

BORDE HILL: See Hayward's Heath.

BOSTON SPA: (Yorks.) Map E. *Bramham Park* (f, ●), reg. days; formal; see p. 100.

BOTANICAL GARDENS: See Birmingham, Bristol, Cambridge, Harrogate, Kew, Leicester, Liverpool, Oxford, Ripley.

BOURNEMOUTH: (Dorset) Map B. *Compton Acres Gardens* (a, ar, f, w, ●), between Bournemouth and Poole. Reg. days. Fine *Municipal Gardens.*

BRADFORD-ON-AVON: (Wilts.) Map B. *The Courts* (f, g, t, w), Natl. Trust. Reg. days; at Holt, E of Bradford. Fine 7-acre gardens, bulbs, flower borders, waterlilies, topiaries, greenhouse. Also at Holt, *Great Chalfield Manor* (f), reg. days; Natl. Trust. Flowers.

BRAMHAM PARK: See Boston Spa.

BRIDGNORTH: (Shrops.) Map B. *Worfield Gardens* (ar, c), reg. days; fine collection of cacti and succulents, also Japanese bonsai.

BRIDLINGTON: (Yorks.) Map E. *Burton Agnes Hall* (f, t), reg. days. Formal topiary garden; modern garden. *Sewerby Hall* (f), reg. days; old walled gardens, choice plants.

BRISTOL: (Glos.) Map B. *Bristol Zoological Gardens* (a, ar, b, c, f, g, r, t, ●) Daily, weekdays from 9 A.M., Sun. from 10. On route A-38, bus, train, or steamer. One part a botanical garden, labeled. Arboretum, rock garden, dahlias, flower borders, rose garden, Tropical House with exotics and butterflies, early bulbs, fall flowers, topiary animals, dwarf conifers.

BROAD CLYST: (Devon) Near Exeter. *Killerton Gardens* (ar, f), reg. days; Natl. Trust. Spring best. Rare trees and shrubs, daffodils.

BROADWAY: (Glos.) Map B. *Snowhill Manor* (f, r), at Snowhill. Walled gardens, old-fashioned roses and flowers.

BROUGHTON CASTLE: See Banbury.

BURFORD HOUSE: See Tenbury Wells.

BURGH-LE-MARSH: (Lincs.) *Gunby Hall* (f), reg. days, formal flower gardens.

BURNBY HALL: See Pocklington.

BURTON AGNES HALL: See Bridlington.

BURWASH: (Sussex) Map C. *Bateman's* (f, r), garden created by Rudyard Kipling; Natl. Trust. Reg. days. Formal gardens, rose garden, bulbs, flowering shrubs and trees.

BURY ST. EDMUNDS: (Suff.) Map C. *Ickworth* (f), reg. days; Natl. Trust. Formal garden, magnolias. Also wonderful *public park* (f, h, r), one circular flower bed a block in diameter; walled rose garden, dahlias, annuals. Scented *Garden for the Blind.*

BUSCOT PARK: See Faringdon.

CAMBRIDGE: (Cambs.) Map C. *Emmanuel College Garden* (f), open daily, fine trees, flowers. The *Fellows' and Scholars' Gardens of Clare College* (f, h, w), Mon.–Fri. 2–5. Fine color-schemed flower gardens on both sides of river; scented garden, lily pool. *Jesus College Garden* (f), open daily. *Cambridge University Botanic Gardens* (a, ar, b, f, g, h, w, •), fine rock garden with geographical divisions, arboretum, bulbs, bog and water gardens, scented garden, collections of bamboos, winter-flowering plants. Greenhouses, orchids. Best in spring.

CANTERBURY: (Kent) *Chilham Castle* (f, r, t), reg. days. Chessmen topiaries, bulbs, flowers, ancient mulberry and wisteria, Banksia rose about 150 years old.

CARK-IN-CARTMEL: (Lancs.) Map D. *Holker Hall* (f), reg. days. Near Grange-over-Sands. Bulbs, magnolias, azaleas, rhododendrons.

CARNFORTH: (Lancs.) Map D. *Leighton Hall* (f, r), near Yealand Convers. Reg. days. Typical 19th-cent. garden, roses, flowers.

CASSIOBURY PARK: See Watford.

CASTLE ASHBY: See Yardley Hastings.

CASTLE HOWARD: See Malton.

CHARD: (Dorset) *Forde Abbey* (a, f, w), reg. days. Park, bulb, rock garden, bog garden, famous flower borders, color-schemed.

CHARLESTON MANOR: See West Dean.

CHASTLETON HOUSE: See Moreton-in-Marsh.

CHATSWORTH: See Bakewell.

CHEVENING: See Sevenoaks.

CHEVITHORNE BARTON: See Tiverton.

CHILHAM CASTLE: See Canterbury.

CHIPPING CAMPDEN: (Glos.) Map B. *Hidcote Manor* (ar, f, r, w, •) Reg. days. Magnif. gardens; see p. 94. Natl. Trust.

CLACTON (Essex) *St. Osyth's Priory* (r, t), reg. days. Formal topiary garden and rose garden.

CLAVERTON MANOR: See Bath.

CLEVEDON: (Som.) *Clevedon Court* (f) Reg. days. Natl. Trust. 18th-cent. terr. garden, flower borders.

CLIVEDEN: See Maidenhead.

COLES: See Petersfield.

COMPTON ACRES GARDENS: See Bournemouth.

COMPTON WYNYATES: See Banbury.

COPPINS: See Uxbridge.

CORPUS CHRISTI COLLEGE: See Oxford.

COTEHELE: See Plymouth.

COTHAY MANOR: See Wellington.

COURTS, THE: See Bradford-on-Avon.

CRAGSIDE GROUNDS: See Rothbury.

CRANBROOK: (Kent) Map C. *Sissinghurst Castle* (ar, f, h, r, •), open reg.; wonderful gardens, see p. 91. *Sissinghurst Place* (a, ar, f), open reg.; old trees, flowering shrubs and borders, rock garden.

CRANFORD: See Ormskirk.

CRAWLEY: (Sussex) Map C. *Nymans* (a, ar, f, r, t, •), near Handcross. Open reg. Very fine, see p. 93.

CREECH GRANGE: See Wareham.

CREWKERNE: (Som.) *Wayford Manor* (a, ar, f), open reg.; series of gardens: rock, water, Japanese; flowering trees and shrubs.

CRITTENDEN HOUSE: See Tonbridge.

CROFT CASTLE: See Leominster.

DEAL: (Kent) *Walmer Castle* (ar, f, i, r), at Walmer, reg. days. Fine trees, 4 walled gardens; roses, iris.

For explanation of symbols and abbreviations, see inside back cover.

DERBY: (Derb.) Maps D and E. *The Arboretum* (ar), public park over cent. old. *Kedleston Hall* (f), reg. days; modern gardens, orangerie.

DERRY AND TOM'S ROOF GARDENS: See London.

DORKING: (Surrey) Maps A and C. *Polesden Lacey* (f), at Bookham. Reg. days. Natl. Trust. Terr., flower borders.

DUNSTER CASTLE: See Minehead.

EAST BUDLEIGH: (Devon) *Bicton Gardens* (ar, c, f, g), reg. days. Wonderful 18th-cent. formal garden; 19th-cent. garden of North American trees and shrubs; fine pinetum; many trees largest of their kind in Britain. Greenhouses, cacti.

EAST GRINSTEAD: (Sussex) Map C. *Gravetye Manor Hotel* (ar, f, •); historic gardens; see p. 93.

EAST LAMBROOK MANOR: See Martock.

EBBERSTON HALL: See Scarborough.

EDENBRIDGE: (Kent) Maps A and C. *Hever Castle* (a, ar, f, t), reg. days. See p. 89.

EGHAM: (Surrey) Maps A and C. *Great Fosters Hotel* (f, r, t), interesting gardens; see p. 85.

ELTHAM: (London) Map A. *Avery Hill Winter Garden* (ar, f, g), Mon.–Fri., 1–5; Sat., Sun., and Bank Hols. Apr. and Sept., 11–5, May–Aug., 11–6. Fine greenhouses; see p. 84.

EMMANUEL COLLEGE: See Cambridge.

EXBURY: (Hants.) Map B. *Exbury Gardens* (f), reg. days. Best spring and fall. Superb rhododendrons. Bulbs, azaleas, flowering shrubs, camellias.

FALMOUTH: (Corn.) *Penjerrick Gardens* (ar, f), at Budock between Falmouth and Mawnan Smith. Reg. days. Great variety subtrop. plants, tree ferns 20 ft. tall, rhododendrons.

FANHAMS HALL: See Ware.

FARINGDON: (Berks.) Map B. *Buscot Park* (f, g), reg. days; Natl. Trust. Formal canal garden, walled kitchen garden, greenhouses, lake.

FARNINGHAM: (Kent) Maps A and C. *Lullingstone Castle* (f, h) at Eynsford. Reg. days. Heathers, herb garden.

FELLOWS GARDEN: See Cambridge.

FENTON HOUSE: See London.

FIELD PLACE: See Horsham.

FORDE ABBEY: See Chard.

FRIARS, THE: See Aylesford.

FROGMORE GARDENS: See Windsor.

FURZEY: See Lyndhurst.

GARDENS FOR THE BLIND: See Birmingham, Bury St. Edmunds, Hastings, Hove, Weston-Super-Mare.

GARDEN HOUSE, THE: See Yelverton.

GARDENS OF REMEMBRANCE: See Stoke Poges.

GILLING CASTLE: See Helmsley.

GLENDURGAN: See Mawnan Smith.

GODALMING: (pron. godd-alming) (Surrey) Map C. *Hascombe Court* (a, ar, f, w), special days only. Large; bulbs, fine rock garden, beautiful trees, flower borders, camellias, magnolias, water garden. *Winkworth Arboretum* (ar, f), 95 acres; Natl. Trust. Many rare trees and shrubs, magnolias, flowering plums, rhododendrons, varieties of mountain ash.

GODINTON PARK: See Ashford.

GORING-BY-SEA: (Sussex) Map C. *Highdown* (a, f, r, w, •), special days only. On Littlehampton Rd.

Wonderful rock and water gardens below a chalk pit, snowdrops, other bulbs, cyclamens, peonies, iris, eremurus, lilies, roses.

GOUDHURST: (Kent) Map C. *Bedgebury National Pinetum* (ar, f), reg. days; best early June. Fine cypress ave.; rhododendrons.

GRAVETYE MANOR HOTEL: See East Grinstead.

GRAYSWOOD HILL: See Haslemere.

GREAT CHALFIELD MANOR: See Bradford-on-Avon.

GREAT DIXTER: See Northiam.

GREAT FOSTERS HOTEL: See Egham.

GREENWICH: (London area) Map A. *Greenwich Park* (f, r), lovely flowers; see p. 84.

GRETTON: (Northants.) Map C. *Kirby Hall,* reg. days; 17th-cent. terr. gardens.

GREYS COURT: See Henley-on-Thames.

GUILDFORD: (Surrey) Maps A & C. *Albury Park* (f), reg. days. Good trees, shrubs, flower borders. *Harvey's* Department Store (f, w), roof garden, pool with flower islands, see p. 91.

GUNBY HALL: See Burgh-le-Marsh.

HADDON HALL: See Bakewell.

HALL'S CROFT: See Stratford-on-Avon.

HAM COMMON: (Surrey) Map A. *Sudbrook Cottage* (f), lovely garden of author Beverley Nichols, see p. 83.

HAMPTON COURT: (Middlex.) Map A. *Hampton Court Palace* (f, h, r, w, ●), reg. days. Superb gardens, see p. 83.

HARDWICK HALL: See Mansfield.

HAREWOOD: (Yorks.) Map E. Regular days. *Harewood House* (f, r),

terr. formal garden, bulbs, rhododendrons, azaleas, roses.

HARROGATE: (Yorks.) Map E. *Harlow Car Gardens* (a, b, f, r, w), reg. days. Fine demonstration gardens; see p. 100. *Ripley Castle* (f), reg. days. Formal walled gardens. *Rudding Park* (f), lovely gardens, reg. days. V*alley Gardens* (a, f, w), beautiful public park; see p. 100.

HARTLEY WINTNEY: (Hants.) Map C. *West Green House* (f, r); Natl. Trust, reg. days. Charming small rose garden and walled kitchen garden.

HARVEY'S: See Guildford.

HASCOMBE COURT: See Godalming.

HASLEMERE: (Surrey) Map C. *Grayswood Hill* (a, ar, f, i), special days only. Famous collection of flowering trees and shrubs, iris, rhododendrons, azaleas, hydrangeas, rock garden. Superb views.

HASTINGS: (Sussex) Map C. *Garden for the Blind* (h), at Leonard's just west of H.

HATFIELD: (Herts.) Maps A and C. *Hatfield House* (f), reg. days; early 17th-cent. garden, maze, parterres.

HAYWARD'S HEATH: (Sussex) Map C. *Borde Hill* (f, g), reg. days; modern informal garden, plants from China, bulbs, camellias, rhododendrons, magnolias, greenhouse.

HELMSLEY: (Yorks.) Map E. *Gilling Castle* (f), reg. days, medium-sized garden.

HENLEY HALL: See Ludlow.

HENLEY-IN-ARDEN: (War.) Map B. *Packwood House* (f, r, t, ●), at Hockley Heath, on A-34, 11 mi. S of Birmingham. Reg. days; Natl.

For explanation of symbols and abbreviations, see inside back cover.

Trust. Wonderful flowers and topiaries, rose garden, see p. 94.

HENLEY-ON-THAMES: (Oxf.) Map B. *Greys Court* (**f, r**), reg. days. Lovely old garden, wonderful peonies and old roses.

HERGEST CROFT GARDEN: See Kington.

HEVER CASTLE: See Edenbridge.

HIDCOTE MANOR: See Chipping Campden.

HIGHDOWN: See Goring-by-Sea.

HODNET: (Shrops.) Map D. *Hodnet Hall* (**f, w, ●**), reg. days. Series of wonderful gardens; see p. 98.

HOLE PARK: See Rolvenden.

HOLKER HALL: See Cark-in-Cartmel.

HOLLAND PARK GARDEN: See London.

HORSHAM: (Sussex) Map C. *Field Place* (**f, r, w**), special days only. Shelley's birthplace. Lovely flower garden, bulbs, lilies, roses, borders. *Leonardslee* (**a, ar, f, w, ●**), at Lower Beeding, reg. days. Wonderful garden, 100 acres, see p. 93. *South Lodge* (**f**), next door to Leonardslee, special days only. Flowering trees and shrubs, rock garden, water garden, rhododendrons, superb azaleas.

HOVE: (Sussex) Map C. *Garden for the Blind* (**h**).

HOWICK: See Alnwick.

HYLAS GARDENS: See London.

HYTHE: (Kent) *Sandling Park* (**ar, f**), special days only. Bulbs, flowering shrubs, lilacs, unusual trees.

ICKWORTH: See Bury St. Edmunds.

ILFRACOMBE: (Devon) *Watermouth Castle* (**ar, c, f**), reg. days. Old terr. gardens, subtrop. trees and shrubs.

ILMINSTER: (Som.) *Barrington Court* (**f, i, r**), reg. days; Natl. Trust.

Best in summer. Walled garden, modern shrub garden, lily garden, rose garden, iris garden, lily pool, dahlias.

JESUS COLLEGE GARDENS: See Cambridge.

KEDLESTON HALL: See Derby.

KENDAL: (Westm.) Map D. *Levens Hall* (**f, r, t, ●**), reg. days; extraordinary topiary garden, flower borders, roses; see p. 101.

KENSINGTON GARDENS: See London.

KEW GARDENS: (Surrey) Map A. (**a, ar, b, c, f, g, i, r, w, ●**) Outstanding botanical gardens, reg. days; see p. 82.

KILLERTON: See Broad Clyst.

KINGSTON BAGPUIZE: (pron. bag-pew-zee) (Berks.) Map B. *Kingston House* (**f, r**), special days only. Bulbs, flowering shrubs and borders, roses.

KINGTON: (Heref.) Map B. *Hergest Croft Garden* (**ar, f**). Reg. days mid-May–mid-June only. Flowering shrubs, rare trees.

KIRBY HALL: See Gretton.

KNIGHTSHAYES COURT: See Tiverton.

KNUTSFORD: (Ches.) Map D. *Tatton Park* (**f**). Reg. days; Natl. Trust. Formal garden, fernery.

LAMBERHURST: (Kent) Map C. *The Owl House* (**f, r**), reg. days. Lovely flowers, rare shrubs, roses. *Scotney Castle* (**h**), reg. days. Small herb garden and park.

LANHYDROCK HOUSE: See Bodmin.

LEICESTER: (Leics.) Map B. *Beaumont Hall Botanic Gardens* (**a, ar, b, f, w**), 10 acres with water and rock gardens, sunken gardens, botanical collections.

LEIGHTON HALL: See Carnforth.

LEOMINSTER: (Heref.) Map B. *Berrington Hall* (**f**), reg. days; Natl.

Trust. Grounds designed by "Capability Brown"; flower borders. *Croft Castle* (f), reg. days; Natl. Trust. Flower gardens.

LEONARDSLEE: See Horsham.

LEVENS HALL: See Kendal.

LILLYWHITES: See Pulborough.

LINTON LODGE HOTEL: See Oxford.

LIVERPOOL: (Lancs.) Map D. *Liverpool Botanic Garden* (a, b, c, f, g, h, w), at Harthill. New 1½ acres of greenhouses, palm house, fernery, medicinal and commercial plants, begonias, orchids. Water and rock gardens, rhododendrons, wildflower garden. In Calderstone Park nearby, cacti collection.

LONDON: Map A. *Derry and Tom's* (f) Roof Garden, Kensington High St.; store hours; three amazing gardens; see p. 82. *Fenton House* (f), reg. hours; Natl. Trust; small walled garden. *Holland Park Garden* (i), iris. *Kensington Gardens* (f), lovely flowers, see p. 81. *Hylas* or *St. John's Gardens* (f, r), near E Gate of Regent's Park; three rose gardens, flower borders. *Regent's Park* (a, f, r), Queen Mary's Rose Garden, rock and begonia gardens, flower borders. *St. James's Park* (f), flowers; see p. 81.

LONGFORD CASTLE: See Salisbury.

LONGLEAT HOUSE: See Warminster.

LONG MELFORD: (Suff.) Map C. *Melford Hall* (ar, f), reg. days; Natl. Trust. Pretty walled gardens, maidenhair tree.

LOUGHBOROUGH: (pron. luff-bra) (Leics.) Map E. *Prestwood Hall* (ar, f, r), special days only. Large gardens, 2000 tree roses, flower borders, cedars centuries old.

LOWESTOFT: (Suff.) *Somerleyton Hall* (f), reg. days; fine garden, famous maze.

LUDLOW: (Shrops.) Map B. *Henley Hall* (a, f, t, w), bulbs, flower borders, lily pool, topiary hedges, rock and water gardens, maze.

LULLINGSTONE CASTLE: See Farningham.

LUTON: (Beds.) Map C. *Luton Hoo* (a, f, r, w), reg. days; rock, water, and rose gardens, formal garden. At Silsoe nearby, *Wrest Park* (f), reg. days, large 18th-cent. walled garden, owned by Natl. Institute of Agricultural Engineering.

LUXMOORE'S GARDEN: See Windsor.

LYME PARK: See Stockport.

LYNDHURST: (Hants.) Map B. At Minstead, *Furzey* (a, ar, f), reg. days; bulbs, heathers, rock garden, winter and summer flowering trees and shrubs.

MAIDENHEAD: (Bucks.) Maps A and B. *Cliveden* (pron. cliv-den) (f, r, w) Reg. days; Natl. Trust. Lovely gardens, see p. 87.

MALTON: (Yorks.) Map E. *Castle Howard* (f), reg. days; grand park, lake, modern gardens.

MANSFIELD: (Derb.) Map E. *Hardwick Hall* (f, h, r), reg. days; Natl. Trust. Lovely flower gardens, fine herb garden, old roses, fruit trees, hornbeam hedges.

MARKET HARBOROUGH: (Northants.) Map C. *Rockingham Castle* (f, r, t), reg. days; near Kettering. Flower borders, rose garden, yew hedge cut as elephant.

MARLBOROUGH: (Wilts.) Map B. *Avebury Manor* (f, t), reg. days; formal topiary garden, thousands of bulbs.

For explanation of symbols and abbreviations, see inside back cover.

MARTOCK: (Som.) Map B. At South Petherton, *East Lambrook Manor* (**f**), special days only or by appointment. Small cottage garden with special color and texture combinations. Rare plants, peat garden.

MAWNAN SMITH: (Corn.) *Glendurgan* (**f**), reg. days; Natl. Trust. Walled and water gardens, wildflower garden, fine trees and shrubs.

MELBOURNE: (Derb.) Map E. *Melbourne Hall*, reg. days, best Fr. style garden in England, old yew tunnel 300 yards long, wrought-iron arbor.

MELFORD HALL: See Long Melford.

MEMORIAL THEATRE: See Stratford-on-Avon.

MERE: (Wilts.) Map B. *Stourhead* (pron. stoor-) (**f**), Reg. days; Natl. Trust. Magnif. landscape garden; see p. 97. Best in May.

MINEHEAD: (Som.) *Dunster Castle* (**f**), reg. days; choice and tender subtrop. plants, mimosas, cork oaks, lemons, olives.

MONTACUTE HOUSE: See Yeovil.

MORETON-IN-MARSH: (Oxf.) Map B. *Chastleton House* (**t**), reg. days; 17th-cent. garden, unusual box topiary.

MORPETH: (Northumb.) Map I. At Cambo, 10 mi. NW of Morpeth, *Wallington* (**f**), reg. days; Natl. Trust. Walled and terrace gardens.

MORRAB GARDENS: See Penzance.

MUCH WENLOCK: (Shrops.) Map B. *Wenlock Abbey* (**f**), reg. days. Charming garden.

MUNCASTER CASTLE: See Ravenglass.

NESTON: (Ches.) Map D. Near Chester. *Liverpool University Botanic Gardens* (**a, b, f, w**) 32 acres, alp., heathers, primulas, water garden, magnif. rhododendrons, flower borders.

NEWBY HALL: See Ripon.

NEW PLACE: See Stratford-on-Avon.

NEWSTEAD ABBEY: See Nottingham.

NORTHIAM: (Sussex) Map C. *Great Dixter* (**f, t**), reg. days; formal and informal gardens, bulbs, fruit trees, dahlias, fine topiaries.

NOSTELL PRIORY: See Wakefield.

NOTTINGHAM: (Notts.) Map E. *Newstead Abbey* (**ar, f**), at Linby, 9 mi. N on Mansfield Rd., reg. days; extensive formal gardens, rare trees and shrubs.

NYMANS GARDENS: See Crawley.

OLD RECTORY, THE: See Plymouth.

OLDWAY: See Paignton.

OLLERTON: (Notts.) Map E. *Thoresby Hall* (**f**), reg. days; large formal Victorian garden.

ORMSKIRK: (Lancs.) Map D. *Cranford* (**f, r**), on Formby Lane, at Aughton, SW of Ormskirk. Reg. days; modern, unusual small garden, shrubs, roses.

OUNDLE: (pron. on-del) (Northants.) Map C. *Barnwell Manor* (**ar, f, r**), special days only. Home of Duke and Duchess of Gloucester. Espaliered pear trees 200 years old, iris, cherry trees, roses, rock garden.

OWL HOUSE, THE: See Lamberhurst.

OXBOROUGH HALL: See Swaffham.

OXFORD: (Oxf.) Map B. *Balliol College* (**f**), daily 2–5. *Corpus Christi College* (**f**), daily 2–4, vacations 10–6. *Linton Lodge Hotel* (**f**), lovely garden. *Rousham House* (**f, r**), at Steeple Aston, 10 mi. N off route 423, reg. days, flower borders, rose garden, large landscape garden with cascades, ponds.

Oxford University Botanic Gardens (b, f, g, i), first botanic garden in England, opened 1621. Closed Sun. 12–2. Best June–Sept. Iris, summer flowers, greenhouse, orchids.

PACKWOOD HOUSE: See Henley-in-Arden.

PAIGNTON: (Devon) *Oldway* (f), municipal gardens, always open. Ital. and grotto gardens.

PARHAM: See Pulborough.

PENJERRICK GARDENS: See Falmouth.

PENSHURST: (Kent) Map C. *Penshurst Place* (f), reg. days. Laid out in 1560. Parterres, yew hedges, pools.

PENZANCE: (Corn.) *Morrab Gardens* (ar, f, w), public parks with tender plants from New Zealand, Australia, South America; palms, tree ferns, pools with rare plants. *Trengwainton* (f, w, ●), splendid garden; see p. 103.

PETERSFIELD: (Hants.) Map C. At Privett nearby, *Coles* (a, f, r, w, ●), special days only. One of loveliest gardens in England, with rock and rose gardens, lily pool, prize azaleas and rhododendrons, primulas, water garden, flower borders.

PETWOOD HOTEL: See Woodhall Spa.

PETWORTH: (Sussex) Map C. *Sutton End* (a, r), special days only; informal, rock garden, roses.

PLYMOUTH: (Corn.) At Calstock, N of Plymouth, *Cotehele* (a, f, w), reg. days; Natl. Trust. Terr. flower garden, alp., stream. At Thurlestone, *The Old Rectory* (f), reg. days; flowering trees, borders, and shrubs.

POCKLINGTON: (Yorks.) Map E. *Burnby Hall* (w), reg. days. Spectacular ponds with 60 varieties waterlilies planted for color effect, summer.

POLESDEN LACEY: See Dorking.

POOLE: (Dorset) Map B. *Yaffle Hill* (ar, f), at Broadstone nearby, special days only. Rhododendrons, azaleas, heathers, unusual trees and shrubs.

PRESTWOOD HALL: See Loughborough.

PUDDLETOWN: (Dorset) Map B. Near Dorchester. *Athelhampton Hall* (ar, f, w), reg. days. Ten acres formal and landscape gardens, water garden, stone-walled flower garden, rare trees.

PULBOROUGH: (Sussex) Map C. At West Burton nearby, *Lillywhites* (f, r), reg. days. Old cottage with garden of white lilies and roses; orchard. *Parham* (f), reg. days. Large walled gardens.

RABY CASTLE: See Staindrop.

RADSTOCK: (Som.) Map B. *Ammerdown Park*, special days only. Famous formal Ital. yew gardens, orangerie, orchards.

RAGLEY HALL: See Alcester.

RAVENGLASS: (Cumb.) Map D. *Muncaster Castle* (ar, f), reg. days. 300 acres; rare, exotic flowering trees and shrubs, fine hydrangeas.

REGENT'S PARK: See London.

RICHMOND: (Surrey) Map A. *Royal Park of Richmond* (f, i, w), always open; see p. 83.

RIPLEY: (Surrey) Maps A and C. *Wisley* (a, ar, b, f, g, i, r, w, ●), Royal Horticultural Society's gar-

For explanation of symbols and abbreviations, see inside back cover.

dens; weekdays 10–7:30; Sun., members only. Superb; see p. 90.

RIPLEY CASTLE: See Harrogate.

RIPON: (Yorks.) Map E. *Newby Hall* (ar, a, f, i, r, ●), reg. days. At Skelton, 4 mi. SE of Ripon. Wonderful gardens; see p. 100.

ROCKINGHAM CASTLE: See Market Harborough.

ROLVENDEN: (pron. rolv-den) (Kent) Map C. *Hole Park* (f), special days only. Formal and natural gardens.

ROTHBURY: (Northumb.) Map I. *Cragside Grounds* (a, f), reg. days; rock gardens, rhododendrons.

ROUSHAM HOUSE: See Oxford.

ROYAL PARK OF RICHMOND: See Richmond.

RUDDING PARK: See Harrogate.

RUGBY: (War.) Map B. *Stanford Hall* (r), reg. days; walled rose garden.

RUGELEY: (Staffs.) Map B. *Blithfield Hall* (r), reg. days; formal rose garden, 18th-cent. orangerie.

ST. JAMES'S PARK: See London.

ST. OSYTH'S PRIORY: See Clacton.

SALISBURY: (Wilts.) Map B. *Cathedral Close* (f), wide flower borders. *Longford Castle* (f, g), reg. days; Ital. garden, greenhouses.

SANDLING PARK: See Hythe.

SANDON: (Staffs.) Map D. *Sandon Hall* (f, g, r), special days only; 50 acres, rose garden, bulbs, greenhouses, flowering shrubs.

SANDRINGHAM: (Norf.) *Sandringham Grounds* (a, f), reg. days, when the Queen is not in residence. Enormous flower borders, rock garden, formal gardens, bulbs.

SCARBOROUGH: (Yorks.) Map E. *Ebberston Hall* (w), reg. days. Formal water garden.

SCOTNEY CASTLE: See Lamberhurst.

SEATON DELAVAL HALL: See Whitley Bay.

SERLBY HALL: See Bawtry.

SEVENOAKS: (Kent) Maps A and C. *Chevening* (pron. chev-ning) (f, r) Special days only; formal gardens, rose garden, flower borders.

SEWERBY HALL: See Bridlington.

SHEFFIELD PARK GARDENS: See Uckfield.

SHIFNAL: (Shrops.) Map B. At Weston-under-Lizard, *Weston Park* (f), reg. days; terr. gardens, deer park.

SHUGBOROUGH: See Stafford.

SISSINGHURST CASTLE: See Cranbrook.

SISSINGHURST PLACE: See Cranbrook.

SNOWHILL MANOR: See Broadway.

SOMERLEYTON HALL: See Lowestoft.

SOUTHAMPTON: (Hants.) Map B. *Southampton University* (a), always open; splendid rock garden.

SOUTH LODGE: See Horsham.

SPETCHLEY: (Worcs.) Map B. *Spetchley Park* (f), reg. days; formal and informal gardens, bulbs, cyclamen, deer park.

SQUERRYES COURT: See Westerham.

STAFFORD: (Staffs.) Map D. *Shugborough* (f), reg. days; landscape, interesting garden buildings, rhododendrons.

STAINDROP: (Durh.) Maps D and I. *Raby Castle* (f), reg. days; 10 acres of gardens, famous sweet peas.

STANFORD HALL: See Rugby.

STOCKPORT: (Ches.) Map D. *Lyme Park* (f, r), at Disley, 6½ mi. SE of Stockport. Reg. days; Natl. Trust. Sunken garden, orangerie, small rose garden.

STOKE POGES: (Bucks.) Maps A and C. *Gardens of Remembrance* (f, w) cemetery; get permission at Church Cottage. Rock, water, parterre, and heather gardens.

STOURHEAD: See Mere.

STRATFORD-ON-AVON: (War.) Map B. *Anne Hathaway's Cottage* (f) at Shottery nearby, reg. days, small flower garden. *Memorial Theatre* (f), flower borders in back. *Hall's Croft* (f), walled garden of Shakespeare's daughter, reg. days. *New Place* (f), reg. days, Elizabethan knot garden of flowers. *Shakespeare's Birthplace* (f); small garden, flowers mentioned in his plays; reg. days.

SUDBROOK COTTAGE: See Ham Common.

SUDELEY CASTLE: See Wynchcombe.

SULGRAVE MANOR: See Banbury.

SUTTON END: See Petworth.

SWAFFHAM: (Norf.) Map C. *Oxburgh Hall* (f), reg. days; Natl. Trust. Fr. parterre garden of 1845, bulbs, flower and shrub borders.

TATTON PARK: See Knutsford.

TENBURY WELLS: (Shrops.) Map B. *Burford House* (f), reg. days; floodlighted at night July and Aug. Formal and informal gardens, flower borders and shrubs (color schemes and continuous bloom). 120 species of clematis.

TETBURY: (Glos.) Map B. *Westonbirt Arboretum* (ar, f), rhododendrons, conifers.

THORESBY HALL: See Ollerton.

TINTINHULL HOUSE: See Yeovil.

TIVERTON: (Devon) *Chevithorne Barton* (f), reg. days; terr. woodland and rose gardens, flowering

shrubs. *Knightshayes Court* (a, f), reg. days in spring; formal garden, alp., rose garden, flowering shrubs.

TONBRIDGE: (Kent) Map C. SE at Matfield, *Crittenden House* (f), special days only; modern labor-saving garden, bulbs, flowering shrubs.

TORQUAY: (Devon) *Torre Abbey* (f, g), reg. days; gardens and greenhouses.

TRELISSICK: See Truro.

TRENGWAINTON: See Penzance.

TRESCO, SCILLY ISLES: (Corn.) *Tresco Abbey* (ar, f, ●), unique subtrop. gardens; see p. 103.

TRURO: (Corn.) *Trelissick* (ar, f), reg. days; Natl. Trust. Best spring and late summer. Spacious subtrop. gardens, tree ferns, bamboos, collection of hydrangeas, early bulbs, flower borders. *Trewithen* (ar, f, r), at Probus NE of Truro; reg. days; rare trees and shrubs, bulbs, formal rose garden.

UCKFIELD: (Sussex) Map C. *Beeches Farm* (f), reg. days; flower borders. *Sheffield Park* (ar, f, w, ●), reg. days; wonderful garden; see p. 93.

UPTON HOUSE: See Banbury.

UXBRIDGE: (Bucks.) Maps A and C. *Coppins* (f), at Iver, 2½ mi. SE of Uxbridge. Special days only. A Royal Garden; see p. 86.

VALLEY GARDENS: See Harrogate.

WAKEFIELD: (Yorks.) Map E. *Nostell Priory* (f, r), reg. days; Natl. Trust. Roses and formal garden.

WALLINGTON: See Morpeth.

WALMER CASTLE: See Deal.

WARE: (Herts.) Maps A and C. *Fanhams Hall*, Westminster Bank

Staff College; special days, or ask permission from Principal of College. Japanese Garden.

WAREHAM: (Dorset) Map B. *Creech Grange* (f), reg. days; patterned flower beds, azaleas, rhododendrons, palms; peacocks. Ponds, cascade.

WARMINSTER: (Wilts.) Map B. *Longleat House* (f), toward Frome. Reg. days. Famous rhododendrons and azaleas, small formal gardens, orangerie.

WARWICK: (War.) Map B. *Warwick Castle*, reg. days; Ital. garden, topiaries; peacocks.

WATERMOUTH CASTLE: See Ilfracombe.

WATERPERRY HORTICULTURAL SCHOOL: See Wheatley.

WATFORD: (Herts.) Maps A and C. *Cassiobury Park* (i), always open, iris.

WAYFORD MANOR: See Crewkerne.

WELLINGTON: (Som.) Map B. *Cothay Manor* (f, r), reg. days. Series of lovely gardens, all seasons: four rose gardens, including old varieties; bulbs, azaleas, iris.

WENLOCK ABBEY: See Much Wenlock.

WEST DEAN: (Sussex) Map C. *Charleston Manor* (r), reg. days; roses.

WEST GREEN HOUSE: See Hartley Wintney.

WESTERHAM: (Kent) Maps A and C. *Squerryes Court* (f), reg. days. Flower borders and shrubs.

WESTONBIRT ARBORETUM: See Tetbury.

WESTON PARK: See Shifnal.

WESTON-SUPER-MARE: (Som.) *Garden for the Blind* (h).

WHEATLEY: (Oxf.) Map B. *Waterperry Horticultural School* (a, f, g), special days only; 38 acres, flowers, veg., alp., herbs, fruits, greenhouses.

WHITLEY BAY: (Northumb.) Map I. *Seaton Delaval Hall* (f), reg. days. Garden in style of 1728.

WIGHTWICK MANOR: See Wolverhampton.

WILTON: (Wilts.) Map B. *Wilton House* (ar, f), reg. days. Magnif. gardens of many periods, one Ital. Finest cedars in Britain.

WINCHCOMBE: (Glos.) Map B. *Sudeley Castle* (ar, f, r), reg. days. Famous formal gardens, double yew hedges 15 ft. high, terr. with clipped trees, flower borders, rose garden.

WINDSOR: (Berks.) Maps A and B. *Frogmore Gardens* (f), Royal Garden of the Queen. Special days only. Flowering shrubs. *Windsor Great Park* (a, ar, f, ●), including Valley Gardens, Kurume Punch Bowl. Reg. days. Magnif.; see p. 85. *Luxmoore's Garden* (f), Eton College, on island in Thames: also nearby Provosts' and Fellows' gardens.

WING: (Bucks.) Map C. *Ascott* (ar, f, t,), reg. days; Natl. Trust. Unusual topiaries, Fr. formal garden, waterlily lake, bulbs, unusual trees.

WINKWORTH ARBORETUM: See Godalming.

WISLEY: See Ripley.

WOBURN: (Beds.) Map C. *Woburn Abbey* (f), reg. days. Vast gardens in the grand manner, begun 17-cent. Camellia House.

WOLVERHAMPTON: (Staffs.) Map B. *Wightwick Manor* (t), reg. days; Natl. Trust. Formal; topiaries.

WOODHALL SPA: (Lincs.) Map E. *Petwood Hotel* (**f, t, w**), about 30 acres; gardens, flowers, topiaries, lily pool, rhododendrons.

WOODSTOCK: (Oxf.) Map B. *Blenheim Palace,* reg. days. Fr.-style formal and water gardens.

WORFIELD GARDENS: See Bridgnorth.

WREST PARK: See Luton.

WYE COLLEGE: See Ashford.

YAFFLE HILL: See Poole.

YARDLEY HASTINGS: (Northants.) Map C. *Castle Ashby,* reg. days. Formal parterre gardens.

YELVERTON: (Devon) *The Garden House* (**f**), glorious bloom spring to fall; rare plants.

YEOVIL: (Som.) Map B. *Montacute House* (**f, r, ●**), reg. days; wonderful garden, see p. 102. *Tintinhull House* (**f, t, w, ●**), reg. days; Natl. Trust; see p. 102.

WHEEL TOURS

GREATER LONDON AREA: Map A. *Inner Circle:* 15-mi. radius: St. James's Park, Fenton House, Regent's Park, Kensington Gardens, Holland Park Gardens, Derry and Tom's, Kew Gardens, Royal Park of Richmond, Ham Common, Hampton Court Palace, Greenwich Park, Eltham. *Outer Circle:* 20-mi. radius: Egham, Windsor, Uxbridge, Stoke Poges, Watford, Hatfield, Ware, Farningham, Sevenoaks, Westerham, Edenbridge, Ripley, Dorking, Guildford.

SALISBURY as hub: Map B. Bradford-on-Avon, Marlborough, Warminster, Wilton, Southampton, Lynd-hurst, Beaulieu, Exbury, Wareham, Poole, Bournemouth, Mere.

BATH as hub: Map B. Berkeley, Tetbury, Bristol, Radstock, Bradford-on-Avon, Marlborough, Warminster, Mere, Wilton.

OXFORD as hub: Map B. Banbury, Moreton-in-Marsh, Woodstock, Wheatley, Kingston Bagpuize, Faringdon. Also Map C: Wing, Henley-on-Thames, Maidenhead.

STRATFORD-ON-AVON as hub: Map B. Birmingham, Rugby, Henley-in-Arden, Warwick, Alcester, Spetchley, Banbury, Chipping Campden, Broadway, Moreton-in-Marsh, Winchcombe, Woodstock.

LEOMINSTER as hub: Map B. Much Wenlock, Bridgnorth, Ludlow, Tenbury Wells, Kington, Spetchley.

HORSHAM as hub: Map C. Egham, Hartley Wintney, Dorking, Westerham, Sevenoaks, Tonbridge, Ripley, Guildford, Godalming, Edenbridge, Penshurst, East Grinstead, Crawley, Haslemere, Petersfield, Petworth, Pulborough, Hayward's Heath, Uckfield, Goring-by-Sea, Hove, West Dean.

TUNBRIDGE WELLS as hub: Map C. Farningham, Aylesford, Sevenoaks, Dorking, Westerham, Edenbridge, Tonbridge, Crawley, Hayward's Heath, Uckfield, Burwash, Northiam, West Dean, Hastings, Penshurst, Cranbrook, Hove.

LUTON as hub: Map C. Yardley Hastings, Woburn, Wing, Ware, Hatfield, Watford, Uxbridge, Stoke Poges, Maidenhead, Windsor.

CAMBRIDGE as hub: Map C. Bury St. Edmunds, Long Melford, Ware.

For explanation of symbols and abbreviations, see inside back cover.

CHESTER as hub: Map D. Ormskirk, Knutsford, Neston, Hodnet, Liverpool. Also in Wales (see "Key to Gardens" for "Wales") Chirk, Llangollen.

DERBY as hub: Map B. Leicester, Rugeley. Map D. Sandon, Stafford. Map E. Bakewell, Mansfield, Nottingham, Melbourne, Loughborough. Ollerton.

KENDAL as hub: Map D. Ravenglass, Cark-in-Cartmel, Carnforth.

YORK as hub: Map E. Helmsley, Ripon, Malton, Harrogate, Boston Spa, Pocklington, Wakefield, Harewood.

FINLAND

There are few flower gardens in this country of long winters, but you can enjoy the lovely little window gardens that jut out from the fronts of many private homes.

ARBORETUM MUSTILA: See Elimäki.

BOTANICAL GARDENS: See Helsinki, Oulu, Turku/Ruissalo.

ELIMÄKI: *Arboretum Mustila* (ar), best in June, July, Sept., Oct. Conifers, rhododendrons, other trees.

HELSINKI: *Botanical Garden* (a, b, f, g), Eläintarha Park, Unioninkatu 44. Best June–Sept. Open Tues. and Fri. Beautiful park, flower borders, greenhouses.

OULU: *Botanical Garden* (a, b, g), Kasarmintie 4. Best June–Aug. Alp. and arctic plants. Greenhouse.

TURKU/RUISSALO: *Botanical Garden* (b, f). Open all year, weekdays all day, Sunday 12–2. Best Apr.–Oct. Greenhouse; 700 kinds of orchids, many species.

FRANCE

To help you in locating these towns on a map, each has been marked with its region in parentheses: North, Central, South, and Île (for Île de France), in the same groupings used in the chapter on "France," and on Maps F and G.

For flower shows and festivals, see chapter "Flower Shows in Europe."

ABBEVILLE: (North) *Château de la Bagatelle,* daily June 15 to October 15, 11–12, 2–7. Formal French.

ALBI: (South) *Palais de la Berbie* (f), scroll parterres.

ALÈS: (South) *Les Jardins au Domaine de Prafrance* (ar, f), 6 mi.

S of Alés. Mar.–Oct., 9–12, 2–7. Arboretum; 32 kinds of bamboos, sequoias, magnolias, rhododendrons, azaleas, etc.

ANGERS: (Central) *Château d'Angers* (f), daily 9–12, 2–6. Flower parterres.

ANSOUIS: (South) *Château d'Ansouis,* daily 2–7 except Mon. Scrolls of box; pools, cascades.

ANTIBES: (South) Station Botanique de la *Villa Thuret* (ar, b, c, f, g), best Apr.–June. Exotic flowers, plants, trees, subtrop. and Mediterranean. Fine arboretum. Greenhouses. 2000 species.

ARBORETUM DES BARRES: See Montargis.

BAGATELLE: See Paris.

BALLEROY: (North) *Château de Balleroy,* Sun., Tues., Thurs., Sat., and hols., 2–6. Parterres.

BESANÇON: (Central) *Jardin Botanique* (a, b, g, h, r, w), 1, Place Maréchal Leclerc. Daily 8–12, Mon.–Fri. also 1:30–5:30. Best May–Nov. Alpinum, ferns, medicinal plants, rosarium with 2000 varieties, Victoria regia, water plants. Greenhouses.

BOIS DE BOULOGNE: See Paris.

BORDEAUX: (South) At Preignac, 25 mi. S of Bordeaux, *Château de Malle,* open Sun. and hols. 3–6. Ital.

BOTANICAL GARDENS: See Jardins Botaniques.

BOUGIVAL: (Île) Le Coq Hardi Restaurant (f), garden.

BOURGES: (South) *Cathedral of St. Étienne.* Formal garden.

BRANTÔME: (South) *Benedictine Abbey* garden.

CAEN: (North) *Jardin Botanique* (a, b, c, f, g, h), 5, Place Blot. Flowers of Normandie, exotic plants, medicinal plants, rock garden, succulents. Greenhouses.

CAP MARTIN: (South) *Villa Roquebrune* (a, ar, c, f, ●) Near Monaco. Best Apr., July, Aug. See p. 149.

CARROUGES, NE of, at St. Christophe-le-Jajolet (North), *Château de Sassy* (f), July 4 to Oct. 15; Thurs. and Sun. 2–6. Terr. flower parterres.

CATHEDRAL OF ST. ÉTIENNE: See Bourges.

CHAMPS-SUR-MARNE: (Île) *Château de Champs-sur-Marne* (f, ●), daily except Tues. 10–6:30. Superb Fr.-style garden by nephew of Le Nôtre, flower parterres.

CHANTILLY : (Île) *Château de Chantilly,* garden; Thurs. 1:30–5:30, Sun. 1:30–6:30. Parterres, etc., by Le Nôtre.

CHAPELLE DE SAINT-GILLES: See Montoire.

CHARTRES: (Île) *Bishopric Gardens* (f, t) behind cathedral; flowers, topiaries.

CHÂTEAU DE LA BAGATELLE: See Abbeville.

CHÂTEAU DE BUSSY-RABUTIN: See Montbard.

CHÂTEAU DE CANON: See Mézidon.

CHÂTEAU DE CLUZEL: See St. Eble.

CHÂTEAU D'EFFIAT: See Lapalisse.

CHÂTEAU DE LAFAYETTE: See Chavaniac-Lafayette.

CHÂTEAU DE MALLE: See Bordeaux.

CHÂTEAU DE MARQUEYSSAC: See Lascaux.

CHÂTEAU DE LA ROCHE-COURBON: See Saintes.

CHÂTEAU DE LA ROCHELAMBERT: See St. Paulien.

CHÂTEAU DE POLIGNAC: See La-voûte-sur-Loire.

CHÂTEAU DE SASSY: See Carrouges.

CHÂTEAU DE VAUX-LE-VICOMTE: See Maincy.

CHAVANIAC-LAFAYETTE: (South) *Château de Lafayette* (f, r), Sat., Sun., Mon., Thurs., and hols., 10–12, 2–6. Birthplace of Lafayette. Rose garden, annuals, woods garden.

CHENONCEAUX: (Central) *Château de Chenonceaux*, daily 9–12, 2–7. Formal garden.

COL DU LAUTARET: (South) *Station Biologique et Alpinum* (a, b), of University of Grenoble; June 15 to Oct. 1. 6150 ft. alt. Accessible by car from Grenoble or Briançon. Best in July. 3000 alpines, many rare.

COURANCES: (Île) *Château de Courances*, Sat., Sun., and hols., Easter to Nov. 1. Famous for great formal pools, cascades; delightful small Japanese garden.

DAMPIERRE: (Île) *Château de Dampierre;* daily except Tues., 2–6. Gardens by Le Nôtre. Formal flower gardens. Greenhouses.

DIJON: (Central) *Jardin Botanique* (a, b, f), 1, Ave. Albert I. Best May–Sept.; 6000 varieties.

EPINAL: (North) *Municipal rose garden* (r).

EVRY-PETIT-BOURG: (Île) between Paris and Melun. *Rosarium* (r).

EZE: (South, near Monaco) *Lou Sueil* (c, f), garden designed by Duchene; exotic plants and flowers, large collection succulents.

FIGEAC: (South) *Château de Loubressac,* daily 9–12, 2–6. Terr. formal gardens; views.

FONTAINEBLEAU, Forest (ar) Many old, named trees; see a French Touring Club map. *Château de Fontainebleau,* parterres by Le Nôtre.

GIVERNY: (Île) Claude Monet's home (f, w); flower garden and lily pond.

HAUTEFORT: (South) *Château de Hautefort* (f, i) Open Easter through Sept., 9–8. Magnif. flower parterres, iris.

JALLERANGE: (Central) *Château de Jallerange;* ask for permission. See p. 139.

JARDIN ALBERT-KAHN: See Paris.

JARDIN BOTANIQUE: See Besançon, Caën, Dijon, Lille, Lyon, Marseille, Metz, Montpellier, Nancy, Nantes, Rouen.

JARDIN DE LA FONTAINE: See Nîmes.

JARDIN DES PLANTES: See Paris.

JARDIN HENRI VINAY: See Le Puy.

JARDINS DU LUXEMBOURG: See Paris.

JARDIN SHAKESPEARE: See Paris.

LA FERTÉ-SAINT-AUBIN: (Central) *Château de La Ferté-Saint-Aubin* (r) Open Easter, Whitsun, and from June through Oct., daily 9–7. Floodlit in evening. Rose garden.

LA JAYSINIA: See Samoëns.

LA NAPOULE: (South) *Château de La Napoule,* June–Oct. daily 3–6; Oct.–June only Thurs., Sat., Sun., 3–6, except closed mid-Nov. to mid-Dec. Formal garden with sculpture by late American, Henry Clewes.

LANGEAIS: (Central) *Château de Langeais,* daily except Mon., 9–12, 2–6:30. Parterres.

LAPALISSE, N. of, at Effiat (South), *Château d'Effiat,* daily 9–12, 2–7. Fine garden by Le Nôtre.

LASCAUX, S of, at Roque-Gageac on Dordogne River (South) *Château de Marqueyssac,* magnif. terr. gardens.

LAVOÛTE-SUR-LOIRE: (South) *Château de Polignac* (there are two, one of them a ruin with no garden!) Daily 9–12, 2–7.

LE LAVANDOU: (South) *Island of Port Cros* (ar) is opposite here, luxuriant national park.

LE PUY: (South) *Jardin Henri Vinay,* daily from 8 A.M. *School Garden for the Deaf and Dumb* (f, t) (Et. Horticole Institution de Sourds-Muets); flowers and vegetables cultivated by the deaf-mutes; topiaries.

LILLE: (North) in suburb of Douai, *Jardin Botanique* (a, b, c, f, g), 39 Blvd. Vauban. Alp.; greenhouses with begonias, bromeliads, orchids, succulents.

LOU SUEIL: See Eze.

LUNÉVILLE: (North) *Château de Lunéville* (f, t), Apr.–Sept., 9–12, 2–6. Formal with flowers, topiaries.

LYON: (South) *Jardin Botanique* (a, ar, b, c, f, g, r, w, ●), in Parc de la Tête d'Or. May–Oct. Alpinum of 2000 varieties, exceptional; rose garden 1200 varieties including historical; 1200 flowering shrubs, many rare; arboretum; subtrop. and trop. flowers, rare water plants including Victoria regia; orchids; succulents. Large park, can drive through. Greenhouses.

MAINCY: (Île) *Château de Vaux-le-Vicomte* (f, ●), garden open only Sat. and Sun. 2–6. Superb, first garden by Le Nôtre. Very extensive. Flower parterres. See p. 135.

MALMAISON: (Île) (ar, f, r) Daily except Tues., 10–12, 2–5. Some flowers, roses; cedar of Lebanon planted by Empress Josephine in 1800.

MARSEILLE: (South) *Jardin Botanique* (g, r), Parc Borély, 52, Ave. Clôt-Bey. Best June–Sept. Rosarium with 2500 plants, 230 varieties. Greenhouses.

MEAUX: (Île) *The Bishop's Garden,* daily. Formal; by Le Nôtre.

MÉNARS: (Central) *Château de Ménars* (ar, f), daily 9–12, 2–7. Flower garden and park, fine old trees.

MENTON: (South) *Serre de la Madone* (f, g), best Apr., June, July. Subtrop. plants. Greenhouses.

METZ: (North) *Jardin Botanique* (b, f, g, r), Rue de Pont-à-Mousson. April–Nov. Bulbs, dahlias, roses, trop. and subtrop. plants. Greenhouses.

MÉZIDON: (North) *Château de Canon* (f), ask permission. Large formal gardens; also walled flower gardens—"Chartreuses."

MONET, home of Claude: See Giverny.

MONISTROL-SUR-LOIRE: (South) *Château de Monistrol,* open in summer.

MONTARGIS: (Central) *Arboretum des Barres* (ar), 10 mi. S of Montargis at Nogent-sur-Vernisson; 700-acre arboretum, conifers from Orient, California redwoods, etc.

For explanation of symbols and abbreviations, see inside back cover.

Rosarium (r), at Bellegarde-du-Loiret, 14 mi. W of Montargis.

MONTBARD: (Central) *Château de Bussy-Rabutin,* daily except Tues., 10–12, 2–6. Copy of Versailles gardens. See p. 140.

MONTOIRE: (Central) *Chapelle de Saint-Gilles,* surrounding gardens.

MONTPELLIER: (South) *Jardin Botanique* (a, ar, b, f, w, ●), Blvd. Henri IV, 8–12, 2–6. Jan.–Mar., orchids; end of May, native flowers; others all summer. Arboretum, fine rock garden, water plants (Egyptian lotus blooms July); greenhouses.

MUSÉE ÎLE DE FRANCE: See St. Jean-Cap-Ferrat.

MUSÉE RODIN: See Paris.

NANCY: (North) *Jardin Botanique* (a, b, f, g, h, i), Rue Ste. Catherine, 8–12, 1:30–5. Alpinum, dahlias, iris, medicinal plants, tulips. Greenhouses. *Parc de la Lignière* (r), rose garden.

NANTES: (Central) *Jardin Botanique* (ar, b, c, f, g, r, ●), Rue Stanislas Baudry, Apr.–Sept. 9–12, 2–6. Arboretum, cacti, 240 varieties camellias; orchids, roses. Greenhouses.

NICE: (South) *Retiro Park* (r), rose garden. *Flower market* (f), on Rue Saint-François-de-Paule.

NÎMES: (South) *Jardin de la Fontaine:* see p. 147.

ORLÉANS: (Central) *Parc Floral d'Exposition Permanente* (f, i, r, ●), 8:30–7:30. Exceptional, see p. 140.

PALAIS DE LA BERBIE: See Albi.

PARC FLORAL D'EXPOSITION PERMANENTE: See Orléans.

PARC GRANDS MURCINS: See Roanne.

PARIS: *Bagatelle* (f, r, ●): on edge of Bois de Boulogne. Outstanding; tulips, roses, etc. See p. 131. *Bois de Boulogne* (f), great park with flower gardens. *Fleuriste Municipal* (a, ar, f, g, i, r, ●), 3, Ave. Porte d'Auteuil. Open all year. 94 greenhouses. Exceptional. See p. 131. *Flower Markets* (f), at Les Halles, 5–8 A.M.; at Quai de Corse and Place Louis-Lépine, near Notre Dame, during day. *Jardin Albert-Kahn* (ar), 6, Quai du 4 Septembre, at St. Cloud. Unusual. See p. 133. *Jardins du Luxembourg* (f, g), 62-acre park, flowers, greenhouses. *Jardin des Plantes* (a, b, c, f, g, h, ●), 57, Rue Cuvier, or Place Valhubert. May–Oct. Fine botanical garden. See p. 130. *Le Jardin Shakespeare* (f), in Bois de Boulogne, au Pré-Catelan. Apr.–Oct. Flowers Shakespeare mentioned. *Musée Rodin* (r), 77, Rue de Varennes. Daily except Tues., 1–6, free weekdays, admission Sun. 2000 rose bushes, 100 varieties. *Roseraie de l'Hay* (r), take bus 186, 187, 192, or Métro line Sceaux, to station Bourg-la-Reine, then bus 192. Fabulous roses. See p. 11. *Tuileries* (f), Place de la Concorde. Flower parterres. *Unesco Building,* Place de Fonteney, 10–12, 2–6, Japanese Garden. *Zoological Garden,* flower beds.

POITIERS: (South) (a) Rock garden on ramparts.

PORT CROS: See Le Lavandou.

PROVINS: (Île) *Château de Provins* (r), roses. City has been famous for roses since the days of the Crusades.

RAMBOUILLET: (Île) *Château de Rambouillet,* daily except Tues. 10–12, 2–6. Formal.

RETIRO PARK: See Nice.

ROANNE: (South) *Parc Grands Murcins* (**ar**), arboretum, conifers, etc. NW of Lyon.

ROSERAIE DE L'HAY: See Paris.

ROSNY: (Île) *Château de Rosny,* daily except Tues. and Wed., unless these fall on hols. Formal.

ROUEN: (North) *Jardin Botanique* (**a, b, c, f, g, w**), 114, Ave. des Martyres de la Résistance. Alpinum, insectivorous plants, exotics, orchids, Victoria regia. Greenhouses. At Clères, nearby, *Château de Clères* (**f**), Apr. through Sept., weekdays 9–12, 1:30–8. Sun. and hols. 9–8. Colorful flower borders.

SAINT-CLOUD (Île) (**f**), Beautiful spring flower mosaics in park. Formal. See also PARIS, Jardin Albert-Kahn.

SAINTES: (South) Nearby at Saint-Porchaire, *Château de la Roche-Courbon* (**i, t**), daily. Large formal garden, iris, topiaries.

ST. EBLE: (South) Near Langeac and Le Puy. *Château de Cluzel,* open all summer. Formal.

ST.-JEAN-CAP-FERRAT: (South) *Musée Île-de-France* (**f**, ●), Ave. Denis-Séméria, daily except Mon. 3–7. 12 acres of gardens: Spanish Garden, Exotic Garden, Italian Garden, etc.

ST. PAULIEN: (South) *Château de la Rochelambert,* 9–12, 2–7. Formal.

SAMOËNS: Jardin Botanique et Alpinum. *La Jaysinia* (**a, b, w,** ●), spring to fall. Near Geneva, Annemasse, Bonneville. Alpines of world arranged geographically; also water plants of mountain area.

SCEAUX: (Île) *Château de Sceaux,* weekdays 2–6, Sat. and Sun. 2–7. Park by Le Nôtre, in eerie setting of overgrown ruins of castle.

SCHOOL GARDEN FOR THE DEAF AND DUMB: See Le Puy.

SERRE DE LA MADONE: See Menton.

STATION BIOLOGIQUE ET ALPINUM: See Col du Lautaret.

TUILERIES: See Paris.

UNESCO BUILDING: See Paris.

USSÉ: (Central) *Château d'Ussé* (**r**), daily 9–12, 2–7. Floodlit Apr.–Sept. Inspired Perrault to write "Sleeping Beauty." Roses.

VERSAILLES: (Île) *Château de Versailles* (**f, r,** ●), daily except Tues. 10–5. Great fountains play first and third Sun. May–Sept. Finest example of Le Nôtre's work; extensive. Flower parterres, rose garden.

VILLANDRY: (Central) *Château de Villandry* (**f, r,** ●), daily mid-Mar. to mid-Nov., 9–12, 2–5:30 or 7. Exceptional; see p. 142.

VILLA ROQUEBRUNNE: See Cap Martin.

VILLA THURET: See Antibes.

WIDEVILLE: (Île) *Château de Wideville,* very fine formal gardens.

ZOOLOGICAL GARDEN: See Paris.

WHEEL TOURS

Paris as hub: Île de France Map F for six excursions from Paris and back. These are sightseeing tours including some gardens, names of which are italicized below:

EXCURSION A: Paris; St. Denis church; Ecouen château; Luzarches churches; *Chantilly;* Senlis cathedral; Compiègne town hall and château; Pierrefonds castle; Villers-Cotterets castle; Vez castle; Crépy; Ermenonville château and Châalis castle; Mortefontaine; Paris.

EXCURSION B: Paris; *Champs, Meaux, Provins, Maincy,* Grosbois château, Ormesson château, Paris.

EXCURSION C: Paris; *Evry-Petit-Bourg, Fontainebleau,* Nemours château, *Courances,* Ballancourt château, Paris.

EXCURSION D: Paris; *Sceaux,* Farcheville château, Mereville château, Etampes churches, etc., Chamarande château, Saint-Sulpice-de-Favieres church, *Dampierre,* Paris.

EXCURSION E: Paris; *Versailles,* Les Mesnuls castle, *Rambouillet,* Maintenon castle, *Chartres,* Dreux town hall and mausoleum, *Wideville, St. Cloud,* Paris.

EXCURSION F: Paris; *Malmaison,* Saint-Germain, Maisons-Lafitte, Poissy, Mantes church, *Rosny,* La Roche-Guyon castles, Gisors castle and town hall, Beauvais cathedral, Paris.

CAEN as hub (North): Balleroy, Mézidon.

NANCY as hub (North): Metz, Lunéville.

ORLÉANS as hub (Central): Blois, La Ferté-Saint-Aubin, Ménars.

TOURS as hub (Central) (or Amboise, Hotel Le Choiseuil): Ménars, Chenonceaux, Langeais, Ussé, Villandry, Montoire.

LE PUY as hub (South) (Hotel du Cygne): Chavaniac-Lafayette, Lavoulte-sur-Loire, St. Eble, Monistrol.

LASCAUX as hub (South): Hautefort.

ARLES as hub (South): Montpellier, Nîmes, Ansouis.

RIVIERA TOUR (South): Marseilles, Le Lavandou, La Napoule, Cannes and Grasse flower fields, Antibes, Nice, St.-Jean-Cap-Ferrat, Menton, Eze, Cap Martin, Monte Carlo.

GERMANY

To help you in locating towns on a map, each has been marked with its region in parentheses: North, Central, South, in the same groupings used in the chapter on "Germany" and on Map J.

ALPINUM AUF DEM SCHACHEN: See Garmisch-Partenkirchen.

ANSBACH: (South) *Hofgarten,* at palace, baroque parterres, lindens lining long walk, orangerie.

ASCHAFFENBURG: (Central) *Park Schoenbusch,* on highway to Darmstadt. Oldest classical landscape garden of Germany. Maze of 1776, revolving bridge to island in lake.

ASCHENDORF: (North) *Haus Altenkamp* (t), SW of Papenburg near Dutch border. Private home, but can be seen by telephoning owner, Herr Dr. Behnes. Unique topiary garden; see p. 163.

AUGSBURG: (South) *Botanischer Garten* (**b, f, g**) Summer flowers, perennials, water garden, greenhouses. *Stadtgarten* (City Park), in SW section of city. Japanese garden; memorial to Rudolf Diesel, inventor of Diesel engine; 56 rocks for it were shipped from Japan as a gift by a Japanese.

BAD PYRMONT: (North) *Kurpark* (**ar, f**), palms from Bordighera, other fine old trees, 1000 azaleas along walk.

BADEN-BADEN: (South) *Lichtentaler Allee* (**ar, f, r**), 150 kinds of rhododendrons along canal, bloom April; rare trees including sequoias, 300-year-old oaks. Flower parterres in front of Kurhaus. Formal *Rose Garden* near tennis courts, Internat. Rose Competition in July.

BERNRIED: (South) *Schloss Hoehenried* (**ar, f**) on the Starnberger See S of Tutzing. A national park donated by an American, Mrs. Woods, to Bavaria. Many flowers, ancient oaks and beeches.

BETHMANNPARK: See Frankfurt.

BOTANISCHER GARTEN: See Augsburg, Dortmund, Essen, Goettingen, Heidelberg, Kiel, Krefeld, Muenchen, Tuebingen, West Berlin.

BREMEN: (North) *Rhododendronpark* and *Botanischer Garten* (**b, f, ●**), on outskirts along Autobahn. Beautifully landscaped, rhododendrons of hundreds of varieties bloom end of May through June.

BRUEHL: (Central) *Schloss Bruehl* (**f, ●**), formal parterres by pupil of Le Nôtre. Flower garden.

BURG GRACHT: See Liblar.

COBURG: (Central) *Rosengarten* (Rose Garden) (**f, i, r**), in S section of city, open May–Oct. Also tulips, dahlias, an Iris Garden.

DARMSTADT: (Central) *Prinz-Georg-Garten*, formal Fr.-style garden, orangerie.

DORTMUND: (Central) *Botanischer Garten* (**a, ar, b, f, g, r**), Alpinum, early bulbs; 14,000 rhododendrons bloom May, June; rose garden, unusual trees; only greenhouses cost admission. *Westfalenpark* (**a, f, i, r, w, ●**), very beautiful, extensive. Annuals, perennials, dahlias, bulbs, ground-cover demonstration; rose, heather, Japanese, and water gardens, etc.

DUESSELDORF: (Central) *Schloss Benrath*, Fr. style, formal.

ESSEN: (Central) *Gruga Park* (**a, f, i, r, w, ●**), very extensive, would take 3 hours to see, walking, less by miniature railway; unique Dahlia Arena. The 1965 German Garden Show here from May to Oct. See p. 169.

Botanischer Garten (**a, b, f, g**), orchids, greenhouses; carpet of gentians blooms Aug.

FLORA: See Koeln.

FRANKFURT/MAIN: (Central) *Palmengarten* (**a, ar, b, c, f, g, i, r, w, ●**), one of finest botanical gardens in Europe, beautiful park. See p. 171. *Bethmannpark* (**f, r**), lovely flower garden; roses, delphinium.

GARMISCH-PARTENKIRCHEN: (South) *Alpinum* (**a, b**) on the Schachen Mountain, open July–Sept. See p. 18.

GOETTINGEN: (Central) *Botanischer Garten* (**a, b, c, f, g, w**), open 7–6,

For explanation of symbols and abbreviations, see inside back cover.

admission fee only for greenhouses. Outstanding "prehistoric" section, large alpinum, bromeliads, ferns, orchids, Victoria regia.

GROSSER TIERGARTEN: See West Berlin.

GRUGA PARK: See Essen.

HAMBURG: (North) *Donners Park* (f, r), has Rose Garden and Dahlia Garden adjacent. *Hirschpark* (f), rhododendrons 180–200 years old. *Planten un Blomen* (a, b, f, h, i, r, w, ●) park, one of finest in Europe; extensive. Roses and iris outstanding. See p. 161. *Volkspark* (f), in Altona suburb, school children's gardens, fine dahlias late summer.

HANNOVER: (North) *Berggarten* (a, b, c, f, g, i, r, ●), open 8 to dusk. Beautiful flower garden, greenhouses; see p. 164. *Herrenhausen* (f, r, ●), open 8 to dusk. Beautiful baroque gardens as in 1680. Concerts and plays, illuminations. See p. 163.

HAUS ALTENKAMP: See Aschendorf.

HEIDELBERG: (Central) *Botanischer Garten* (b, c, f, g), Hofmeisterweg 4, open only Sun. and hols. 9–1, May–Sept. Fine collection cacti and succulents; orchids; greenhouses.

HERRENHAUSEN: See Hannover.

HILDESHEIM: (North) *Mariendom* (cathedral) (r) unique "1000-year-old" climbing rose on apsis. Tours 9–12, 3–5 include this. See p. 166.

HOBBIE GARTEN: See Westerstede.

HOHENHEIM: (South) *Exotischer Garten* (ar), between Stuttgart and Esslingen, 1000 varieties of trees, many planted by King Fred-erick in 1813. Grouped by plant families, labeled.

HOEHENPARK KILLESBERG: See Stuttgart.

HUMBOLDTHAIN: See West Berlin.

KARLSAUE: See Kassel.

KARLSRUHE: (South) *Stadtgarten* (city park) 7 to dusk. S section near entrance, a rock garden. N section, dahlia garden, iris garden, rose garden. The 1967 German Garden Show will be held here, May–Oct.

KASSEL: (Central) *Karlsaue* (ar, f) Main garden always open, but the Blumeninsel (Flower Island), with rare flowers and trees, open only 9–12. Combination of Fr. formal, Eng. park, Dutch canals. *Schlosspark Schoenfeld* (b, f, r), on S edge of city. Botanical garden, rose garden. *Schlosspark Wilhelmshoehe* (ar, c, g, ●), extensive park always open; greenhouses weekdays 10–12, 1–5, Sun. 10–5:30. Fountains play Sun., Wed., and hols. in summer, 3:30–4:45. Over 400 kinds old trees.

KIEL: (North) *Botanischer Garten* (a, ar, b, c, f, g, ●), Duesternbrookerweg 17, 9–5 Mon. through Fri., 9–12 Sat., 9–1 Sun. and hols. Exceptional; geographical landscapes, 10,000 cacti and succulents, 1000 alp., etc. See p. 20.

KOELN: (Central) *Rheinpark* (f, i, r, w), specialized gardens of bulbs, iris, roses, water plants. Cable car to view from above. On Sun. and hols., miniature railway tour. *Flora* (a, b, c, f, w), created by Linnaeus, includes botanical garden. Landscaped. Azaleas, rock garden, greenhouse with cacti, orchids, palms, Victoria regia.

KREFELD: (Central) *Botanischer Garten* (b, f, t), flowers of lower Rhine region; small farmer's garden (Bauerngärtchen) with topiary figures of yew, beech arbor.

LEVERKUSEN: (Central) *Bayer-Leverkusen* factory (f), big Japanese garden, and flower garden, open to public after business hours.

LIBLAR: (Central) *Burg Gracht,* W of Bruehl, old baroque garden, fine trees.

LIETZENSEEPARK: See West Berlin.

LINDERHOF: (South) W of Oberammergau, *Schloss* (f) Extensive formal park, cascades, parterres, terr., etc.; 3000 feet alt.

LUDWIGSBURG: (South) *Schlosspark* (a, f, ●), 7 A.M.–11 P.M. Flower parterres, perennial garden; see p. 174.

MAINAU: (South) *Park und Blumeninsel* (Park and Flower-Island) (a, ar, f, i, r, ●) 7 to dusk. Fabulous garden and arboretum; see p. 176.

MUENCHEN (Munich): (South) *Botanischer Garten* (a, b, c, f, g, h, w, ●), extensive. Arboretum, alpinum, begonias, cacti and succulents, commercial plants, ferns, orchids, palms, rhododendrons, water plants; 6000 varieties. Large greenhouses. *Schlossgarten Schleissheim,* formal Fr. type. *Schlosspark Nymphenburg,* dawn to dusk, Fr. style by pupil of Le Nôtre, Eng. park around it.

OLDENBURG: (North) *Schlosspark,* wonderful rhododendrons.

PAGODENBURG: See Rastatt.

PALMENGARTEN: See Frankfurt.

PARK SCHOENBUSCH: See Aschaffenburg.

PFAUENINSEL: See West Berlin.

PFORZHEIM/WUERM: (South) *Alpengarten* (a), weekdays 8–6, Sun. and hols. 7–7. Over 5000 alpines. See p. 17.

PLANTEN UN BLOMEN: See Hamburg.

PRINZ-GEORG-GARTEN: See Darmstadt.

RASTATT: (South) *Pagodenburg* (f, r), charming flower garden, roses. See p. 173.

RASTEDE: (North) *Schlosspark* (f), famous for rhododendrons planted 150 years ago, also azaleas.

RHEINPARK: See Koeln.

RHODODENDRONPARK: See Bremen.

SAARBRUECKEN: (South) Park der Deutsch-Französischen Gartenschau (*Garden of German-French Cooperation*), (f, r) On a fortified area of World War II with bunkers still there, France and Germany built a flower park in 1960. Roses, individual natl. gardens. See p. 174. *Schlossgarten* (f, r), many secluded individual gardens, perennial garden, rose garden, baroque garden. *Theatergarten* (f), opposite the theater, acres of flower beds.

SCHLOSS BENRATH: See Duesseldorf.

SCHLOSS HOEHENRIED: See Bernried.

SCHWETZINGEN: (Central) *Schlossgarten,* formal Fr. Long allee of lindens.

STUTTGART: (South) *Hoehenpark Killesberg* (f, r, ●), displays of newest flowers, collections of begonias, dahlias, primulas, tulips, perennials.

TUEBINGEN: (South) *Botanischer Garten* (a, b, f, g, w), weekdays 7–5, Sun. 10–5. Regional wildflow-

For explanation of symbols and abbreviations, see inside back cover.

ers, water plants, alp.; greenhouses.

UETERSEN: (North) NW of Hamburg, *Rosarium* (**f, r**), includes other flowers also. Center of a rose-growing district.

VEITSHOECHHEIM: (Central) *Landesanstalt fuer Wein-Obst-und-Gartenbau* (agricultural station) (**f, i**); large collection of iris in the display gardens (Sichtungsgarten).

WEST BERLIN: (North) *Botanischer Garten* (**a, ar, b, c, f, g, h, w, •**), in Dahlem suburb; 105 acres, one of largest in Germany. Daily 10 to dusk. Admission charged weekdays, but free from 1 to dusk Sat., Sun., and hols., including greenhouses. Beautifully landscaped, outstanding rock garden. See p. 167. *Brixplatz* (**f**), in Charlottenburg section, school gardens with wild-flowers. *Grosser Tiergarten* (Zoo) (**f, •**) Thousands of rhododendrons and other flowers; see p. 166. *Humboldthain* (**r**), 18,000 roses of 75 varieties, also collection of wild roses. *Lietzenseepark* (**f**), in Charlottenburg section; perennial gardens. *Pfaueninsel* (Peacock Island) (**ar**), near Potsdam. Many exotic trees planted by Linnaeus. Apr. and Sept. 9–6, May–Aug. 8–8, March and Oct. 9–5. *Schlosspark Charlottenburg* (**f**), baroque garden; see p. 167. *Schlosspark am Humboldtschloss* (**ar**), in Tegel section, Wed. 12 to dusk, Sat. and Sun. 2 to dusk. Ancient trees, including two oaks 500 years old. *Viktoriapark* (**h**), herb garden. *Volkspark Glienicke*, landscape park designed by Linnaeus.

WESTERSTEDE: (North) *Dietrich Hobbie's Garden* (**f**), midway between Oldenburg and Leer, just outside Westerstede, at 2911 Linswege. Telephone (04481) 2294. Thousands of rhododendrons, many developed by Herr Hobbie. End of May through June. Open to public.

WIESMOOR: (North) (**f**) Tour of flower fields, greenhouses. Ask Tourist Office in Bremen for details. See p. 163.

WUERZBURG: (Central) *Residenz* (Palace) garden (**f, r**) Dawn to dusk. Formal gardens; rose garden.

ZWEIBRUECKEN: (South) *Rosengarten* (**r, •**), one of finest rose gardens in Germany, best mid-June into early July; 60,000 bushes of 700 varieties, collection of Fr. roses. Newest ones in internatl. display each year.

IN EAST GERMANY: SANGERHAUSEN: (**r**) World-famous rose garden.

WHEEL TOURS

BREMEN as hub (North): Rastede, Oldenburg.

DUESSELDORF as hub (Central): Krefeld, Essen, Leverkusen, Koeln, Liblar, Bruehl.

FRANKFURT as hub (Central): Darmstadt, Aschaffenburg.

ETTLINGEN as hub (South): Hotel Erbprinz, best food in Germany. Karlsruhe, Rastatt, Baden-Baden, Pforzheim, Schwetzingen.

STUTTGART as hub (South): Ludwigsburg, Hohenheim, Tuebingen, Pforzheim.

MUENCHEN as hub (South): Bernried.

HOLLAND

Gardens marked with * are historically interesting land-scape gardens.

AALSMEER: *Seringen Park* (f), 7½ acres, scientific collection of lilacs, landscaped. *Flower Auction.*

AMERONGEN: *Renswoude,* 17th-cent. castle. Landscape garden.

AMSTERDAM: *Botanical Garden* (Hortus Botanicus) (b, c, f, g) established 1682; 3 acres, greenhouses include one for Victoria regia, blooms evenings late summer. Cacti, succulents, ferns. Cycad (Encephalartos Altensteinii) about 600 years old.

ARBORETUM POORT-BULTEN: See Oldenzaal.

ARBORETUM SCHOENHORST: See Putten.

ARBORETUM TROMPENBURG: See Rotterdam.

ARNHEM: *Sonsbeek,* 250 acres, landscape garden, 17th-cent., small water wheel. *Zijpendaal,* 150 acres, hunting lodge 1760, landscape garden, pools.

BAARN: *Cantonspark* (a, ar, b, f, g, ●), Botanical Garden, largest in Holland, 12½ acres. Large geographical rock garden, arboretum, greenhouse, over 1000 varieties orchids, plants from West Africa, Himalayas, etc.

BENNEBROEK: *De Hartekamp,* on the Herenweg; 70 acres. Early 19th-cent. landscape garden, orangerie, admission on request. *Linnaeushof* (a, ar, f, g, r, ●), Apr.–Oct., bulbs, perennials, etc.; see p. 153.

BOTANICAL GARDENS: See Amsterdam, Baarn, Groningen, Leyden, Utrecht, Wageningen.

BREDA: *Park Valkenbos,* 19th-cent. landscape garden; also Renaissance garden at castle.

BREUKELEN: *Gunterstein,* 19th-cent. landscape garden.

CANTONSPARK: See Baarn.

CLINGENDAAL: See Hague.

DE BEUKENHOF RESTAURANT: See Oegstgeest.

DELDEN: *Kasteel Twickel* (a, ar, f, r, ●), most beautiful flower garden in Holland; see p. 154.

DELFT: *Prinsenkelder Restaurant,* old formal garden.

DENEKAMP: (Overijssel) *Singraven,* mansion 1661, landscape garden with stream, double waterwheel of 1544.

DE WIERSEE: See Vorden.

DOORN: *Von Gimborn Arboretum* (a, ar, f, w, ●), 50 acres; about 620 kinds of conifers, flowering trees and shrubs. Large heath garden, water and bog garden, bamboos, ornamental grasses, rhododendrons, azaleas. Admission on request.

DRIEBERGEN: *Heidentuin,* 300 varieties heather, bloom all year.

EERDE: (Overijssel) Near Ommen, on right side of road from Ommen to Almelo, *castle,* landscape garden.

GEMEENTEMUSEUM: See Hague.

GOOR: (Overijssel) *Weldam.* Man-

For explanation of symbols and abbreviations, see inside back cover.

sion 1644 with moats, formal garden, yew hedges, landscape garden.

GRONINGEN: *Botanical Garden* (Hortus Botanicus) (**b, g**), Grote Rozenstraat 31. Open 9–12, 2–4, closed Sun. European wild plants, greenhouse, ferns. *Prinsenhof,*° small 15th-cent. walled garden, geometric design.

HAGUE: Nearby, *Clingendaal,* fine Japanese Garden, also landscape garden 140 acres. *Gemeentemuseum* (**f, w**), waterlily pools in front, flower borders in back, tea terr. *Peace Palace* (**f, r,** ●), rhododendrons, azaleas, rose garden, flower borders. *Rosarium* (**f, r**), Josef Israelsplein, fine rose garden, phlox and dahlias later. *Westbroekpark* (**f, r,** ●), roses and mixed flower borders; see p. 154. *Zuiderpark* (**ar, r**), entrance at Soestdyksekade. Over 1000 kinds ornamental trees and shrubs, rose garden.

HEERENVEEN: *Oranjewoud,*° 19th-cent. landscape garden.

HEIDENTUIN: See Driebergen.

HILLEGOM: *Restaurant Treslong* (**f**), beautiful spring bulbs.

HILVERSUM: *Pinetum Blydenstein* (**ar**), 5 acres; one of best collections of conifers on Continent.

KASTEEL DE GELDERSCHE TOREN: See Spankeren.

KASTEEL TWICKEL: See Delden.

KEUKENHOF: See Lisse.

LEERSUM: *Broekhuizen,*° on S side of road from Doorn to Leersum, near Hotel De Donderberg. 19th-cent. landscape garden, 600 acres, classical orangerie.

LEYDEN: *Botanical Garden,*° (Hortus Botanicus) (**ar, b, f, g, h**), 9–

12 weekdays, Sun. and hols. 9–12, 1:30–5. Oldest botanical garden in Holland, founded 1587 by Prof. Carolus Clusius of University of Leyden; see laburnum near entrance, planted 1601; 15 acres. Greenhouse for trop. plants, orchids, herbs. Old trees.

LINNAEUSHOF: See Bennebroek.

LISSE: *Keukenhof* (**f,** ●), superb bulb garden; see p. 152.

MAARSSEN: *Goudestein,*° 18th-cent. landscape garden.

MENCKEMABORG: See Uithuizen.

MIDDACHTEN: See Rheden.

OEGSTGEEST: (near The Hague) *De Beukenhof Restaurant* (**f**), lovely bulb garden. *Oud Pollgeest,*° 17th-cent. estate, 19th-cent. landscape garden, 23 acres.

OLDENZAAL: *Arboretum Poort-Bulten* (**ar, f**), near German border; 2542 varieties trees and shrubs, many conifers; European beech.

OVERVEEN: (near Haarlem) *Elswout,*° 19th-cent. house, park 1775, 200 acres.

PEACE PALACE: See Hague.

PINETUM BLYDENSTEIN: See Hilversum.

PRINSENHOF: See Groningen.

PRINSENKELDER RESTAURANT: See Delft.

PUTTEN: (Geld.) *Arboretum Schovenhorst,* near S end of Zuiderzee. Open Mar.–Nov.; 700 acres. Write for appointment. Testing conifers for use in Holland. (Douglas fir from Oregon found useful.) Seeds from country of origin sown in mixed groups.

RHEDEN: *Middachten,*° 19th-cent. Fr. garden in Le Nôtre style, 18th-cent. orangerie; 2500 acres. In summer, castle also open.

RIJPERKERK: *Vijversberg* (f, g),° between Groningen and Leeuwarden. Small 19th-cent. house, small park, parterre flower beds, greenhouses with orchids.

ROTTERDAM: *Arboretum Trompenburg* (ar, c, f, g, r, ●), Honingerdijk 64. Write for tickets to: Stichting Trompenburg, Groenewetering 46, Rotterdam. Mon.–Sat. 9–12, 1–5; 1000 varieties trees and shrubs from Europe, Africa, Asia, and America. Superb group of cedars, Atlas, Himalaya, Lebanon; 80 varieties oaks. Greenhouse with succulents, flower garden; rose garden. *Lijnbaan* (f), modern shopping area with flowers everywhere. *Zoo* (b, f, g), botanical section, greenhouses with orchids, trop. and subtrop. plants.

SERINGEN PARK: See Aalsmeer.

SLOCHTEREN: *Fraelemaborg*,° 18thcent. park; get tickets at Hotel Het Hogehuis.

SPANKEREN: *Kasteel de Geldersche Toren* (f), open only last weekend of July or first in Aug., for flower-arrangers' festival.

UITHUIZEN: *Menckemaborg* (r),° 15th-cent. estate; building is museum. Gardens with statues, sundial, rose garden.

UTRECHT: *Botanical Garden* (Hortus Botanicus) (b) Weekdays during business hours.

VALKENBOSCH: See Zeist.

VELP: (Geld.) *Biljoen*,° on right side of road from Velp to Dieren, just outside village. 16th-cent. castle with moats, landscape garden, ponds. *Rosendaal*,° 3 miles NE of Arnhem near village of Rosendaal. Formal 17th-cent. garden, shell-decorated cave, water jokes, statues, terr. In castle, Museum of the Internatl. Castle Institute.

VELSEN: *Beeckesteyn*,° 18th-cent. estate, formal landscape park 1774, pond, terr. *Groenendaal* and *Meerenberg*,° country house, 18th-cent. landscape garden, 225 acres.

VIJVERSBERG: See Rijperkerk.

VON GIMBORN ARBORETUM: See Doorn.

VOORSCHOTEN: *Duivenvoorde*,° Left side of Veurseweg from Voorburg to Voorschoten. Medieval hall altered in 1625. 18th-cent.-style garden, later park, 800 acres. Museum in house open in summer.

VORDEN: (near) *De Wiersee* (f, r),° between Vorden and Ruurlo. 650 acres park, rhododendrons, formal rose garden.

WAGENINGEN: *Botanical Garden and Belmonte Arboretum* (a, ar, b, f, r), 50 acres. Flowering shrubs, roses, rhododendrons, rock garden, fine trees.

WESTBROEKPARK: See Hague.

ZEIST: *Valkenbosch* (f), flowering shrubs and flower borders.

ZUIDERPARK: See Hague.

ZUILEN: *Castle*,° medieval, interesting interior, simple park.

Flower Parades (Bloemencorsos) and Flower Festivals

FRIESLAND: Lippenhuizen, last Sun. in Aug.

DRENTHE: Eelde-Paterswold, first Sat. in Sept. Frederiksoord, second Sat. in Sept.

GELDERLAND: Eibergen, mid-Aug., in odd years. Winterswijk, last Fri. and Sat. in Aug.

UTRECHT: Leersum, first or second Sat. in Aug.

NORTH HOLLAND: Aalsmeer, first Sat. in Sept.; wagons exhibited day before.

SOUTH HOLLAND: Hillegom, April 30, Children's Flower Parade, Kat-wijk aan Zee, about 3rd week in Aug. Leyden, first Sat. in Aug. Lisse, Apr. 30, Children's Flower Parade. Westland, about first week in Sept. Rotterdam, 3rd Sat. in Aug. Warmond, Apr. 30, Children's Flower Parade.

NORTH BRABANT: Valkenswaard near Eindhoven, 2nd Sun. in Sept. Zundert, first Sun. in Sept.

ZEELAND: Goes, 3rd Sat. in Sept.

IRELAND

(Counties are in parentheses.)

ADARE: (Limerick) *Dunraven Arms Hotel* (f, r), lovely garden. Also small front gardens of thatched cottages opposite.

ANNESGROVE: See Castletownroche.

ASHFORD: (Wicklow) *Mt. Usher* (ar, f, i, w, ●), property of Mr. R. B. Walpole; Mon.–Fri. 9–6, except hols. Buy booklet at entrance. Beautiful river garden, everything labeled. See p. 64.

BALLYOWEN HOUSE: See Drumbeg.

BANTRY: (Cork) *Bantry House*, daily except Sunday, 10–6. Ital. style, terr.

BELFAST: (Ulster) *Botanic Gardens* (a, b, f, g, r), daily from 7:30, at Stranmillis. Rock gardens, rose terr., greenhouses.

BIRR CASTLE: (Offaly) (ar, f, r, w, ●), Apr.–Sept., 2–6; Oct.–Mar., 2–5. Famous magnolias and other trees, flowers; see p. 62.

BOTANIC GARDENS: See Belfast, Dublin.

CASTLETOWNROCHE: (Cork) *Annesgrove* (a, ar, f, w, ●), Natl. Trust. Write or phone Mr. R. G. Annes-ley at Annesgrove, Castletownroche, Co. Cork, Ireland, for appointment. Walled garden, river garden; see p. 50.

CASTLEWELLAN: (Down) *Fota Island Garden* (ar), owned by Mr. Gerald Annesley; phone or write him for appointment. Fine arboretum, see p. 56.

COBH (pron. cove): (Cork) *Fota House* (ar, f), phone owners for appointment. Maj. and the Hon. Mrs. Bell, Fota House, Cohh, Co. Cork, Ireland. 18-acre arboretum, walled garden. See p. 49.

CREEVY ROCKS: See Saintfield.

DRUMBEG: (Down) *Ballyowen House* (f), private garden owned by Mrs. P. E. J. Anderson. Open once or twice a year; ask Natl. Trust office in Belfast for dates. (See "Useful Information," end of chapter on "Ireland.")

DUBLIN: (Dublin) *Glasnevin Botanical Gardens* (a, ar, b, f, g, ●), 47 acres; weekdays 9–6, Sun. 11–6; greenhouses weekdays 10–6, Sun.

2–6; 25,000 plants, flowering shrubs, dwarf conifers, orchids.

DUNRAVEN ARMS HOTEL: See Adare.

ENNISKERRY: (Wicklow) *Powerscourt* (ar, ●), Natl. Trust. Easter–Oct. daily 11–6. Fabulous terr. Ital. garden, Japanese garden; see p. 62.

FOTA HOUSE: See Cobh.

FOTA ISLAND GARDEN: See Castlewellan.

GARINISH ISLAND: See Glengarriff.

GLASNEVIN BOTANICAL GARDENS: See Dublin.

GLENGARRIFF: (Cork) *Garinish Island* (ar, f, ●), 19-acre garden. Hire motorboat to take you there, a 10-min. ride. Daily 10–5:30. Ital. garden, walled garden, etc. See p. 52.

GLEN VEAGH ESTATE: See Veagh.

HELEN'S BAY: (Down) *Guincho* (a, f), private garden of Mrs. Frazer Mackie, open once or twice a year; ask Natl. Trust in Belfast for dates (see "Useful Information," end of chapter on "Ireland"). See p. 60.

KILLARNEY: (Kerry) *Muckross House* (a, ar, f,), formal sunken garden, rock garden; rhododendrons behind house. Part of Vincent Memorial Park.

LEITRIM ESTATE: See Mulroy.

MITCHELLSTOWN: (Cork) *Mitchellstown Technical School* (f, r); fine rose garden July–Aug., then dahlias. See p. 51.

MT. CONGREVE: See Waterford.

MT. STEWART: See Newtownards.

MT. USHER: See Ashford.

MUCKROSS HOUSE: See Killarney.

MULROY: (Donegal) *Leitrim Estate* (f) Phone owner, Lady Leitrim, for appointment. Fine display of Hooker rhododendrons in May. Near Mulroy Bay, north of Letterkenny.

NEWTOWNARDS: (pron. newton-ards) *Mt. Stewart* (f, t, w, ●), Natl. Trust. Mon., Wed., Sat., Sun., and Bank Hols., 2–6. Buy booklet at entrance. Series of beautiful gardens; see p. 57. Also, *The Whins* (a), Tullynagardy, private garden of Capt. W. J. Miller, open a few days a year; ask at Natl. Trust in Belfast for dates (see "Useful Information," end of chapter on "Ireland"). Charming small rock gardens; see p. 61.

POWERSCOURT: See Enniskerry.

RATHFARNHAM: (Dublin) *Willbrook House* (a, f, ●) Write or phone owner, Lady Moore, for appointment. A garden of rare treasures, for the connoisseur.

RATHKEALE: (Limerick) *Community Garden* (f), on right side of highway going N to Limerick. Early bulbs; delightful varied planting of shrubs.

ROWALLANE: See Saintfield.

SAINTFIELD: (Down) *Creevy Rocks* (a, f), private garden of Maj. D. Anderson, open only a few days a year; ask Natl. Trust office in Belfast for dates (see "Useful Information," end of chapter on "Ireland"). Extensive rock plantings; see p. 61. Also *Rowallane*, (pron. row-allan) (a, ar, f, ●) Natl. Trust, daily 2–6 in Apr.–June; after that, Wed., Sat., Sun., and Bank Hols., 2–6. Especially fine in May, rhododendrons and azaleas. Walled garden, rock garden. See p. 58.

For explanation of symbols and abbreviations, see inside back cover.

TEMPO: (Fermanagh) *Wayside Shrub Demonstration* (a, f) of Pubble Park Nursery, Ministry of Agriculture. On route from Enniskillen toward Tempo. Fine rock garden, heathers, shrubs, all labeled.

TULLY: (Kildare) *Japanese Garden* at Tully House, daily 2–6 or by appointment. Best in May and Sept. Designed by a Japanese.

VEAGH: (Donegal) *Glen Veagh Estate* (pron. vay) (ar, f, w, •), NW of Letterkenny. Write to Estate Agent, Glen Veagh Estate, Veagh, Co. Donegal, Ireland, for permission to visit. Open only Wed. 3–5 in May, June, and July when owner is away. Owned by American Henry P. McIlhenny. See p. 54.

WATERFORD: (Waterford) *Mt. Congreve* (f, g •), Sun. 2:30–5:30, Apr.–Sept.; other days by phoning agent for appointment; phone Kilmeaden 15; 4 acres of gardens, music. See p. 51.

WHINS, THE: See Newtownards.

WILLBROOK HOUSE: See Rathfarnham.

————

CLOCKWISE CIRCLE TOUR OF IRELAND'S GARDENS: Cobh, Castletownroche, Waterford, Mitchellstown, Bantry, Glengarriff; Killarney; Rathkeale, Adare; Veagh, Mulroy; Tempo; Castlewellan, Saintfield, Newtownards, Belfast; Dublin, Rathfarnham, Enniskerry, Ashford, Tully, Birr.

WHEEL TOURS

CORK as hub (Cork): Castletownroche, Mitchellstown, Cobh.

CO. DOWN AREA: Stay at The Old Inn, Crawfordsburn (charm, wonderful food and service): Newtownards, Saintfield, Castlewellan, Belfast.

DUBLIN as hub: Rathfarnham, Enniserry, Ashford, Tully.

ITALY

To help you in locating towns on a map, each has been marked with its region in parentheses: North, Central, South, in the same groupings used in the chapter on "Italy."

AGLIÉ: (North) 21 mi. from Turin. *Park of Castello* (f), 17th-cent. garden, terr., flowers.

ALPINIA: See Stresa.

ARCUGNANO: (North) *Villa Pasini Salasco* (f); ask for permission. Formal, flowers.

ASSISI: (Central) *San Damiano Monastery* (f), charming cloister garden, flowers.

BAGNAIA: See Viterbo.

BASSANO DEL GRAPPA: (North) *Villa Bianchi Michiel.*

BISUSCHIO: See Lake Lugano.

BOBOLI GARDENS: See Florence.

BOTANICAL GARDENS: See Orto Botanico.

BREGANZA: (North) *Villa Diedo, Malvezzi* or *Tadini.*

≫ 268 ≪

BRISSAGO: See under "Switzerland" in "Key to Gardens."

CAGLIARI, SARDINIA: (South) *Orto Botanico* (**b, c**), Viale Fra Ignazio da Laconi 13. Closed Sun. and hols. Best Apr.–June. Succulents.

CAMERINO: (Central) between Rome and Florence. *Orto Botanico* (**b, f, g**), best June–Sept. Ornamental plants, greenhouse.

CAPRAROLA: (Central) north of Rome toward Viterbo. *Villa Farnese* (**f, ●**); 2 beautiful gardens; ask permission. Villa (most magnif. ever built in Italy) always open.

CAPRI, ISLAND OF: (South) At Anacapri, *Atrium of San Michele,* charming use of vines. At Capri, magnif. *gardens* of Augustus.

CARDUCCI GARDENS: See Perugia.

CASERTA: (South) Near Naples. *Royal Palace Gardens* (**●**), vast 18th-cent. garden, formal. Ask permission at any local tourist office.

CASTELGOMBERTO: (North) *Villa Piovene* or *Da Schio.*

CASTELLO: (North) Near Florence. *Villa Medici* (**f**), flower parterres.

CASTELLO DI URIO: See Lake Como.

CASTELLO MARCELLO GRIMANI GIUSTINIAN: See Montegalda.

COLLODI: (North) NE of Lucca. *Villa Garzoni* (**t, ●**), spectacular baroque garden, formal, topiaries. Nearby is children's "Pinocchio Garden."

COSTABISSARA: (North) *Villa Bissari,* Conte Dalle ore.

FLORENCE: (North) *Boboli Gardens;* see p. 197. *Giardini di Marignolle* (**f, g, i, w**), Via di Marignolle 65. Owned by Marchese Pierro Grossi. Greenhouses. Best May, June,

Sept. Open 9–12, 2–6. Anthurium, iris, orchids, water plants. *Iris Garden* (**i, ●**) (Giardino dell' Iris), Piazzale Michelangelo. End of Apr. through May; best May 5–20. Over 1000 varieties. See p. 193. *Orto Botanico* (**ar, b, g**), Via Lamarmora 4. Thurs., 9–12, 3–5:30. Best June–Sept. Collection of Cyadaceae, palms, agave, old Mediterranean trees. *Pitti Palace,* open daily; ask local tourist office, see Boboli Gardens above. *Villa Bellosguardo* (**f**), a Renaissance garden often on Florence Garden Tour. *Villa Capponi* (**f, t**), also on Garden Tour; flowers, topiaries. *Villa I Collazzi,* also on Garden Tour. *Villa La Pietra* (**●**), beautiful series of gardens, including green theater; also on Garden Tour. *Villa Palmieri,* extensive formal garden, delightful oval lemon garden; on Garden Tour. *Villa San Leonardo* or Villa Brocklebank; on Garden Tour. *Villa Torri di Gattaia;* on Garden Tour.

FRASCATI: (Central) Near Rome. *Villa Aldobrandini* (**●**), ask tourist office or local guide to get permission. Magnif. Baroque garden, well restored. *Villa Muti* (**f**), building now commercial, but small charming flower garden with box parterres.

GARDENS OF AUGUSTUS: See Capri.

GENOA: (South) *Orto Botanico Hanbury* (**ar, b, g**), open 8:30–12, 2:30–6; arboretum, flowers in pots, greenhouse. Ferns and Cyadaceae. *Park* has interesting flower bed designed as Columbus' three ships

For explanation of symbols and abbreviations, see inside back cover.

and anchors. *Villa Pallavicino* (f), vast formal garden, flowers.

GIARDINI DI MARIGNOLLE: See Florence.

GIUSTI GARDENS: See Verona.

IDANIA: See Lake Garda.

IRIS GARDEN: See Florence.

ISOLA BELLA: See Lake Maggiore.

ISOLA MADRE: See Lake Maggiore.

LA FAVORITA: See Palermo.

LAKE COMO: (North) at Urio, *Castello di Urio* (f); for permission ask Opus Dei, Via Alberto da Giussano, 6, Milan, Italy; or Opus Dei, Via Pompeo Magno, 9, Rome, Italy. Formal garden on three levels, parterre of colored pebbles, rose arbors. *Grand Hotel Serbelloni* (f), modern garden. *Villa di Balbianello* (f), near Lenno, open once a week; ask local tourist office; American owner. *Villa Carlotta* (ar, f), at Cadenabbia, famous for azaleas; see p. 189. *Villa D'Este Hotel* at Cernobbio, once home of Queen Caroline of England; fine terr. garden. *Villa Melzi* (ar, f, w, •) at San Giovanni, open certain days; ask tourist office in Bellagio. Exotic trees, spectacular azaleas; see p. 190. *Villa Monastero* (f), near Varenna, garden along lake, rare and exotic plants. *Villa Olmo,* spacious gardens. *Villa Passalacqua,* at Moltrasio, stately terr. gardens. *Villa Serbelloni* (f), open at certain times; ask tourist office in Bellagio. Profusion of flowers; see p. 190.

LAKE GARDA: (North) *Idania* (a, f, r, •), famous garden at Garda. Write Mrs. Ida Noble Borletti for permission to visit. Beautiful Eng. flower borders, rock and rose gardens, etc. See p. 191. *Villa Hruska* (a, f, g), at Gardone Riviera, famous rock garden of Dr. Arturo Hruska. Go by train to Desenzano, then 1½ hr. steamer. Or from spring to fall, quicker by hydrofoil boat or bus from Milan. Alp.; greenhouse.

LAKE LUGANO: (North) *Villa Cicogna* (•) near Bisuschio. Magnif. formal garden, water staircase, terr.

LAKE MAGGIORE: (North) *Isola Bella* (ar, f, g, •) 9–12, 1:30–5. Greenhouse closed Oct.–Mar. Spectacular island garden; 10 terraces; see p. 187. Best April and Sept. *Isola Madre* (ar, f, •) closed Oct.–March. Arboretum, rhododendrons, azaleas, etc. See p. 187. *Villa Taranto* (ar, f, •), at Verbania-Pallanza. Apr. through Oct.; 100 acres of flowers, exceptional; see p. 185.

LA MORTOLA: See Ventimiglia.

LONGARE: (North) *Villa Garzadori* or *Da Schio a Costozza.*

LONIGO: (North) *Villa Giovanelli* or *dei Gesuiti.*

LUCCA: (North) *Villa Reale de Marlia* (f, •), historic; see p. 195.

LUGO VINCENTINO: (North) *Villa Godi Valmarana* or *Malinverni a Lonedo;* weekdays 9:30–12, 4–7; Sun. 9:30–12. Fine, formal, *Villa Piovene Porto Godi a Lonedo.*

MILAN: (North) *La Fiorera,* Via Agnello 18, unusual flower shop, flower-arranging courses.

MIRAMAR: See Trieste.

MONTECCHIO MAGGIORE: (North) *Villa Cordellina* or *Lombardi.*

MONTEGALDA: (North) *Castello Marcello Grimani Giustinian.* Also *Villa Fogazzaro* or *Roi.*

MONTEGALDELLA: (North) *Villa Conti* or *Lampertico "La Delicioza"*.

MONTEVIALE: (North) *Villa Loschi* or *Zileri dal Verme a Biron*.

MUSSOLENTE: (North) *Villa Negri* or *Piovene Porto Godi*.

OROIANO: (North) *Villa Fracanzan* or *Piovene Porto Godi*.

ORTO BOTANICO: See Cagliari, Camerino, Florence, Genoa, Padua, Palermo, Pavia, Pisa, Torino, Trieste.

PADUA: (North) *Orto Botanico* (ar, b, f, ●), daily 9–12, 2–6. Closed Sun. and hols. Best Apr.–Sept. 6000 varieties of plants, ⅓ in greenhouses. Extensive, interesting also historically; see p. 193.

PALACE OF STUPINIGI: See Torino.

PALAZZO RUFOLO: See Ravello.

PALERMO, SICILY: (South) *La Favorita,* formal garden with arabesque parterres. *Orto Botanico* (ar, b, c, g, h, w, ●), best Apr.–Sept. Beautiful, lush, great variety; see p. 201. *Villa Igea Hotel,* Piazza Acquasanta; fine gardens.

PARADISIA: See Valnontey-Cogne.

PAVIA: (North) Orto Botanico (r), Via S. Epifanio 12. Sun. and hols. 9–12, 2–7. Best spring and fall. Specialty: roses.

PERUGIA: (Central) *Carducci Gardens.*

PIENZA: (North) *Piccolomini Castle* (f, r), open at certain times; ask local tourist office. Small, beautifully designed, 14th-cent. spectacular views, roses, flowering shrubs.

PINCIO GARDENS: See Rome.

PISA: (North) *Orto Botanico* (b, f, g), Via Luca Ghini 5. Open 8–12, 2–5. Best May, June, Sept. Green-house. Overgrown, old specimens from far countries. Ferns, orchids.

POMPEII: (South) Ask guide to show you the interesting reconstructed gardens.

RAVELLO: (South) *Palazzo Rufolo* (f), private but garden open to public. Unique surviving example of medieval secular garden.

ROMANO DI EZZELINO: (North) *Villa Cornaro.*

ROME: (Central) *Villa Aurelia* (t), at American Academy; ask an American student to obtain permission for you. Topiaries. Church of *Santi Quattro Coronati* (f), charming cloister garden. *Lateran,* cloister garden with roses, peonies. *Municipal Rose Garden* (Il Roseto all' Aventino) (r) Very fine, see p. 197. *Museo Nazionale,* cloister garden, with ancient cypress near central basin perhaps planted by Michelangelo. *Pincio Garden* (ar, f), immense old trees, flower beds, flowering shrubs. *Protestant Cemetery* (f), in San Paolo district. Lovely garden where Keats and Shelley are buried; roses, jasmine, carnations. *St. Paul's Without the Walls,* cloister garden. *Spanish Steps* (f), massed azaleas at Easter; other seasonal flowers, beautiful effect. *Vatican Gardens* (f, t, ●), get permission from the Segreteria della Commissione Pontificia per la Città Vaticano, telephone 555.-251. Beautiful parterres of flowers, topiaries. *Villa Barberini* at Castelgondolfo, can drive around grounds in car. *Villa Borghese* (ar, f, ●), magnif. formal gardens, flower parterres, borders; masses of

For explanation of symbols and abbreviations, see inside back cover.

cinerarias, azaleas, etc. Many trees labeled. *Villa Celimontana,* fine avenues of pines, palms. *Villa di Papa Giulio,* especially lovely when floodlit for ballets, etc. *Villa Doria Pamphilj* (**a, f, ●**), open ten days in Oct. for chrysanthemum display; also beautiful perennials and rock garden. Arabesque parterres. *Villa Medici* (**f**), on Pincio Hill. Open to public Wed. and Sat. afternoons. Fine example of 16th-cent. garden; flower parterres. *Villa Sciarra,* or *Wurts,* now a public park; floral displays here sometimes.

ROSA: (North) *Villa Dolfin Boldù.*

ROYAL PALACE GARDENS: See Caserta.

SAN DAMIANO MONASTERY: See Assisi.

SAN DOMENICO HOTEL: See Sicily.

SANTI QUATTRO CORONATI: See Rome.

SARDINIA: See Cagliari.

SCHIAVON: (North) *Villa Chiericati, Mugna* or *Tamaro a Longa.*

SETTIGNANO: (North) near Florence. *Villa di Castello.* Beautifully restored Renaissance garden, terr., parterres, orangeries. *Villa Gamberaia* (**f, ●**), lovely, formal garden of 17th cent. See p. 194. *Villa I Tatti,* former property of Bernard Berenson, now owned by Harvard. Fine modern garden in spirit of old Ital. villa gardens. *Villa La Petraia,* a magnif. fountain, winding canal, 400-year-old oak.

SICILY: (South) At Taormina, *San Domenico Hotel* (**f**), former monastery, lovely flower gardens. Also gardens at *Greek Theater,* and at *Hotel Timeo.*

SPANISH STEPS: See Rome.

STRÀ: (North) *Villa Pisani,* 18th-cent., long canal, fine vistas, maze.

STRESA: (North) *Alpinia* (**a, f**), along highway above town. Best May–Sept. Fine alp. garden, 2000 small and 1000 woody varieties.

TIVOLI: (Central) Outside Rome. *Villa d'Este* (**●**), famous for many fountains, cascades. Floodlit. See p. 199.

TORINO: (North) *Orto Botanico* (**b**), Viale Mattioli 25. Open 9–12, 2–6. Best May–Sept. 3000 varieties. Greenhouse. *Palace of Stupinigi,* belongs to Order of San Naurizio; open to public. Formal Fr. garden, maze.

TRIESTE: (North) *Civico Orto Botanico* (**b, g**), Via Marchesetti 2. Sun. 9–12, 2–6; hols. 9–1. Best Apr.–June. Plants of Adriatic area. Greenhouse. *Miramar* (**ar, r**), designed by Archduke Maximilian of Austria. Exotic trees, formal garden, rose garden.

TRISSINO: (North) *Villa Trissino Marzotto;* large pool, long avenues, gardens.

VALNONTEY-COGNE: (North) just S of Aosta; take bus or train to Cogne, then on foot or by car about 1½ mi.; 5100 ft. alt. *Paradisia* (**a**), Alpine Garden of the national park Gran Paradiso. Open June–Sept., 8–12:30, 2–6:30. Best June and July. Plants from W Alps.

VALSANZIBIO: (North) *Villa Barbarigo;* private, but can get permission at tourist office in Padua or other cities. Beautiful Fr.-style gardens, superb views.

VATICAN GARDENS: See Rome.

VENTIMIGLIA: (North) *La Mortola* (**ar, f, h, ●**), garden of Villa Hanbury. Glorious trop. garden; see p. 184.

VERONA: (North) *Giusti Gardens* (f), formal garden, some flowers, some of oldest cypresses in Italy.

VICENZA: (North) *Villa Capra* or *Valmarana "La Rotonda." Villa Ghislanzoni* or *Curti a Bertesina. Villa Guiccioli* or *Museo del Risorgimento. Villa Imperiali* or *Lampertico ad Anconetta. Villa Rinaldi "La Commenda." Villa Valmarana "Ai Nani."*

VILLA ALDOBRANDINI: See Frascati.

VILLA AURELIA: See Rome.

VILLA BARBARIGO: See Valsanzibio.

VILLA BARBERINI: See Rome.

VILLA BELLOSGUARDO: See Florence.

VILLA BIANCHI MICHIEL: See Bassano del Grappa.

VILLA BISSARI: See Costabissara.

VILLA BORGHESE: See Rome.

VILLA CAPPONI: See Florence.

VILLA CAPRA: See Vicenza.

VILLA CARLOTTA: See Lake Como.

VILLA CELIMONTANA: See Rome.

VILLA CHIERICATI: See Schiavon.

VILLA CICOGNA: See Lake Lugano.

VILLA CONTI: See Montegaldella.

VILLA CORDELLINA: See Montecchio Maggiore.

VILLA CORNARO: See Romano di Ezzelino.

VILLA D'ESTE: See Tivoli.

VILLA D'ESTE HOTEL: See Lake Como.

VILLA DI BALBIANELLO: See Lake Como.

VILLA DI CASTELLO: See Settignano.

VILLA DIEDO: See Breganze.

VILLA DI PAPA GIULIO: See Rome.

VILLA DOLFIN BOLDÙ: See Rosa.

VILLA DORIA PAMPHILJ: See Rome.

VILLA FARNESE: See Caprarola.

VILLA FOGAZZARO: See Montegalda.

VILLA FRACANZAN: See Oroiano.

VILLA GAMBERAIA: See Settignano.

VILLA GARZADORI: See Longare.

VILLA GARZONI: See Collodi.

VILLA GHISLANZONI: See Vicenza.

VILLA GIOVANELLI: See Lonigo.

VILLA GODI VALMARANA: See Lugo Vicentino.

VILLA GUICCIOLI: See Vicenza.

VILLA HRUSKA: See Lake Garda.

VILLA I COLLAZZI: See Florence.

VILLA IGEA HOTEL: See Palermo.

VILLA IMPERIALI: See Vicenza.

VILLA I TATTI: See Settignano.

VILLA LA PETRAIA: See Settignano.

VILLA LA PIETRA: See Florence.

VILLA LANTI DI BAGNAIA: See Viterbo.

VILLA LOSCHI: See Monteviale.

VILLA MEDICI: See Castello; Rome.

VILLA MELZI: See Lake Como.

VILLA MONASTERO: See Lake Como.

VILLA MUTI: See Frascati.

VILLA NEGRI: See Mussolente.

VILLA OLMO: See Lake Como.

VILLA PALLAVICINO: See Genoa.

VILLA PALMIERI: See Florence.

VILLA PASINI SALASCO: See Arcugnano.

VILLA PASSALACQUA: See Lake Como.

VILLA PIOVENE: See Castelgomberto.

VILLA PIOVENE PORTO GODI A LONEDO: See Lugo Vicentino.

VILLA PISANI: See Strà.

VILLA REALE DE MARLIA: See Lucca.

VILLA RINALDI "LA COMMENDA": See Vicenza.

VILLA SAN LEONARDO: See Florence.

VILLA SCIARRA or WURTS: See Rome.

VILLA SERBELLONI: See Lake Como.

VILLA TARANTO: See Lake Maggiore.

VILLA TORRI DI GATTAIA: See Florence.

VILLA TRISSINO MARZOTTO: See Trissino.

VILLA VALMARANA "AI NANI": See Vicenza.

VITERBO: *Villa Lante di Bagnaia* (●), open at certain times; ask local tourist office. Beautifully designed and restored, 17th-cent.

WHEEL TOURS

See lists for LAKE COMO; LAKE GARDA; LAKE LUGANO; LAKE MAGGIORE.

VICENZA as hub: Arcugnano, Bassano del Grappa, Breganze, Castelgomberto, Costabissara, Longare, Lonigo, Lugo Vicentino, Montecchio Maggiore, Montegalda, Monteviale, Mussolente, Oroiano, Romano di Ezzelino, Rosa, Schiavon, Trissino. For details and hours, ask for the Marchese Giuseppe Roi, president of the regional tourist office, Ente Provinciale per il Turismo, Piazza Duomo 5, Vicenza.

FLORENCE as hub: Castello, Collodi, Lucca, Settignano.

ROME as hub: Frascati, Tivoli.

NAPLES as hub: Caserta, Pompeii, Ravello.

MONACO

MONTE CARLO: *Exotic Garden* (c), extraordinary collection of cacti and succulents; see p. 149. *Casino Gardens* (ar, c, f), among oldest subtrop. gardens of Riviera. Palms, water gardens, cacti, flowering trees, sunken garden with large flower beds. On Mont Agel, 2500 ft. alt., *Alpine Botanical Garden* (a), around Monte Carlo Golf Club.

NORWAY

Write to the Norwegian Horticultural Society (Det Norske Hagelskap, Motzfeldtsgate 1,V,Oslo, Norway) for introductions to visit interesting gardens on private estates.

ARBORETUM: See Vollebek.

BERGEN: *Botanical Garden* (a, b, f), a public park, with general and alp. collections. Many primulas, lilies, heathers, rhododendrons, etc. Best May and June.

BOTANICAL GARDENS: See Bergen, Oslo.

KONGSVOLL: In the Dovre Mountains. *Kongsvoll Alpine Garden* (a, f), 1800 ft. alt. Many rare and interesting alp. Best beginning of June, end of July.

MOLDE: This is called the "Rose City"; see their parks.

OSLO: *Botanical Garden* (a, ar, b, f, g), Trondheimsveien 23. Weekdays 7–6, Sun. 10–6, except Wed. only until 3. In summer open until 10 P.M. Greenhouses: May through

Aug., Sun., Tues., Fri., 12–3. Sept. through April, Wed. 6–8. Alpine flowers of Norway, about 2300 species outdoors. 1000 trop. and subtrop. in the 2 greenhouses. Rock garden of plants from Asia and North America. Large arboretum.

In one greenhouse: rice, sugarcane, tea, coco, bananas, citrus fruits, various spices, Victoria regia. Landscaped, terr., pool.

VOLLEBEK: *Arborteum* and park, Norw. Hort. College (ar).

PORTUGAL

Gardens marked with * are historic, for students of Portuguese gardens. Ask for permission at local tourist office or garden itself.

ARRABIDA: *Conventinho* * (16th-cent.)

BARCELOS: (N of Oporto) (f) Fine *Municipal Gardens.*

BEMFICA: (suburb of Lisbon) (f, ●) *Casa de Marquês de Fronteira,* formal 17th-cent. garden and tiling; see p. 221. Ask at Lisbon Tourist Office whether open reg., or only by telephoning for permission.

BOTANICAL GARDENS: See Coimbra, Lisbon, Oporto.

BRAGA: *Casa dos Biscaínhos* * (17th-18th-19th-cent.) *Bom Jesus do Monte* * (17th-18th-19th-cent.)

CARTAXO: *Os Chavões* (17th-cent.)

CASTELO BRANCO: (E of Leiria) (●) *Episcopal Palace Garden,* formal; see p. 226. Also garden, *Belvedere of S. Gens.*

COIMBRA: *Cerca de Santa Cruz de Bussaco* * (17th-18th-19th-cent). *Cerca de Convento de Santa Cruz* * (18th-cent.). *Jardim Botânico,* lovely gardens, fine trees; see p. 228. *Conimbriga* * (before 5th cent.). *Jardim da Manga* * (16th-cent.). *Portugal dos Peque-*

ninos, The Children's Portugal, miniature plantings; see p. 226.

CRYSTAL PALACE: See Oporto.

ENGLISH CEMETERY: See Lisbon.

EPISCOPAL PALACE: See Castelo Branco.

ESTRELA PARK: See Lisbon.

ESTUFA FRIA: See Lisbon.

FOREST OF BUSSACO: (N of Coimbra) (ar) Marvellous forest preserve; S entrance from Penacova, N one from Luso; see p. 228. *Palace Hotel* (f) in forest, deluxe, fine gardens; see p. 228.

JARDIM BOTÂNICO: See Coimbra, Lisbon, Oporto.

JARDIM COLONIALE DO ULTRAMAR: See Lisbon.

LISBON: *English Cemetery* (ar, f) near Jardim da Estrela; climbing geraniums, trees. *Estufa Fria* (ar, g, ●), unique open-air greenhouse, see p. 220. *Jardim Botânico da Faculdade de Ciências* (ar, f), exotic park, labeled plants. *Jardim Coloniale do Ultramar* (ar, w), at Belem suburb, plants of the colonies, see p. 222. *Jardim da Estrela* (f), flower beds. *Royal Park of*

Ajuda (**ar**), 300 years old; arboretum. *Tapada da Ajuda* (**ar, f**), botanical garden. *Zoological Garden* (**r**), rose garden, water garden.

LOURES: *Quinta do Correio Mor* * (17th-cent.). *Quinta dos Pinteus* * (18th-cent.).

MANGUALDE: *Casa de Mangualde* * (19th-cent.). *Quinta da Ínsua* * (18th-19th-cent.).

MARGARIDE: *Casa de Simaes* * (17th-cent.).

MONSERRATE: See Sintra.

OEIRAS: *Quinta e Palácio do Marquês* * (18th-cent.).

OPORTO: (Sometimes called Porto) *Crystal Palace* (**r**), fine rose garden. *Jardim Botânico* (**f, r**), includes formal garden, flowers, see p. 230. *Jardim dos Viscondes de Villar d'Allen* * (19th-cent.). *Quinta da Meio* (**ar, f, •**), private garden; write Miss M. R. Tait, 219 Rua Entre Quintas, Oporto, Portugal, for permission to visit. Wonderful English flower garden, see p. 229. *Quinta da Prelada* * (18th-cent.). *Quinta de Freixo* * (18th-cent.). *Villa Nova de Gaya* (**ar, f, •**), private garden, write to Conde Campo Bello, Villa Nova de Gaya, Oporto, Portugal, for permission to visit. Marvelous camellias and unusual trees. See p. 230.

PALÁCIO DA PENA: See Sintra.

PENACOVA: (S of Forest of Bussaco) (**f**) Elaborate *Municipal Garden.*

PORTUGAL DOS PEQUENINOS: See Coimbra.

QUELUZ: (near Lisbon) (**f, •**) *Royal Palace* gardens, beautiful, formal 18th-cent.; flowers: see p. 223.

QUINTA DA BACALHOA: See Villa Fresca de Azeitao.

QUINTA DA MEIO: See Oporto.

SINTRA: *Casa dos Ribafrias* * (16th-cent.). *Convento dos Capuchos* * (16th-cent.). *Monserrate* (**ar, •**), wonderful park of fine trees, and tree ferns (18th-19th-cent.). *Paco Real da Vila* * (11th-19th-cent.). *Palácio da Pena* (**ar, f**), over 400 species of trees, flowering shrubs; sunken garden (16th-19th-cent.). *Palácio de Seteais* * (18th-19th-cent.). *Parque de Dr. Oliveira Salazar* (**ar, f**) trees, flowers. *Quinta da Penha Verde* * (16th-cent.).

TAPADA DA AJUDA: See Lisbon.

TIBÃES: *Convento* * (11th-18th-cent.).

TORRES NOVAS: (N of Santarem) (**f**) Fine *Municipal Garden.*

TORRES VEDRAS: *Quinta das Lapas* * (17th-cent.). *Solar do Espanhol* * (17th-cent.).

VILLA FRESCA DE AZEITAO: (25 mi. S of Lisbon on road to Setubal) *Quinta da Bacalhoa* (**f, •**), private garden, write to Mrs. Herbert Scoville (an American), Quinta de Bacalhoa, Villa Fresca de Azeitao, Portugal, for permission to visit. Lovely restored gardens, see p. 223.

VILLA NOVA DE GAYA: See Oporto.

VILLA VICOSA: *Paco dos Duques de Braganca* * (17th-cent.).

VIZEU: *Paco do Fantelo* (16th-17th-cent.).

WHEEL TOUR

From Lisbon, visit Queluz, Sintra, Villa Fresca de Azeitao.

SCOTLAND

For up-to-date information about days and hours of admission, see the booklet, *Historic Houses, Castles and Gardens*, mentioned in "Useful Information," end of chapter on "England."

ABERDEEN: (Aberdeen) *Cruikshank Botanic Garden* (**a, g**), St. Machar Dr., Old Aberdeen. Alp., greenhouses. *Parks* (**r**), are famous for roses. At Drumoak, just W of Aberdeen, is *Drum Castle* (**ar, f**); reg. days, June–Aug. Rare flowering shrubs and trees, water garden.

ACHAMORE: See Isle of Gigha.

AIRLIE CASTLE: See Kirriemuir.

AN CALA: See Easdale, Isle of Seil.

BALLATER: (Aberdeen) *Balmoral Castle* (**ar, f**), May–July only, reg. days, when Royal Family not in residence. Queen Mary's sunken garden; rare trees.

BANCHORY: (Kinc.) *Crathes Castle* (pron. crath-ease) (**ar, f, r, ●**), Natl. Trust, reg. days. Wonderful trees, flower gardens; see p. 114.

BENMORE, THE YOUNGER BOTANIC GARDEN: See Dunoon.

BIRKINSHAW: See Traquair.

BLACKHILLS: See Elgin.

BOTANIC GARDENS: See Aberdeen, Dunoon, Edinburgh, Glasgow, St. Andrews.

BRODICK CASTLE: See Isle of Arran.

CALLANDER: (Perth.) *Roman Camp Hotel* (**f**), delightful formal parterre garden.

CASTLE DOUGLAS: (Kirk.) *Threave School of Practical Gardening* (**f, g**), Natl. Trust. Gardens open daily all year, 9 to dusk. Walled garden and greenhouses.

CAWDOR: (Nairn) *Cawdor Castle* (**f, w, ●**), special days only. Lovely flower garden. See p. 118.

CRARAE LODGE: See Minard.

CRATHES CASTLE: See Banchory.

CRIEFF: (Perth.) *Drummond Castle* (**t**), reg. days. Formal Ital.; topiary; see p. 111.

CULLEN: (Banff.) *Cullen House* (**ar, f**), reg. days. Fine trees, rhododendrons.

CULROSS (pron. coo-ross): (Fife) *Palace* (**f**), small charming garden.

CULZEAN CASTLE: See Maybole.

DIRLETON: (East Lothian) W of N. Berwick. *Dirleton Castle* (**f**), week days 10–7, Sun. 2–7. Attractive flower gardens with 17th-cent. bowling green, ancient yews.

DRUM CASTLE: See Aberdeen.

DRUMMOND CASTLE: See Crieff.

DUNBLANE: (Perth.) *Keir* (**f, w**), near Stirling Castle. Reg. days, G.S. Spring bulbs, rhododendrons, azaleas, flower borders, water garden, woodland garden.

DUNFERMLINE: (Kin.) *Pittencrieff Glèn* (**a, f, g**), public garden donated by Andrew Carnegie.

DUNOON: (Arg.) *Eckford* (**f**); reg. days Apr.–June, G.S. Daffodils, rhododendrons. Also *Benmore, The Younger Botanic Garden* (**a, ar, b, f, w**), 7 mi. N of Dunoon. Rare trees, shrubs, plants, fine rhododendrons; formal, water, and rock gardens.

DUNS: (Berw.) *Manderston* (f, g), special days. Narcissus, rhododendrons, sunken garden, greenhouse.

EARLSHALL: See Leuchars.

EASDALE, ISLE OF SEIL: (Arg.) (a, ar, f, r, w) *An Cala,* reg. days, G.S. Azaleas, cherry trees, roses; rock and water gardens.

ECKFORD: See Dunoon.

EDINBURGH: (pron. Edin-boro) (Midloth.) *Prestonfield House* (r), hotel with large garden of tree roses, late June. *Royal Botanical Garden* (ar, a, b, f, g, w, •), Inverleith Row; 60 acres; weekdays 9 to sunset, Sun. 11 to sunset; greenhouses weekdays 1–5, Sun. 11–5. World-famous, especially rock garden, see p. 109. Also *Floral Clock,* in park on Princes Street.

EDZELL: (Angus) *Edzell Castle* (f) regular days. Unique formal patterned garden of 1604. See p. 113.

ELGIN: (Moray) *Blackhills* (f), private garden, special days; species rhododendrons.

FALKLAND: (Fife) *Falkland Palace* (a, ar, f, r, •), reg. days, Natl. Trust. Glorious flower garden; see p. 111.

FINLAYSTONE: See Glasgow.

FORRES: (Moray) *Kinkorth* (f, r), reg. days, G.S. Roses, mixed borders.

GLAMIS: (Angus) *Glamis Castle* (f), reg. days. Formal gardens, yew hedges, park. See p. 113.

GLASGOW: (Glasgow) *Botanic Gardens* (a, b, f, g, h), daily 7 to dusk; most greenhouses 1–4:45. Herb, rock, and woodland gardens; ferns,

orchids, trop. plants. Near here at Langbank (Renfrew), 2½ mi. from Port Glasgow, *Finlaystone* (a, ar, f, w), special days. Azaleas, flower borders, ancient yew; see p. 124.

GLENARN: See Rhu.

GORDON: (Berw.) *Mellerstain* (f, r), reg. days. Ital. garden, fine collection of old and modern roses.

GUTHRIE: (Angus) *Guthrie Castle* (f, r), reg. days. Lovely flower gardens, roses; see p. 113.

HUMBIE: (E. Lothian) *Johnstounburn Hotel* (f), SE of Edinburgh. Lovely gardens.

INSCH: (Aberdeen) *Williamston* (f), reg. days, G.S. Flower borders, shrubs, woodland garden.

INVERESK LODGE: See Musselburgh.

INVEREWE: See Poolewe.

ISLE OF ARRAN: (Bute) 17 mi. off Ayrshire coast. *Brodick Castle* (ar, f, r, •), Natl. Trust, reg. days. Beautiful gardens, rare trees and shrubs; see p. 123.

ISLE OF GIGHA: (Arg.) *Achamore* (ar, f, r). Take bus from Glasgow to Tayinloan, ferry by request, phone two hours in advance, Gigha 217; or steamer from West Loch Tarbert. Reg. days. Extensive, lovely. See p. 123.

JOHNSTOUNBURN HOTEL: See Humbie.

KEIR: See Dunblane.

KENNETHMONT: (Aberdeen) *Leith Hall* (a, f), reg. days, Natl. Trust. Famous flower borders, rock garden; see p. 116.

KINKORTH: See Forres.

KINROSS: (Kin.) *Kinross House* (f, r), special days only. Fine borders, rose garden.

KIRRIEMUIR: (Angus) *Airlie Castle* (t), near Craigton; ask for appointment from owner, Earl of Airlie, Airlie Castle, Craigton. Topiaries representing battle of Waterloo.

LEITH HALL: See Kennethmont.

LEUCHARS: (Fife) *Earlshall* (f, t), special days only. Topiaries, flower gardens.

LOGAN GARDENS: See Port Logan.

MANDERSTON: See Duns.

MAYBOLE: (Ayr.) *Culzean Castle* (ar, f, r, ●), Natl. Trust, reg. days. Beautiful gardens, rare trees; see p. 125.

MELLERSTAIN: See Gordon.

MINARD: (Arg.) 10 mi. SW of Inveraray. *Crarae Lodge* (ar, f, ●), daily dawn to dusk. Bus from Glasgow goes to door. Wonderful glen garden and arboretum; see p. 121.

MUSSELBURGH: (Midloth.) NE of Edinburgh. *Inveresk Lodge* (f), reg. days.

PENCAITLAND: (E. Loth.) E of Ormiston. *Winton Castle* (ar, f), special days or by appointment with owner, Sir David Ogilvy. Daffodils, terr. gardens, fine trees.

PITMEDDEN HOUSE: See Udney.

PITTENCRIEFF GLEN: See Dunfermline.

POOLEWE: (Ross and Cromarty) *Inverewe* (a, ar, f, w, ●), weekdays 10 to dusk, Sun. 1 to dusk. Natl. Trust. Fabulous subtrop. garden; see p. 119.

PORT LOGAN: (Wig.) *Logan Gardens* (a, ar, f, ●), reg. days. Lovely subtrop. garden; see p. 125.

PRESTONFIELD HOUSE: See Edinburgh.

RHU: (Dunbarton) *Glenarn* (a, f), reg. days. Over 500 different rhododendrons, other shrubs, flowers, rock garden.

ROMAN CAMP HOTEL: See Callander.

ROYAL BOTANICAL GARDEN: See Edinburgh.

ST. ANDREWS: (Fife) *Rufflets Hotel* (f), lovely gardens. *University Botanical Garden* (a, c, f, g), closed Sat. afternoon and Sun. Alp., plants from Himalayas, cacti, succulents.

STIRLING: (Stirling) *Stirling Castle* (f), garden.

TARBERT: (Arg.) *Stonefield Castle Hotel* (f), fine rhododendrons.

THREAVE SCHOOL OF PRACTICAL GARDENING: See Castle Douglas.

TRAQUAIR: (Peeble.) *Birkinshaw* (f), near Innerleithen, reg. days. Small hillside garden, views.

UDNEY: (Aberdeen) *Pitmedden House* (f, r, ●), daily 9:30 to dusk, Natl. Trust. Reconstructed 17th-cent. garden; see p. 117.

UNIVERSITY BOTANICAL GARDEN: See St. Andrews.

WILLIAMSTON: See Insch.

WINTON CASTLE: See Pencaitland.

WHEEL TOURS (See Map I)

EDINBURGH as hub: Musselburgh, Pencaitland, Dirleton, Humbie, Traquair, Gordon, Dunfermline, Kinross, Falkland, St. Andrews, Culross, Stirling, Leuchars.

DUNFERMLINE as hub: Dunblane, Callander, Crieff, Kinross, Falkland, Leuchars, St. Andrews, Stirling, Culross, Musselburgh, Dirleton, Pencaitland, Humbie.

For explanation of symbols and abbreviations, see inside back cover.

DUNDEE as hub: Crieff, Glamis, Kirriemuir, Guthrie, Edzell, Leuchars, St. Andrews, Falkland, Kinross.

ABERDEEN as hub: Banchory, Kennethmont, Cullen, Forres, Cawdor.

ELGIN as hub: Kennethmont, Cullen, Forres, Cawdor.

GLASGOW as hub: Dunoon, Rhu, Callander, Dunblane, Stirling, Culross.

SPAIN

ALCAZABA: See Málaga.

ALCÁZAR: See Sevilla.

ALFABIA: See Majorca.

ALGECIRAS: *Hotel Reina Cristina* (f), flower garden.

ALHAMBRA: See Granada.

ANDALUCÍA PALACE HOTEL: See Sevilla.

ANDÚJAR: (NE of Córdoba) *Palace of Carlos III* (r), Fr. type, formal, roses.

ARANJUEZ: (S of Madrid) *Palacio Real* (ar, f, r, ●), Ital. gardens, roses, flowers, fine trees. See p. 216.

BARCELONA: *Jardín Botánico* (ar, b, c, f), daily 10–2. Arboretum, plants from Balearic Islands, North Africa, Morocco. *Parque de la Ciudadela* (f), flower beds. *Parque de Montjuich,* formal Ital., fountains, illumination. *Plaza de Cataluña,* formal gardens, cascades. *Rambla de San José* (f), flower markets, mornings. *Restaurant Miramar* (f), near Parque de Montjuich, gardens.

BLANES: (Costa Brava) *Marimurtra, Jardín Botánico* (a, b, c, f, w, ●), daily 9–7. Height of bloom May–June. See p. 203. *Pinya de Rosa* (c), private garden of Don Fernando Rivière-Caralt. Phone Mr. Rivière for permission to visit. Entirely cacti and succulents.

BOTANICAL GARDENS: See Jardín Botánico.

CANARY ISLANDS: At Orotava, *Jardín de Aclimitación* (ar, b, c, f), 220 varieties from 80 plant families, including 30 different palms. At Tenerife, *Icod de los Vinos* (ar), dragon tree (Dracaena draco) 3000 years old.

CÓRDOBA: *Casa de Don Gome* (f), Calle de Santa Isabel, 14 flower-filled patios; see p. 213. *Las Ermitas* (Hermitages) (f) Flower gardens; see p. 213. *Museo Arqueológico Provincial* (f), Calle Comedias. Flower-filled patio. *Museo Provincial de Bellas Artes* (Fine Arts Museum) Patio with pebble mosaic. *Museo Romero de Torres;* ask permission there to see the formal Renaissance gardens, semitrop. *Parador la Arruzafa* (hotel), on outskirts, terr. gardens. *Sementales Barracks* (r), tree roses.

DUKE OF ALBA'S GARDEN: See Sevilla.

ELCHE: (S coast) *El Palmeral* (ar), fabulous palm grove; see p. 208. *Huerto del Cura* (Curate's Garden (ar).

EL ESCORIAL: (W of Madrid) *San Lorenzo* (f, r, ●), fabulous formal gardens, 88 fountains, roses; see p. 216.

EL PALMERAL: See Elche.

GENERALIFE: See Granada.

GRANADA: *Alhambra* and *Generalife* (f, r, •), finest gardens in Spain, see p. 210. *Parador de San Francisco,* hotel in the Alhambra; patio garden. *Parque de Alhambra* (ar), elms planted by Wellington.

HOTEL BAHIA PALACE: See Majorca.

HOTEL FORMENTOR: See Majorca.

HOTEL REINA CRISTINA: See Algeciras.

HUERTO DEL CURA: See Elche.

ICOD DE LOS VINOS: See Canary Islands.

JARDÍN BOTÁNICO: See Barcelona, Blanes, Madrid.

JARDÍN DE ACLIMATACIÓN: See Canary Islands.

JARDÍNES DEL REAL or VIVEROS: See Valencia.

JARDÍN DE MONFORTE: See Valencia.

JARDÍN REAL: See Madrid.

LA GRANJA: (•) (7 mi. from Segovia) at 3795 ft. alt. One of finest gardens in Spain; formal Fr.; fountain display Thurs. at 5 P.M. See p. 216.

LAS ERMITAS: See Córdoba.

MADRID: *Ciudad Universitaria* (University City); formal gardens. *Jardín Botánico* (ar, b, c, f, •), Plaza de Murillo near the Prado. Best Apr.–July. About 30 acres; 30,000 varieties of trees and plants. See p. 215. *Jardín Real* (Royal Garden), clipped formal hedges. *Parque del Oeste* (r), fine rose garden; see p. 215. *Parque del Retiro* (r), small rose garden.

MADRID HOTEL: See Sevilla.

MAJORCA: Gardens at *Alfabia, Hotel Bahia Palace* at Palma; *Hotel Formentor* at Formentor; at *Raxa;* and at *Valldemosa,* see p. 207.

MÁLAGA: *Alcazaba* (f), subtrop. flower gardens. *Parque de Puerta Oscura* (f), along the waterfront. See p. 210.

MARIA LUISA PARK: See Sevilla.

MARIMURTRA: See Blanes.

PALACE OF CARLOS III: See Andújar.

PALACIO REAL: See Aranjuez.

PARADOR DE SAN FRANCISCO: See Granada.

PARADOR LA ARRUZAFA: See Córdoba.

PARQUE DE MONTJUICH: See Barcelona.

PINYA DE ROSA: See Blanes.

RAXA: See Majorca.

RONDA: (W of Málaga) Home of *Marqués de Salvatierre,* garden open to public.

SAN LORENZO: See El Escorial.

SANTA CLOTILDE: (N of Blanes near Lloret de Mar) Gardens of Marqueses de *Santa Clotilde* (ar); unique; thousands of cypresses, terr.

SEVILLA: *Alcázar* (f, •), fascinating gardens; see p. 214. *Andalucía Palace Hotel,* gardens. *Duke of Alba's garden* (f), charming; flowers. *Madrid Hotel* (f, r), Menendez Peleyo 2. See amusing garden story, p. 213. *Maria Luisa Park,* many small fountain gardens; has interesting tilework benches and pools.

UBEDA: (N of Granada) *Municipal rose garden* (r).

VALENCIA: JARDÍN DE MONFORTE, at #1, Llano de Real, no sign on door. Ring bell for admission. Mid-19th-cent. formal green garden. *Jardínes del Real* (r), or *Viveros*

For explanation of symbols and abbreviations, see inside back cover.

(the gardens go by either name);
rose garden, fine restaurant. *Terraza Jardín Rialto Restaurant* (r) in the Internatl. Trade Fair Hall; rose garden.

VALLDEMOSA: See Majorca.

WHEEL TOUR

With Madrid as hub, go to El Escorial and Aranjuez; also, a little more than 30 miles away, to La Granja.

SWEDEN

BÅSTAD: *Norrviken Gardens* (ar, f, t, w, •), daily mid-May–mid-Sept., 9:30–6; during July 9:30–7. English-speaking guides available. Refreshment area open all day. Designed by famous landscape architect Rudolf Abelin. Baroque Garden, pools, cypresses; Japanese Garden; Medieval Cloister Garden; Renaissance Garden, box parterres; Romantic Garden, a natural park; Water Garden, terr. and ponds; Oriental Garden, with "prayer-rugs" of flowers.

BOTANICAL GARDENS: See Göteborg, Lund, Stockholm, Uppsala.

DROTTNINGHOLM PALACE: See Stockholm.

GÖTEBORG: *Botanical Garden* (a, ar, b, f, g, •), Frölundagatan 22. Garden daily 8–8:30; greenhouses Mon.–Sat. 8–4, Sun. 1–3. Vast arboretum, rhododendrons, rock garden, orchids. About 10,000 species. Wildflowers and mosses in woodland section. *Kungsparken Arboretum* (ar), conifers. *Liseberg Amusement Park* (f), lovely gardens. *Trädgårdsföreningen Gardens* (Swedish Horticultural Society), beautiful flower display, palm house, restaurant. Ask at Tourist Office for garden tours.

HÄLSINGBORG: *Botanical Garden* (b, w), 14½ acres, 500 species. Specialize in plants that like water, salt, or sand. *Sofiero Castle* (f, g, h, r, w, •), the King's own garden; 1–2 daily. Rose and herb gardens; primrose dell, English perennial border, greenhouses with grapes, etc.; famous rhododendrons (over 300 species plus many hybrids), waterlily pool. Espaliered apple orchard, the top of each tree grafted to the next. Ask at Tourist Office about tours to estate gardens in S Sweden.

HAMMARBY, HOME OF LINNAEUS: See Uppsala.

KARLSTADT: 25 mi. from here, *Rottneros;* beautiful flower beds and park.

KIVIK: *Arboretum* (ar) of conifers at Kiviks Esperod.

KUNGSPARKEN ARBORETUM: See Göteborg.

LUND: *Botanical Garden* (a, ar, b, f, g), daily 7 A.M.–9 P.M.; 7500 species. Scandinavian flora, African flowers, herbs, crab-apples, mountain ash, cacti.

MALMÖ: Ask at tourist office about trips to castles with gardens.

MILLES GARDEN: See Stockholm.

NORRVIKEN GARDENS: See Båstad.

SOFIERO CASTLE: See Hälsingborg.

STOCKHOLM: *Botanical Garden* (Hortus Botanicus Bergianus) (**b, f, g, w, ●**) daily to dusk; greenhouses Apr.–Sept. 10–11:30, 2–4:30 (Victoria regia house only June–Sept.). Best in May–June. 8800 species, many Asiatic plants, especially from China. *Drottningholm Palace*, May–Sept. 11–5, Apr. and Oct. 1–3, Sun. 1–5. Beautiful 17th-cent. Fr.-style gardens, scroll parterres. Fountains play daily 1–6. *Milles Garden*, in suburb Lidingo, daily May–Oct., 12–5; during June and July also Tues. and Fri. 7–9. Formal garden setting for sculptures. *Town Hall* (**f**), terr. garden. *Waldemarsudde*, Djurgården, former residence of Prince Eugen, gardens Tues.–Sun. 11–4, evenings 8–10. Lovely terr. gardens overlooking the water, flowers and statuary.

TRÄDGÅRDSFÖRENINGEN GARDENS: See Göteborg.

UPPSALA: *Botanical Garden* (**a, b, f, g**), Apr.–Sept. 7 A.M.–9 P.M.; Oct.–Mar., to 8:30. 10,000 species, especially hosta, mountain ash, Scandinavian plants, annuals. Temperate garden of ornamental and commercial plants. Greenhouses. *Hammarby* (**a, f**), Svartbäcksgatan 27, home of Linnaeus. Small formal garden, much as he left it, and wildflower garden.

VISBY: (**r**) Called the "City of Ruins and Roses." Rose displays even at the airport, sometimes bloom in Dec. and Jan.

WALDEMARSUDDE: See Stockholm.

SWITZERLAND

ALBERGO: See Brenscino.

ALP GRUEN: *Alpengarten* (Alpine Garden) (**a**) on the Bernina Line of the "Raetische Bahn" railroad. 6270 ft. alt. Best June–Aug.

AROSA: (Canton Grisons) *Maran* (**a**), Alpine Garden.

BASEL: *Botanical Garden* (**a, b, c, f**), Schoenbeinstr. 6. Best May–June. Alp., orchids, succulents, greenhouses.

BERN: *Botanical Garden* (**a, b, f, g**), Altenbergrain 21. Best June–Sept. Alp. divided geographically. Greenhouse. *Municipal Rose Garden* (**r**), also Eng. Garden, in park.

BOTANICAL GARDENS: See Basel, Bern, Brissago, Fribourg, Geneva, Lausanne, St. Gallen, Zuerich.

BOURG.-ST.-PIERRE: (Valais) *Linnaea*, Alpine Garden.

BRENSCINO: Albergo (inn) near Brissago, nice garden.

BRISSAGO: Island on Lake Maggiore. *Botanical Garden* (**a, r, f, ●**) Take boat from Brissago, Locarno, or Ascona in Switzerland; or from Stresa, Italy. Luxuriant subtrop. garden; see "ITALY," p. 187.

CASTLE BRESTENBERG: See Zuerich.

CASTLE GERZENSEE: See Lake Thun.

CASTLE HEIDEGG: See Gelfingen.

CASTLE OBERHOFEN: See Lake Thun.

CASTLE ST. ANDREAS: See Cham.

CASTLE SCHADAU: See Lake Thun.

CASTLE VON REDING: See Schwyz.

CHAM: *Castle Andreas* (**f**), fine garden.

FLORALPE: See Lac Champex.

FRIBOURG: *Botanical Garden* (**a, b, g**), best June–July. Alp. of various soils in Switz. Greenhouse.

GELFINGEN: (Lucerne) *Castle Heidegg* (**f**), 25 mi. from Lucerne. Fine garden.

GENEVA: *Botanical Garden* (**a, b, c, f, g, w**), 192, Route de Lausanne. Best Apr.–May. Closed Fri. Alp., arboretum, greenhouses with trop. and subtrop. plants, rare water plants. Eng. Garden, park with *Floral Clock* (**f**). *Parc de la Grange* (**r**), wonderful rose garden, see p. 13. *Parc des Eaux Vives* (**f**), formal, flowers.

GWATT: Near Thun. Garden of estate *Von Bonstetten-de-Rothschild* (**f**), open to public.

INTERLAKEN: Gardens of Kursaal, *Floral Clock*.

LA THOMASIA: See Pont de Nant sur Bex.

LAC CHAMPEX: (Valais) *Floralpe* (**a, ●**) Alpine Garden, 4500 ft. alt., on Mont Blanc. Open May through Oct., 11–12 except Sun. Best June, July. Along road from Martigny to St. Bernard, 40 min. from Martigny by car. On railroad line from Paris to Milan via Lausanne. One of finest alp. gardens in Europe; see p. 16.

LAKE THUN: *Castle Gerzensee* (**f**), fine garden. *Castle Oberhofen* (**f**), very colorful flower garden; same for *Castle Schadau* (**f**). *Von Selve* estate (**f**), fine garden.

LAUSANNE: *Botanical Garden* (**a, b, h**), Palais de Rumine. Daily Apr.

through Oct. except Mon. Alp. and medicinal plants.

LINNAEA: See Bourg-St.-Pierre.

LUGANO: At Castagnola nearby, *Villa Favorita;* formal garden, palms, clipped hedges, statues. Famous art collection inside.

MARAN: See Arosa.

MONTREUX: At Rochers de Naye, *Alpine Garden* (**a**), alt. 6700 ft.; reach by cog railway from Montreux. Also nearby, *Rambertia* (**a, f**), private, open to public daily June–Oct. Some exotic and some native plants.

PARC DE LA GRANGE: See Geneva.

PONT DE NANT SUR BEX: (Vaud) *La Thomasia* (**a, b**), large botanical garden, open May through Oct., best June–July. Alpines.

RAMBERTIA: See Montreux.

ST. GALLEN: *Botanical Garden* (**a, b, c, f, g, ●**), Brauerstr. 69. Open all year, 8–12, 1:30–6; greenhouses 9:30–12, 2–5. Many small specialized flower gardens, plants grouped by homelands, families, soil, etc. Greenhouse with 400 varieties alp., 700 kinds orchids, 800 cacti and succulents. Some changing flower shows.

SCHWYZ: *Castle Von Reding*, fine garden.

SCHYNIGE PLATTE: *Alpengarten* (**a, ●**), mid-June through Sept. 6000 ft. alt.; reach by cog railway from Wilderswil near Interlaken. Swiss alp., over 300 varieties, from various altitudes.

VILLA FAVORITA: See Lugano.

VON BONSTETTEN-DE-ROTHSCHILD: See Gwatt.

VON SELVE ESTATE: See Lake Thun.

ZUERICH: *Botanical Garden* (**b, g**), Pelikanstr. 40. Best in May and Aug.–Sept. Greenhouse with Mediterranean plants, etc. *Castle Brestenberg* (**f**), fine garden. *Staedtische Sukkulentensammlung* (City Succulent Collection) (**c, g**), Mythenkai 88. Open all year. Collection and show place of Internatl. Succulent Society; 7 greenhouses, 13 outdoor display cases. Succulents from whole world, in 30 plant famiiles.

WHEEL TOURS

BERN as hub: Fribourg.

CHAMPEX as hub: Bourg-St.-Pierre.

INTERLAKEN as hub: Schynige Platte.

LAKE THUN as hub: Gwatt.

LOCARNO or LUGANO as hub: Brissago, Brenscino; also see Lake Maggiore gardens in chapter on "ITALY."

LUCERNE as hub: Gelfingen.

MONTREUX as hub: Lausanne, Pont de Nant sur Bex.

WALES

Note: The double "ll" in Welsh is pronounced with a throaty "h."

ABERGAVENNY: (Monm.) *Llanvihangel Court* (pron. hlan-vee-angle) (**ar, f**) Sun. and Bank Hols. 2:30–6. Informal stone-walled flower garden; ave. of old sweet chestnuts.

ARBORETUM: See Leyton Welshpool.

BANGOR: (Caern.) *Bible Garden* (**f**), small section of public park, plants mentioned in the Bible. *Penrhyn Castle* (**f**), Natl. Trust. Apr., May, and Oct., Mon., Wed., Thurs.; Bank Hols., 2–5. June–Sept., weekdays including Bank Hols., 10:30–12:30, 2–5; also Sun. in Aug. 2–5. Walled and formal gardens, choice plants.

BLACKALDERN: See Narberth.

BODNANT: See Tal-y-Cafn.

CARDIFF: (Glam.) *Roath Park* (**r**), fine roses. St. *Fagan's Castle* (**f, h**), cent.-old terr., fountain garden, mulberry grove, herb garden.

Daily (except Mon.) and Bank Hols., Apr.–Sept., 11–7; Sun. 2:30–7.

CHIRK: (Denb.) Map D. *Chirk Castle* (**f, t, •**); inquire locally about hours. Flowers, topiaries; see p. 71.

GILFACH: See Roewen.

GWYDYR CASTLE: See Llanwrst.

GWYLLT GARDENS: See Portmeirion.

HAVERFORDWEST: (Pemb.) *Picton Castle* (**f**); special days only; see Garden Scheme booklet. Shrubs and walled garden.

LEYTON WELSHPOOL: (Montg.) *Arboretum,* Royal Forestry Society; small.

LLANGOLLEN: (pron. hlan-goh-len) (Anglesey) Map D. *Plas Newydd* (pron. plass new-eth) (**t**) Amusing topiaries; see p. 70.

LLANVIHANGEL COURT: See Abergavenny.

LLANWRST: (pron. hlan-roost) (Denb.) *Gwydyr Castle* (pron. gwee-dor) (**r, t**) Daily 10–6. Formal gardens, topiaries, roses, peacocks.

NARBERTH: (Pemb.) *Blackaldern* (**f**), special days only; see Garden Scheme booklet (see end of chapter on ENGLAND). Rhododendrons, azaleas.

PENRHYN CASTLE: See Bangor.

PICTON CASTLE: See Haverfordwest.

PLAS NEWYDD: See Llangollen.

PORTMEIRION: (Merion). *Gwyllt Gardens* (**f**), Daily 10–7. Rhododendrons, azaleas, 30,000 hydrangeas, subtrop. flora. Whole village full of flowers.

POWIS CASTLE: See Welshpool.

ROATH PARK: See Cardiff.

ROEWEN: (Caern.) *Gilfach* (**f**) Daily 10–10 except Sun. Delightful private garden, see p. 67.

RHYL: (pron. roy-el) (Flint.) *Royal Floral Hall* (**c, f, g, ●**) Daily 10–8. Wonderful greenhouse; see p. 70.

ST. FAGAN'S CASTLE: See Cardiff.

TAL-Y-CAFN: (pron. tally-cown) (Denb.) *Bodnant* (**a, ar, f, i, r, ●**) Natl. Trust. Tues., Wed., Thurs., Sat., 1:30–4:45; entrance at Eglwysbach Rd., E of A–496. One of the loveliest gardens in the world; see p. 67.

WELSHPOOL: (Montg.) *Powis Castle* (pron. po-iss) (**a, f, ●**) Due W of Shrewsbury, Eng. Road to Newtown A–483. Daily except Mon. and Tues., 1–6. Striking gardens; see p. 72.

WHEEL TOUR MAPS

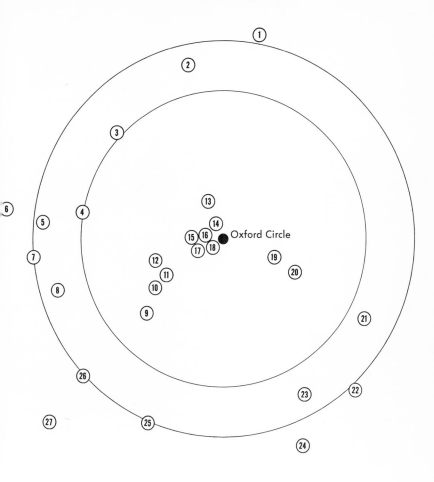

MAP A: GREATER LONDON AREA, 15 and 20 mile radius from Oxford Circle.

1. Ware	10. Ham Common	19. Greenwich
2. Hatfield	11. Royal Park of Richmond	20. Eltham
3. Watford	12. Kew Gardens	21. Farningham
4. Uxbridge	13. Fenton House	22. Sevenoaks
5. Stoke Poges	14. Regent's Park	23. Westerham
6. Maidenhead	15. Holland Park Gardens	24. Edenbridge
7. Windsor	16. Kensington Gardens	25. Dorking
8. Egham	17. Derry & Tom's	26. Ripley
9. Hampton Court	18. St. James's Park	27. Guildford

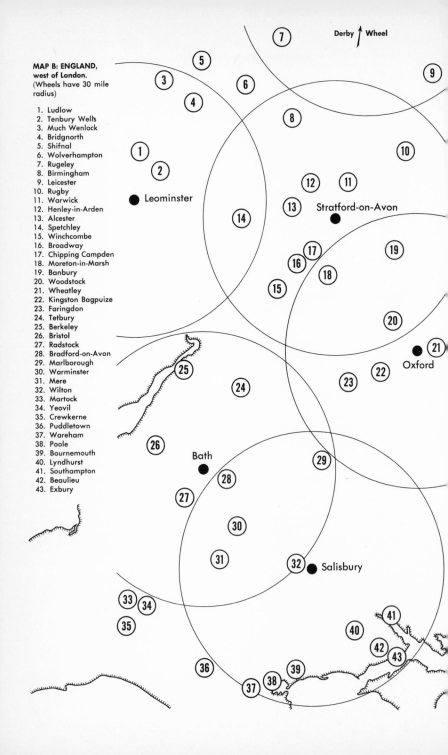

MAP B: ENGLAND,
west of London.
(Wheels have 30 mile
radius)

1. Ludlow
2. Tenbury Wells
3. Much Wenlock
4. Bridgnorth
5. Shifnal
6. Wolverhampton
7. Rugeley
8. Birmingham
9. Leicester
10. Rugby
11. Warwick
12. Henley-in-Arden
13. Alcester
14. Spetchley
15. Winchcombe
16. Broadway
17. Chipping Campden
18. Moreton-in-Marsh
19. Banbury
20. Woodstock
21. Wheatley
22. Kingston Bagpuize
23. Faringdon
24. Tetbury
25. Berkeley
26. Bristol
27. Radstock
28. Bradford-on-Avon
29. Marlborough
30. Warminster
31. Mere
32. Wilton
33. Martock
34. Yeovil
35. Crewkerne
36. Puddletown
37. Wareham
38. Poole
39. Bournemouth
40. Lyndhurst
41. Southampton
42. Beaulieu
43. Exbury

Derby ↑ Wheel

Leominster

Stratford-on-Avon

Oxford

Bath

Salisbury

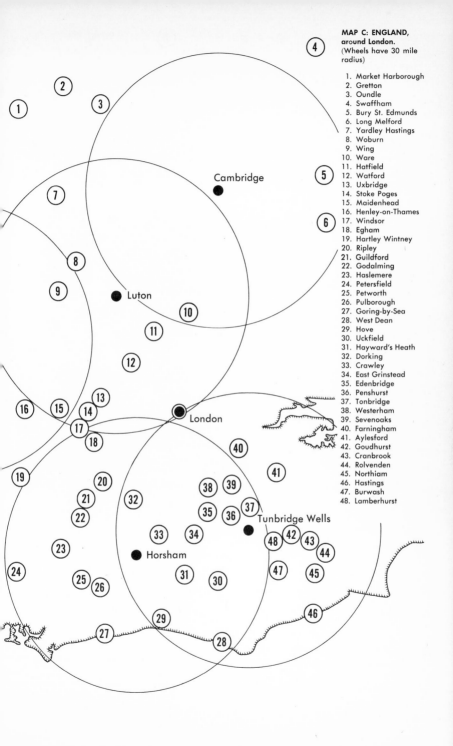

MAP C: ENGLAND, around London.
(Wheels have 30 mile radius)

1. Market Harborough
2. Gretton
3. Oundle
4. Swaffham
5. Bury St. Edmunds
6. Long Melford
7. Yardley Hastings
8. Woburn
9. Wing
10. Ware
11. Hatfield
12. Watford
13. Uxbridge
14. Stoke Poges
15. Maidenhead
16. Henley-on-Thames
17. Windsor
18. Egham
19. Hartley Wintney
20. Ripley
21. Guildford
22. Godalming
23. Haslemere
24. Petersfield
25. Petworth
26. Pulborough
27. Goring-by-Sea
28. West Dean
29. Hove
30. Uckfield
31. Hayward's Heath
32. Dorking
33. Crawley
34. East Grinstead
35. Edenbridge
36. Penshurst
37. Tonbridge
38. Westerham
39. Sevenoaks
40. Farningham
41. Aylesford
42. Goudhurst
43. Cranbrook
44. Rolvenden
45. Northiam
46. Hastings
47. Burwash
48. Lamberhurst

Cambridge

Luton

London

Tunbridge Wells

Horsham

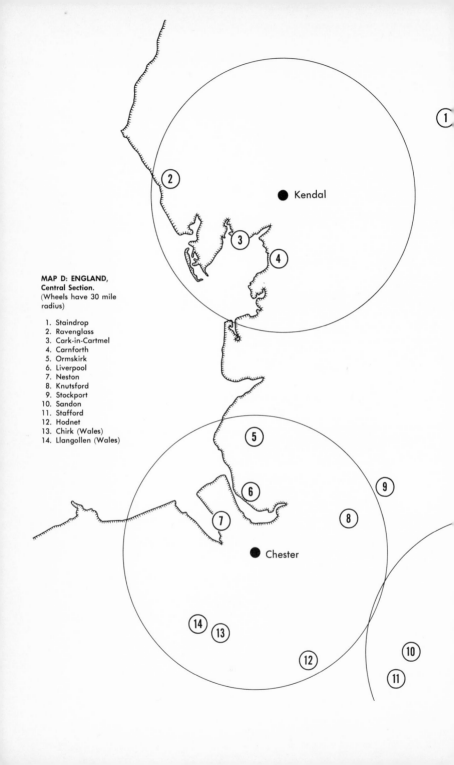

MAP D: ENGLAND,
Central Section.
(Wheels have 30 mile
radius)

1. Staindrop
2. Ravenglass
3. Cark-in-Cartmel
4. Carnforth
5. Ormskirk
6. Liverpool
7. Neston
8. Knutsford
9. Stockport
10. Sandon
11. Stafford
12. Hodnet
13. Chirk (Wales)
14. Llangollen (Wales)

Kendal

Chester

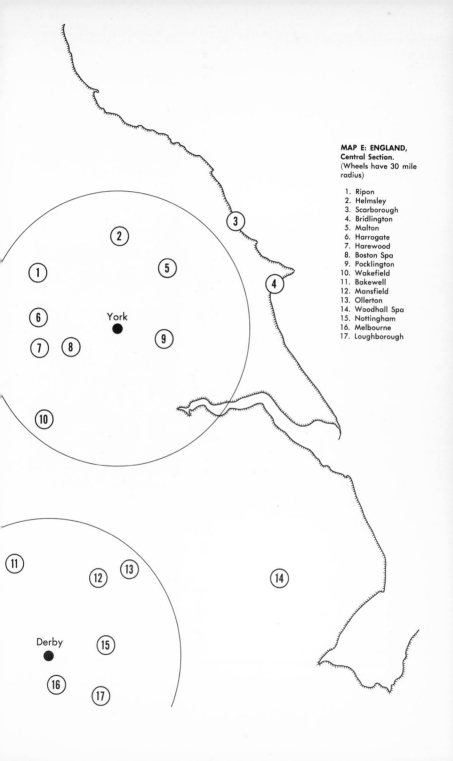

MAP E: ENGLAND,
Central Section.
(Wheels have 30 mile
radius)

1. Ripon
2. Helmsley
3. Scarborough
4. Bridlington
5. Malton
6. Harrogate
7. Harewood
8. Boston Spa
9. Pocklington
10. Wakefield
11. Bakewell
12. Mansfield
13. Ollerton
14. Woodhall Spa
15. Nottingham
16. Melbourne
17. Loughborough

York

Derby

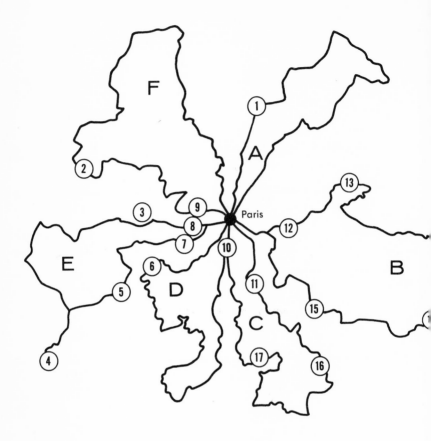

MAP F: ÎLE DE FRANCE (Area around Paris)

1. Chantilly
2. Rosny
3. Wideville
4. Chartres
5. Rambouillet
6. Dampierre
7. Versailles
8. Saint-Cloud
9. Malmaison
10. Sceaux
11. Evry-Petit-Bourg
12. Champs
13. Meaux
14. Provins
15. Maincy
16. Fontainebleau
17. Courances

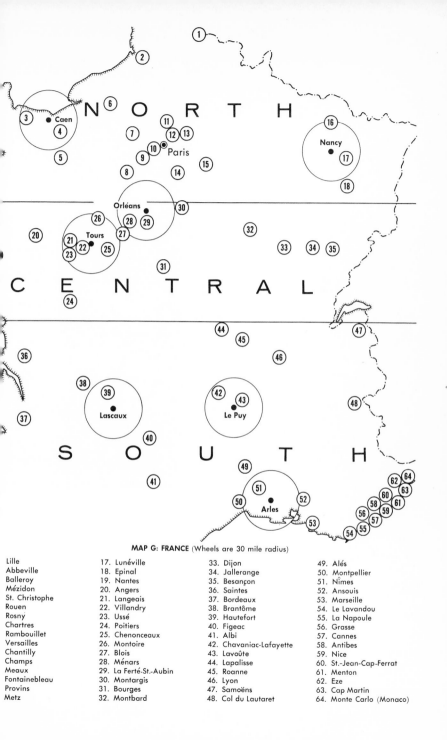

MAP G: FRANCE (Wheels are 30 mile radius)

Lille	17. Lunéville	33. Dijon	49. Alés
Abbeville	18. Epinal	34. Jallerange	50. Montpellier
Balleroy	19. Nantes	35. Besançon	51. Nîmes
Mézidon	20. Angers	36. Bordeaux	52. Ansouis
St. Christophe	21. Langeais	37. Bordeaux	53. Marseille
Rouen	22. Villandry	38. Brantôme	54. Le Lavandou
Rosny	23. Ussé	39. Hautefort	55. La Napoule
Chartres	24. Poitiers	40. Figeac	56. Grasse
Rambouillet	25. Chenonceaux	41. Albi	57. Cannes
Versailles	26. Montoire	42. Chavaniac-Lafayette	58. Antibes
Chantilly	27. Blois	43. Lavoûte	59. Nice
Champs	28. Ménars	44. Lapalisse	60. St.-Jean-Cap-Ferrat
Meaux	29. La Ferté-St.-Aubin	45. Roanne	61. Menton
Fontainebleau	30. Montargis	46. Lyon	62. Eze
Provins	31. Bourges	47. Samoëns	63. Cap Martin
Metz	32. Montbard	48. Col du Lautaret	64. Monte Carlo (Monaco)

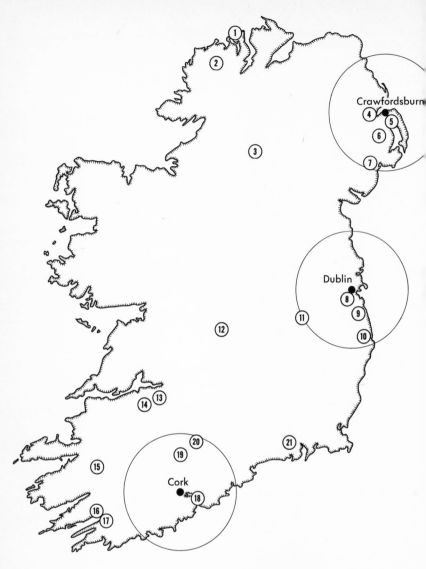

MAP H: IRELAND (Wheels have 30 mile radius)

1. Mulroy	8. Rathfarnham	15. Killarney
2. Veagh	9. Enniskerry	16. Glengarriff
3. Tempo	10. Ashford	17. Bantry
4. Belfast	11. Tully	18. Cobh
5. Newtownards	12. Birr	19. Castletownroche
6. Saintfield	13. Adare	20. Mitchellstown
7. Castlewellan	14. Rathkeale	21. Waterford

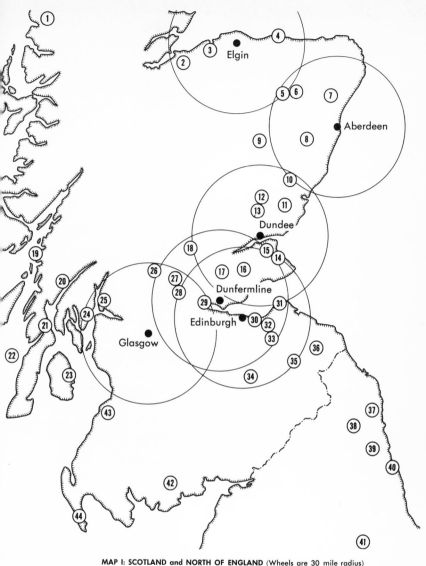

MAP I: SCOTLAND and NORTH OF ENGLAND (Wheels are 30 mile radius)

SCOTLAND

1. Poolewe
2. Cawdor
3. Forres
4. Cullen
5. Kennethmont
6. Pitmedden
7. Pitmedden
8. Banchory
9. Ballater
10. Edzell

11. Guthrie
12. Kirriemuir
13. Glamis
14. St. Andrews
15. Leuchars
16. Falkland
17. Kinross
18. Crieff
19. Easdale
20. Minard
21. Tarbert
22. Isle of Gigha

23. Isle of Arran, Brodick
24. Dunoon
25. Rhu
26. Callander
27. Dunblane
28. Stirling
29. Culross
30. Musselburgh
31. Dirleton
32. Pencaitland
33. Humbie
34. Traquair

35. Gordon
36. Duns
42. Castle Douglas
43. Maybole
44. Port Logan

ENGLAND

37. Alnwick
38. Rothbury
39. Morpeth
40. Whitley Bay
41. Staindrop

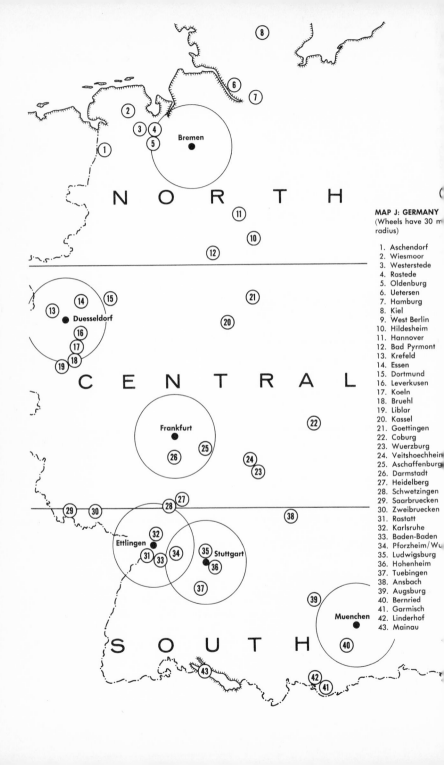

MAP J: GERMANY
(Wheels have 30 m
radius)

1. Aschendorf
2. Wiesmoor
3. Westerstede
4. Rastede
5. Oldenburg
6. Uetersen
7. Hamburg
8. Kiel
9. West Berlin
10. Hildesheim
11. Hannover
12. Bad Pyrmont
13. Krefeld
14. Essen
15. Dortmund
16. Leverkusen
17. Koeln
18. Bruehl
19. Liblar
20. Kassel
21. Goettingen
22. Coburg
23. Wuerzburg
24. Veitshoechhein
25. Aschaffenburg
26. Darmstadt
27. Heidelberg
28. Schwetzingen
29. Saarbruecken
30. Zweibruecken
31. Rastatt
32. Karlsruhe
33. Baden-Baden
34. Pforzheim/Wu
35. Ludwigsburg
36. Hohenheim
37. Tuebingen
38. Ansbach
39. Augsburg
40. Bernried
41. Garmisch
42. Linderhof
43. Mainau

INDEX

Alpine gardens, arboretums, and botanical gardens will be found in the "Key to Gardens."

Båstad, 282
Bateman's (Burwash), 240
Bath (Map B), 239
Bawtry, 239
Beaulieu (Map B), 239
Beaumont Hall (Leicester), 244
Bedgebury National Pinetum (Goudhurst), 243
Beeches Farm (Uckfield), 249
Belfast (Map H) area, 56 ff., 266
Bellecourt, 235
Bemfica, 221 f., 275
Bennebroek, 154, 263
Bergen, 274
Berkeley (Map B), 239
Bern, 283
Bernried (Map J), 259
Berrington Hall (Leominster), 244 f.
Besançon (Map G), 140, 253
Bethmannpark (Frankfurt), 172, 259
Bicton Gardens (East Budleigh), 242
Birkinshaw (Traquair), 279
Birmingham (Map B), 240
Birr (Map H), 62, 266
Blackaldern (Narberth), 286
Blackhills (Elgin), 117 f., 278
Blenheim Palace (Woodstock), 94, 251
Blanes, 203 ff., 280
Blickling Hall (Aylsham), 239
Blithefield Hall (Rugeley), 248
Boboli Gardens (Florence), 269
Bodmin, 240
Bodnant (Tal-y-Cafn), 67 ff., 286
Bois de Boulogne (Paris), 256
Bokrijk, 235 f.
Bordeaux (Map G), 146, 253
Borde Hill (Hayward's Heath), 243
Boston Spa (Map E), 100, 240
Bougival, 253
Bourges (Map G), 253
Bournemouth (Map B), 240
Bradford-on-Avon (Map B), 240
Bramham Park (Boston Spa), 100, 240
Brantôme (Map G), 146, 253
Breda, 263
Bregentved Castle (Køge), 237
Bremen (Map J), 162 f., 259
Bridgnorth (Map B), 240
Bridlington (Map E), 240
Brissago (Lake Maggiore), 187 ff., 283
Bristol (Map B), 240
Broad Clyst, 240
Broadway (Map B), 240
Brodick Castle (Isle of Arran), 123, 278
Broughton Castle (Banbury), 239
Bruehl (Map J), 170 f., 259
Brussels, 236

Burford House (Tenbury Wells), 21, 249
Burg Gracht (Liblar), 261
Burgh-le-Marsh, 240
Burnby Hall (Pocklington), 23, 247
Burton Agnes Hall (Bridlington), 240
Burwash (Map C), 240
Bury St. Edmunds (Map C), 240
Buscot Park (Faringdon), 242

C

Caen (Map G), 138, 253
Cagliari, Sardinia, 269
Callander (Map I), 111, 277
Cambridge (Map C), 240 f.
Camerino, 269
Canary Islands, 217 f., 280
Canterbury, 241
Cap Martin (Map G), 149, 253
Caprarola, 269
Capri, 269
Cardiff, 285
Cark-in-Cartmel (Map D), 241
Carnforth (Map D), 241
Carrouges, 138, 253
Caserta, 198 f., 269
Cassiobury Park (Watford), 87, 250
Castello, 269
Castello di Urio (Lake Como), 270
Castelo Branco (photo, 227), 226, 275
Castle Ashby (Yardley Hastings), 251
Castle Douglas, (Map I), 126, 277
Castle Howard (Malton), 245
Castletownroche (Map H), 50, 266
Castlewellan (Map H), 56, 266
Cathedral of St. Étienne (Bourges), 253
Cawdor (Map I), 118, 277
Cham, 284
Champs-sur-Marne (Map F & G), 135, 253
Chantilly (Maps F & G), 133 ff., 253
Chapelle de St.-Gilles (Montoire), 256
Chard, 241
Charleston Manor (West Dean), 250
Chartres (Map F & G), 137, 253
Chastleton House (Moreton-in-Marsh), 246
Château d'Attre (Ath), 235
Château de Beloeil (Brussels), 236
Château de Bussy-Rabutin (Montbard), 140, 256
Château de Canon (Mézidon), 138, 255
Château de Chimay (Brussels), 236
Château de Cluzel (St. Eble), 145, 257
Château d'Effiat (Lapalisse), 144, 255
Château de Gaesbeek (Brussels), 236

306

SYMBOLS AND ABBREVIATIONS

used in the Key to Gardens

● — especially fine garden
a — alpines, rock garden
ar — arboretum, unusual trees
b — botanical garden
c — cacti and succulents
f — flowers
g — greenhouse
h — herb garden
i — iris
r — rose garden
t — topiaries
w — water plants

alp. — alpine; alpines
alt. — altitude
ave. — avenue; avenues
cent. — century; centuries
E — east; eastern
Eng. — English; England
ft. — foot; feet
Fr. — French
G.S. — Garden Scheme
hol., hols. — holiday; holidays
internatl. — international
Ital. — Italian; Italianate
magnif. — magnificent
mgr. — manager

mi. — mile; miles
min. — minutes
N — north; northern
natl. — national
pron. — pronounced
rd. — road
reg. — regular; regularly
S — south; southern
subtrop. — subtropical
supt. — superintendent
terr. — terrace(s); terraced
trop. — tropical
veg. — vegetable(s)
W — west; western